AN IMPROBABLE LIFE

AN IMPROBABLE LIFE

The Autobiography

Trevor McDonald

WEIDENFELD & NICOLSON

First published in Great Britain in 2019
by Weidenfeld & Nicolson

3 5 7 9 10 8 6 4 2

A CIP catalogue record for this book
is available from the British Library.

HB ISBN   978 1 4746 1 4757
TPB ISBN 978 1 4746 1476 4
eBook 978 1 4746 1478 8

Typeset by Input Data Services Ltd, Somerset

Printed and bound in Great Britain by Clays Ltd, Elcograf S.p.A.

Weidenfeld & Nicolson

The Orion Publishing Group Ltd
Carmelite House
50 Victoria Embankment
London, EC4Y 0DZ
An Hachette UK Company
www.weidenfeldandnicolson.co.uk
www.orionbooks.co.uk

For my parents, Geraldine and Lawson, who enveloped me – their firstborn – in the warmth of their deep affection.

For my family, whose love and affection sustained me, and for the army of friends and colleagues without whose generosity I may never have survived as a journalist.

Contents

Preface   ix

1   A New Age in America   1
2   A Trinidad Apprentice   25
3   Between Two Worlds   58
4   The Arch of Experience   88
5   Under Fire   112
6   Foreign Correspondent   134
7   A New Birth of Freedom   184
8   Looking Beyond the Past   209
9   Facing Saddam   240
10   Encounters on Death Row   278
11   The Politics of Black and White   303

Acknowledgements   310
Index   317
Picture Credits   323

Preface

'Think where man's glory most begins and ends,
And say my glory was I had such friends.'
W.B. Yeats, 'The Municipal Gallery Revisited'

'The journalist is a stranger who moves in the opposite direction from the crowd, toward danger, leaving the settled
majority perplexed. Why, they ask, are you going over the
lines? Why do you choose such a lonely existence? In search of
a fair understanding, you say, and they shake their heads. There
is nothing to understand, they insist, just write the truth! But
truths are many and that is the problem.'
Roger Cohen, *International New York Times*

If it were left to me Roger Cohen's words would be stamped
on the heart of every journalist and engraved on tablets of
stone at the entrance to every news organisation. They describe the basic difficulties faced by all journalists and remind
us about the professional standards we must maintain.

The key observation is: TRUTHS ARE MANY.

There is a resonance to that line in the irresistible explosion
of social media, in the politics of contemporary populism
and in the urge to label anything not entirely favourable to a
political leader's cause, however accurate and well founded,
as fake news.

It is troubling to observe how popular that description has become in politics today. The practice of running bogus campaigns on social media platforms is now commonplace. Given the internet and the infinite variety of ways to command the attention of its users there is now probably no way to stop that entirely.

What is entirely new is how readily unscrupulous politicians reach for the label 'fake news' to describe anything which attempts to hold them to account. Openly contemptuous of the very concept of a free press, they see unbiased reporting as the enemy of the state. Faced with incontrovertible evidence of their lies and deceit they shamelessly describe reported facts as fake news.

There is a dark, revealing history about this. It goes back to the 1930s. The Nazis, fearful of having their gross inhumanity disclosed to the German people and to the world, came up with a plan to destroy the credibility of the mainstream media. To reports they didn't like they applied the term *Lügenpresse*, or lying press. It worked for a time, enabling the Nazi propaganda machine to distribute its message and successfully conceal the unpleasant truth of their despicable actions.

It bears an uncomfortable resemblance to what happens in our politics today. Be on your guard whenever you hear the words 'fake news': it may be nothing more than the new term of abuse for inconvenient facts. In a variation on the theme the Egyptian government has taken action against opposition activists for 'publishing false news'.

But back to Cohen's words.

The thought that 'truths are many' encapsulates the challenge I have faced throughout my life as a journalist – cutting through a thicket of interlocking political and social issues and trying to find the truth frequently buried in a mass of deliberate falsehoods. It has always been difficult. It is terribly easy to be misled and to get things wrong.

One of the first things I discovered in my cub reporting

days is that journalism is riddled with complexity. The simplest stories may not be that simple after all! We learn to spot some false leads almost by instinct. No one today, for example, would seriously argue that all official government statements should be taken at face value. The difficulty has always been to try to find out why they have been made and what lies behind them. In time, it is to be hoped, the ability to do that becomes second nature to a journalist. Even so, complications occur when we least expect them. We stumble into the trap of ignoring the difficulties of reporting, not only significant political shifts, but the subtle changes in the way local council meetings are conducted.

Go one step further as a reporter and try, as I have for more years than I care to remember, to look into the dimly lit corners of the international political world. The problems of making any sense of it loom larger. I cannot recall a time when I have not been baffled by the complexities of some political issues. That remains true today.

Here's the first rule of that side of the trade.

The politics of the most open countries defy easy analysis. Coming to a view about what governments do or what a president or prime minister means on the basis of what he or she says, and understanding it sufficiently well to explain it to readers, listeners or television viewers, can be rhetorical torture. The pitfalls awaiting those who choose the casual approach become craters seething with dangerous misapprehensions.

First impressions can be misleading and invariably are. In politics as in life truth, real truth, hides its face in a confusion of disguises. A life in journalism is terribly destructive of certainty. Sadly, there's nothing to suggest it gets better with the greater time spent doing the job.

Think of the changes to the world order brought about by the fall of the Berlin Wall, the collapse of the old Soviet Union, the rise of authoritarian regimes in Russia, Hungary,

Thailand, the Philippines, Kyrgyzstan and even more recently in Turkey, where journalists face terrorism charges merely for being critical of the government, and the fact that leaders in some of the most open democracies are guilty of the most shameless acts of dishonesty.

There were times when we thought it would be all so different.

I say this partly to explain why the inherent problem of attempting to reflect objectively on a career in journalism cannot be overstated. Looking back does not always provide crystalline clarity or rock-solid analysis. Our ability to hit false notes is enormous. We journalists get things wrong. We misread would-be leaders and the honesty of their promises. We misunderstand the true nature of some political campaigns.

Something else makes the task of looking back in a memoir problematical.

Consciously or not, we create glowing images of ourselves and insist we did what we did with the best intentions and for the loftiest reasons. We are desperate to have our work seen in the best possible light. We crave self-justification. We spend our lives, as the eighteenth-century French philosopher Diderot suggested, trying to make ourselves into a version of what we imagine ourselves to be. The reality is frequently different and facing up to that fact is the primary challenge when embarking on a personal account of any kind.

To be credible, a book like this must be rooted in an honest attempt to confront one's true self, failings and all, and it must do all it possibly can to ignore the idealised version that floats around in the alluring realms of our own imagination. And I am conscious of the fact that 'the eye sees not itself, but by reflection'.

So with all those qualifications here's my story clothed in the hope that, however slanted, it shines some light on who I am, what I chose to do and the manner in which I chose to do it.

1

A New Age in America

'Making a living is nothing; the great difficulty is making a point, making a difference – with words.'

Elizabeth Hardwick, 'Grub Street, New York'

I remember the cold.

I had dragged myself out of bed before dawn. There was nothing unusual about that. It was what we had to do when working in Washington to cope with the five-hour time difference between DC and London. By the time I was barely awake, my office on the other side of the Atlantic was well into its working day.

Drawing back the blinds and looking out of my hotel window down onto the street below I was amazed at the sight of streams of people making their way up towards Capitol Hill. From my room high up on the tenth floor they seemed like a procession of Lowry-like figures, shuffling along wordlessly in the semi-dark, in heavy overcoats, thick scarves and gloves. It was, after all, a January winter's day in Washington DC.

The event that had brought them to the nation's capital was hours away, but everyone expected the crowds to be large and getting there early would be the only way to find a good spot to watch the ceremony. Only on venturing outside myself much later did I discover how cold it was. A freeze had set in. First light revealed a clear day and a sky of faultless blue, but when the wind rose it showered icicles across the Mall. They hit you in the face with the sting of burning needles. Toes and fingers went numb.

And yet the weather discouraged no one.

Spirits were high. The mood was celebratory. It was as if the warmth of expectation had blunted the effects of the cold.

The early risers had done the right thing. By late morning the largest number of people ever to assemble in Washington had occupied every square inch of the two-mile-long grass runway from Capitol Hill to the Lincoln Memorial to witness the final act in a political drama that had transfixed America and the world.

Picking my way through the gathering multitude that day I could almost taste the excitement. A black man with the unlikely name of Barack Hussein Obama had defied political orthodoxy and was about to be sworn in as president of the United States. It was happening in a country where black Americans had only been legally guaranteed the right to vote a little over forty years earlier after a campaign as bruising and turbulent as the Civil War.

Now this junior senator from Illinois was about to enter the White House of Jefferson, Lincoln and Roosevelt, of JFK, Reagan, Clinton and Bush – a White House built by slaves. As tradition required, a huge cast of political and civic dignitaries had made its way stageside up at the far end of the Mall – decked out in style and living up to its name as America's Front Yard.

Everything slotted into place for a presidential inauguration like no other and I was there to watch an extraordinary moment in American history. It was one of the thrills of my life as a journalist and as a black man.

I had followed the noisy carnival of the presidential election campaign with its twists and turns, its frothy controversies and its spasms of political spite. Those memories were already passing into history. They had been superseded by the election result.

Watching the president elect's victory speech at Grant Park in Chicago late on election night from my hotel in Washington, I strained to believe what my eyes were telling me. I had telephoned friends in London to share the excitement but also as a way of checking that I had not been transported to a distant planet at a time in the distant future. That evening in Chicago, Obama struck all the right notes in describing to an ecstatic crowd and to the American nation the historic nature of his victory.

My conversations with friends across the Atlantic had all ended in tears of high emotion and glorious incredulity.

As I walked through the crowds on Inauguration Day I did wonder what Martin Luther King would have made of it. When he delivered his famous speech on the very Washington ground on which Obama would take the oath of office, did his American dream ever go as far as seeing a black man walk the last few yards up Pennsylvania Avenue to enter the White House as president and commander in chief?

I thought of my mother. I had learned a lot about the world as a child by glimpses of the prisms through which she saw it. From the little she knew – by reading, I suppose, because she'd never been to the United States – she bristled with anger at racial segregation. She understood, she told me, why Jesse Owens was slighted by Hitler at the Olympic Games in Berlin in 1936 but found the discrimination he faced when he returned to his native America unforgivable. And she talked endlessly about how in the majority of American hotels the great Joe Louis was not allowed to book a room. He had become the undisputed heavyweight champion of the world but that changed little in the eyes of those who ran a bigoted system without shame. Joe Louis was still consigned to the terrible fate of being black.

Now, though, here was a black president of the United

States. My mother would be doing handstands in her grave.

Sitting at my mother's feet I grew up to believe that race discrimination was an abomination, especially in a country where the framers of the constitution placed such emphasis on liberty, equality and democracy. Countless stains on human decency that marked so much of American life were about to be brushed aside on Inauguration Day in 2009, at least for one bright, shining moment.

I had watched the pre-inauguration atmosphere build from the preceding weekend.

Washington was on high-octane. The city was buzzing.

Its broad, elegant avenues, lit by a pale winter sun and usually sedate on a non-working day, throbbed with vitality. By early Sunday evening, roads leading to and from the White House and the Capitol were clogged by a seemingly endless, slowly moving human mass. Clumps of people spilled out of every side street going everywhere and nowhere. It was impossible to ignore the sense that we were on the cusp of something big.

Getting to the lobby of any downtown hotel was possible only by picking a path through snaking lines of limousines, which appeared even absurdly longer than usual, and a cacophony of noisier Washington taxis disgorging passengers or waiting to whisk new clients away.

The chaos in the foyer of my hotel could easily have been the work of a prankster who had scheduled several large conventions for the same time, on the same evening, at the same venue. In a suffocating crush I spent ten minutes trying to reach the reception desk. People waved their arms and shouted in order to be heard by friends and connections at the furthest points of overcrowded rooms.

No one complained. Resigned good nature prevailed and in the spirit of a rollickingly successful party the bars and restaurants off the main foyer heaved and groaned under the burden of coping with ceaseless demand.

I had never seen the lobby of a Washington hotel so crowd-ed – and never with such a wide cross-section of the variety of peoples who make up the population of the United States. In 1961 Tom Wolfe described Washington on the eve of the Kennedy inauguration as a 'gilt-edged, mink-lined, silk-hatted, 10-gallon, 100-proof' celebration. He speculated that if you fell out of any city hotel window you would 'hit nothing but minks and bouffant hairdos'.

By 2009 mink had largely slipped out of fashion and what the crowds lacked in bouffant hairdos they made up for in size and effervescence.

I found it oddly amusing that the only Washingtonians un-touched by the festive buzz were the immigration officers at Dulles Airport. Visitors flooding into the city that weekend found rows of desks unmanned. Queues of travellers waiting to present their documents stretched further into the distance than I'd seen before and the act of formally being allowed into the United States took hours. Surely, I thought, Homeland Security officials were aware of the big deal about to take place in downtown DC and had adjusted their shift patterns accordingly.

We travellers from across the pond stared at each other in astonishment. We spoke only in whispers. To betray impatience or the slightest sign of irritation in a queue at immigration anywhere in United States is not advisable. In any event the waiting confirmed that Washington was the place to be that Sunday. The tedium of shuffling along inch by excruciating inch was, we wearily agreed, a price worth paying to watch history being made in less than forty-eight hours.

By the morning of Tuesday 20 January 2009, Inauguration Day, the memory of those Dulles Airport queues had van-ished. Throughout the afternoon a moving wall of noise rose on the wind and when it peaked seemed to shake the very foundations of imposing buildings ringing the Mall.

Walking through the crowd from early morning to

mid-afternoon and talking to some of those milling around, beating their hands together and stamping their feet to banish the cold from their extremities, I was surprised to find people still struggling, as I was, to come to terms with what they'd actually come to see. One woman who had grown up during the segregation years in the Southern state of Mississippi told me with tears coursing down her cheeks: 'This is all too much. It's too difficult for me to imagine this is happening. If I'm dreaming I pray I never wake up. This is a new age in America. I never thought I'd live to see this day.'

Neither did I, but the truth was beginning to sink in. It was difficult to escape. It had been hailed in the breathless prose of newspaper headlines. The *New York Times*, the Grey Lady and the Grande Dame of American newspapers, where the house style is to refer to the successful presidential candidate by his full name in the main story on the morning after the election, wrote on 5 November: 'Barack Hussein Obama was elected forty-fourth president of the United States on Tuesday, sweeping away the last racial barrier in American politics.'

The *New Yorker* magazine was even more pointed about what had occurred. Encapsulating the moment in language unmatched by any other publication, it mixed amazement with delight at the fact that 'sixty-five million Americans turned a liability – a moniker so politically inflammatory that the full recitation of it was considered foul play – into a global diplomatic asset, a symbol of America's ability to astonish and inspire'. It went on to explain that the United States had elected 'a person whose first name is a Swahili word derived from the Arabic and whose middle name is not only that of a grandson of the Prophet Muhammad but also the original target of an on-going American war, and whose last name rhymes nicely with "Osama"'. That's not a name concluded the *New Yorker* ironically, 'it's a catastrophe'.

Catastrophe indeed!

My thoughts went back to incidents during the campaign.

In Ohio I had been repeatedly told by voters that 'Obama' was not 'an American name'. Not that anyone rushed to explain what an American name is. That was only one of Obama's problems. There was a greater impediment to the possibility of his winning the race. One caller to an early morning radio phone-in programme in West Virginia on which I was a guest told me emphatically that the Democratic candidate is 'a Moslem'. I remember attempting to suggest rather feebly that so far as I knew he was a practising Christian. It cut no ice. 'That's what he says,' came the sharp retort, 'but I tell you he's a Moslem.'

On the Ohio–Kentucky border voters had other concerns. They were worried that if that this 'un-American' candidate were ever allowed anywhere near 1600 Pennsylvania Avenue he would in one legislative sweep abolish that blessed Second Amendment right to carry guns. Customers I talked to at one gunsmith doing a brisk mid-morning trade could barely contain their disbelief when, in reply to a discourse on the many virtues of high-velocity guns, I said that such weapons were not commonplace in London houses. But how do you manage to survive, their facial expressions seemed to ask. Then, as if to underline the degree to which a wide variety of lethal weapons were part of the fabric of everyday life, one man explained his opposition to Obama's candidacy by telling me, almost in the manner of someone sharing a family confidence, that on hearing of the terrorist attacks on New York and Washington on 11 September 2001, he had locked his front door securely and had sat bolt upright in his living room with his AK-47 on his lap ready to repel any terrorist intruder.

I was lost for words. I've always found the American passion for gun ownership disturbing. That story did little to change my view. I tried to convince the storyteller that if Obama ever got to the Oval Office he'd be engulfed by so many of the problems facing the American economy that he might struggle to find time to get congressional approval to outlaw the right of Americans to cradle AK-47s in their living rooms.

But to voters in parts of rural America, views about guns, about Obama's name and allegations about his religion had become toxic issues. Even when pollsters gave him a sporting chance of beating his Republican rival John McCain, a significant majority of black Americans in the Southern states continued to doubt he would ever be elected.

I spent a weekend in Selma, Alabama, meeting people whose lives had been bruised by the horrors of segregation. Some had been in the vanguard of the struggle for civil rights. With enviable bravery and courage they had staged protests, organised boycotts and joined marches to pursue their cause. I thought of the avuncular, ageing pastor of one evangelical church who recalled how he'd ignored warnings of the state authorities and joined one of the famous marches from Selma to the state capital, Montgomery. On the Edmund Pettus Bridge leading out of the city – named with striking irony after a Confederate general who later became a Grand Dragon of the Alabama Ku Klux Klan – the marchers were met by more than 150 armed men: state troopers and a posse ordered on to the bridge by Sheriff Jim Clark. The governor of Alabama, George Wallace, wanted the march to be stopped at all costs. The state troopers had come equipped to do the governor's bidding. They wore gas masks and carried night-sticks. The sheriff's men, some on horseback, were armed with clubs, whips and cattle prods. Watched by a sizeable crowd of white Alabamans, the marchers were given two minutes to go back to their houses and to their churches. When they stood their ground, the troopers charged. Then came the horses and the tear gas. The pastor told me: 'We were beaten, and I fell to the ground. When I looked up, I saw a number of others on the ground around me and I saw blood.' That final word '*blood*' was rendered with all the rhetorical flourish of Southern Baptist preachers.

On the morning of Obama's inauguration my mind went

back to reports of those marches. I recalled the gallows humour of one protester who said that the horses were more humane than the troopers; they stepped over fallen victims!

Although the marches had taken place more than forty years ago, the memories of those who were a part of them were chilling and painful. I won't forget that visit to Selma before the presidential election because of something else. At the end of almost every formal interview my interlocutors would turn the tables on me, to ask as an observer but also, I'm sure, as a black man, what I thought about the race. I, too, had been plagued by doubts about the possibility of an Obama victory and my record of political predictions has never been good. But for the life of me I couldn't quite imagine John McCain being elected president, especially after he and his campaign team came up with the zany idea of choosing the unknown and politically untutored, rabble-rousing governor of Alaska, Sarah Palin, as his running mate. Whenever I expressed that view, my interviewees, especially if they happened to be black Americans, would retreat into contemplative silence and then quietly opine that it was too big an imaginative leap for them to think that a black man might be the next president of their country. They were convinced that Obama was the better candidate and that by any objective measure he should win. They would even agree with me that some opinion polls were beginning to point steadily in his direction. But given the country's history, how could they be sure what their fellow Americans would do in the privacy of the voting booths? This, after all, was the same country where only a few decades ago patriots who had put their lives on the line to help make the world safe for democracy in two world wars were made to sit at the back of the bus.

One evening while I was sitting in a hotel bar with other journalists someone pointed out a poignant historical quirk in the doubts about a possible Obama presidency expressed or implied by the black Americans we had met. In the 1960s some Catholic Americans felt that the country was not yet prepared to elect the Catholic John Kennedy to the White House. Indeed, Cardinal Richard Cushing, a close Kennedy friend and benefactory, had openly said so. Some black Americans convinced themselves that a campaign to elect a black president might backfire and ultimately harm the cause of improving race relations.

My failure to find adequate responses to those doubts encouraged points to be made with greater emphasis. I would be reminded that as recently as 1965 black Americans in the eleven Southern states were unable to vote, let alone be a candidate in a presidential race. Only four years earlier, in July 1961, white supremacists had rained blows down on Freedom Riders seeking to desegregate interstate routes in the South.

It all came back to me when I was taken to a museum on the outskirts of Selma, where permanent displays recalled how oppressive life was for black Americans in the segregated South. Keeping segregation alive was only possible if black men and women were denied the right to vote, because in many Southern states African Americans made up a large percentage of the population; in some they were in the majority.

By boycotting city services black Americans had demonstrated that as a constituency they possessed economic power and were not afraid to use it. Real change, though, could only be achieved if people were given the opportunity to choose their elected political representatives to sit in city halls or state houses. That's why in places like Selma every effort was made to ensure that blacks were given no such chance. Voter suppression was state policy. Voter registration offices were open for a few unspecified hours every week. There were random late starts and officials had unpredictable lunch hours. If would-be black voters did manage to find an office open for business, they were ritually humiliated in the presence of panels whose members asked questions like the infamous

'How many bubbles are there in a bar of soap?' Nor was that all.

Those who got their names on a Voter List were beaten up or sacked by their employers if they attempted to cast a ballot. Stopping the black vote was the key to keeping power in white hands. It had a profound effect, too, on the way justice was administered. Juries were chosen from voter registration lists and if black people were prevented from getting their names on those lists then it was left to all-white juries to give verdicts on defendants hauled before the courts. It meant that those accused of organised lynching, or of the murder of black churchmen or civil rights workers, were invariably allowed to walk free. It was a time when the white suprema-cist marauders of the Ku Klux Klan roamed the countryside in Southern states, staining the night with unspeakably vile deeds.

Just to make sure I got the point whenever I suggested that even so Obama might still win, I was told that in the American South some memories are long and bitter. I was fully aware of that. But listening to the voices of those who had been involved in some of those events, and who in the general course of their lives had endured the slings and arrows of outrageous state law, was always a chastening experience. William Faulkner observed that in the American South the past is never dead; it isn't even past, he concluded.

All those thoughts kept swimming through my mind as I walked among the crowds on the Mall, talking to people on Inauguration Day. It seemed that everyone wanted to talk, especially when I said I worked for British television.

I came across one group of black and white Americans who were reflecting on the fact that Barack Obama had played no part in the battle for civil rights in the 1960s. That marked him out from the handful of black Americans who had chanced their arm in previous presidential races. When Martin Luther King was preaching about that glorious day when black

Americans would be able to say 'Free at last, free at last, thank God we're free at last' and when civil rights activists were being tear-gassed and clubbed in Selma, Montgomery and Memphis, Obama was not even of school age.

His father had been a visiting student from Kenya when he met and married a white teenager from Wichita, Kansas, in Hawaii. Obama senior abandoned his wife soon after the birth of his son and went off to Harvard. Young Barack spent much of his early years with his mother, who married a second time and went to live in Indonesia, and with his maternal grand-parents in Hawaii. Not surprisingly his book *Dreams from My Father* is essentially about a search for identity. He knew what it is to be different. That didn't shield him from the indignity of racial slurs, but it helped him to deal with them. It gave him the confidence to confront the race issue with the honesty and pragmatism that few others in a similar battle for votes could match.

To me that explained his ability to defuse perhaps the big-gest threat to his election when, in March 2008, the Reverend Jeremiah Wright, the pastor who married him and Michelle and at whose church they had worshipped for twenty years, made an inflammatory and widely reported speech denoun-cing racism in America.

Responding to those comments, gleefully seized upon by his opponents, Obama made it absolutely clear that he disagreed strongly with his pastor. He went on to explain, however, that he could no more disown him than he could his white grandmother who had occasionally crossed to the other side of the street on seeing a black man coming towards her. He added: 'I have spent my entire adult life trying to bridge the gap between different kinds of people. That's in my DNA.' It was a response that went to the heart of Obama's run for the presidency. He had embarked on what commentators de-scribed as a 'post-racial' campaign, not as a black man running for president but as a man well-suited to be president who happened to be black. It was his way of attempting to take his candidacy beyond the question of race.

I was at the Democratic Convention in Denver, Colorado, in August 2008 when Obama's nomination faced other questions. He had defeated Senator Hillary Clinton in the Democratic Party's primary contests, but a vocal band of her supporters believed that misogyny had played a part in her defeat, claiming that she was clearly the better standard-bearer for Democrats. So would the Denver convention throw its weight unambiguously behind Obama and anoint him as the nominee or would Senator Clinton and her husband, former President Bill Clinton, and their supporters cause trouble and force the convention to a divisive delegate tally? In that event, Barack Obama might still get the nomination, but a fight for delegates on the convention floor would provide an unedifying spectacle for the television cameras and would hurt his chances in the general election.

The day before the convention in a jostling clutch of reporters I managed to shout a question to Michelle Obama who was familiarising herself with the convention stage. Would there be too much political tension at the convention? Would what should be her husband's coronation turn out to be an uninspiring fight for delegates? Mrs Obama responded calmly. She assured me that the convention would be the image of political unity, and that her husband's nomination would be a formality.

The tension about what the Clintons would do was evident right up to the moment they made their speeches. And then cheered to the rafters by delegates hugely relieved that the party would fight the election totally committed to Obama, Bill and Hillary Clinton left the convention in no doubt that they would campaign unstintingly for the Democratic Party and for Barack Obama. Fortified by his success, Obama chose to make his acceptance speech not in the convention hall but in the much larger Broncos Stadium a few miles away.

Now, four months later, the time had come to speak to the American people as their president.

Incoming presidents probably have more time to work on their inaugural address than they will have to work on speeches at any other time in a four-year term. The speech must rise above party, reach out to the nation at large and set the tone for the new administration. It should also pay due regard to the fine tradition of great inaugurals.

Obama went to the podium with one big advantage. He is a brilliant speaker.

He began by stating the obvious. His administration faced formidable problems. The atmosphere on the Mall could not disguise the state of the American economy. Banks had collapsed, the financial system was in crisis, factories were closing all over the country, millions of jobs were being lost and people were defaulting on their home mortgages in unprecedented numbers. And, of course, gobbling up billions of dollars were the wars against what the new president called the 'far-reaching network of violence and hatred'. That was euphemistic shorthand for America's war in Iraq, which Obama had always described as a war of choice, and, the one he favoured, the military commitment to Afghanistan.

The economic outlook was bleak, but the president summoned Americans to emulate the spirit of the men and women who, in the earliest years of the nation's founding, had sacrificed much and given their lives to help make America 'the most powerful nation on Earth'. He spoke in praise of that nation's patchwork heritage as a source of strength not weakness, shaped, he said, by every language and culture and drawn from every part of the world. He challenged the Muslim world to join him in seeking a new way forward based on mutual interest and mutual respect and in a soaring passage he said what his election symbolised. 'This is the meaning of our liberty and our creed – why men and women and children of every race and every faith can join the celebration across this magnificent mall, and why a man whose father less than sixty years ago might not have been served at a local restaurant can now stand before you to take a most sacred oath.'

We had been waiting to hear how the new president would address the race issue. He had done it in a sweep of grand oratory, and it won him one of the biggest ovations of the afternoon.

In the final part of his speech Obama quoted George Washington who, at the lowest point of the Revolutionary War in 1776, told his troops: 'Let it be told to the future world . . . that in the depth of winter, when nothing but hope and virtue could survive . . . that the city and the country, alarmed at one common danger, came forth to meet it.'

Obama had chosen to end his speech not on a note of triumph, but by adopting a more sombre tone, invoking the spirit of 1776, to prepare America for the austerity of the economic winter ahead. That theme found an amusing echo in the satirical paper *The Onion*. Its post-inauguration headline read: BLACK MAN GIVEN NATION'S WORST JOB. Perhaps the new president secretly felt the same.

Obama's inauguration address was perfectly pitched. In the sweep of American political history the result of the election described an arc which went all the way back to those attempts by marchers in Selma to cross the Edmund Pettus Bridge and confront the state authorities in Montgomery. That simple proposition of walking across a bridge to demand the basic rights of citizens produced images that stunned the world. Now a presidential election had done the same and it had come to symbolise 'what comes at the end of that bridge'. I kept hugging myself partly to keep out the cold but also because I was there to see that end.

Inauguration Day 2009 was my last Washington trip as an ITN journalist. The beginning of the Obama presidency marked the end of my career in television news. I was overcome by a strange melancholy walking away from the Mall that day and leaving Washington. I had relished every moment as a working journalist in the United States and was sad to think I would not be returning to the nation's capital in that capacity again.

I have always felt that no other country on earth proclaims such an attachment to the ideals of freedom and liberty. Frequently and conspicuously, the United States falls short of applying those principles to the lives of all its peoples, and yet there is something magnificent about a country that welcomed many of its new immigrants with a Statue of Liberty, a 'mighty woman with a torch' who according to Emma Lazarus's poem cries 'with silent lips':

> Give me your tired, your poor,
> Your huddled masses yearning to breathe free . . .
> Send these, the homeless, tempest-tost to me . . .

However many times I've heard them I have always been moved to tears by the eloquent humanity of these words. They express a hope, and a belief in a glorious vision. They embody the finest spirit of what all nations should strive to be. They grace the shoulders of what is still a great country.

In no other place I know do senior politicians and government officials see it as part of their duty to be accessible to journalists. That for me goes to the heart of democratic responsibility. But then, too, where else in the world could reporting politics be such fun? With what can you compare being given a seat, however far back, on Air Force One as President Ronald Reagan campaigned for re-election on a swing through North and South Carolina and the Rocky Mountain states? In Washington President Clinton once agreed to see me at the White House for ten minutes, turned up late and stayed talking for thirty, and just before the second fateful war with Iraq, President Bush the younger, much preferring to walk rather than to talk about why he was so determined to take America into another Middle East war, took me, cameras in tow, for part of my allotted time with him, on a tour of the West Wing and the Oval Office. The president understood the value of the privilege I had been given.

Nearing the end of what turned out to be, much to my surprise, a memorable afternoon in the company of the president, I suggested that he was referring to me, a little too frequently, as 'Sir Trevor'. He did it repeatedly and in every sentence. Half in jest, I felt I should remind him that such titles were no part of life in a republic such as the United States. Attempting to convince him to call me only by my first name, I went on to say that titles like mine were not always merited and that in some cases they were worthless. His response was immediate and emphatic, 'No, no, you mustn't say that. My father has one.' I had forgotten entirely that President George Herbert Walker Bush had some years earlier been given an Honorary Knighthood by her Majesty the Queen. I found no words to hide my embarrassment at such a clumsy blunder.

As I left, he told me with a huge guffaw that I would be the envy of every White House correspondent. For a short time I was. And for a much longer time I wished I could tell my mother about those moments I shared with the president of the United States.

I've been asked a hundred times what I've enjoyed most about my career as a reporter and I've always fallen back on a stock reply. It has given me front-row seats at some of the biggest international political events of my time. Watching Barack Hussein Obama take the oath of office as forty-fourth president of the United States was, as I have said before, one of those and one I never thought I'd see in my lifetime.

My mind kept drifting back to how far America had travelled.

In his book about John Kennedy, Thurston Clarke noted that at Roosevelt's 1933 inauguration African Americans had danced at a 'Colored People's Ball', and that at the Truman and Eisenhower inaugurations black people were tokens. In 1961 five hundred African Americans served on inaugural committees and five thousand attended an inauguration that *Ebony* praised for having 'more Negro participation than any other in history'.

Now a black man had become more than a participant. He had stolen the show and taken over the shop as president and commander in chief.

Perhaps for the first time I felt a little cheated that I had not been in America to report earlier phases of the battle for racial equality, the partial success of which had resulted in what we had seen in Washington on that emotionally charged afternoon. I was giving in to a journalistic fallacy. We like to believe we reported events in their totality, to think we saw the beginning and the end. But I was never in Selma or Memphis or Montgomery at the time of the marches and I thought how amazing it would have been to be able to say that I had witnessed the events of those hate-filled years and was now able to report the dawn of a more hopeful future. I would have completed that journalistic circle. I might even have glimpsed the mountain top.

Somewhat greedily, I suppose, I envied those who had been part of the life of those strife-torn cities and who were alive on that day in 2009. I understood those who speculated about what Martin Luther King would have made of Obama's victory. Would Dr King have thought it possible when, in March 1965, Lyndon Johnson, who had voted against every civil rights bill – even those aimed at ending lynching – changed tack and urged Congress in uncompromising language to pass a voting rights act? That night on Capitol Hill, Johnson adopted the great civil rights anthem as his own and, recalling the clashes between state troopers and marchers, said: 'What happened in Selma is part of a far larger movement which reaches into every section and state of America.' Their cause, said Johnson, 'must be our cause too, because it is not just Negroes, but really it is all of us who must overcome the crippling legacy of bigotry and injustice'.

According to an account of that evening given by Johnson's biographer Robert Caro, the president paused for effect, and then stunned his audience by saying: 'And we shall overcome.' Johnson then walked down the aisle acknowledging the out-stretched hands of members of Congress while at the same time leaving them in no doubt that he meant what he had said and that they should sit day and night if necessary to enact the legislation.

Here was the occasion, surely, when a few of those dazzling points of light pierced the darkness of the road to racial equal-ity and made an Obama presidency possible. I could not stop myself thinking back to those stages on the journey. I had read an account of the Johnson speech when I was still a reporter in Trinidad. I could hardly believe that the old Texan politi-cal operator had ended his speech with the words of Martin Luther King.

Almost a hundred years before Obama's election, President Woodrow Wilson hailed America's uniqueness, its exceptional qualities. Talking to a group of newly naturalised citizens from all over Europe, he described America as the only country that experiences a 'constant and repeated rebirth'. Wilson was re-ferring to the way successive waves of immigrants from every corner of the world had added a new dynamism to the pulse of American life. Those words conveyed a meaning perhaps even deeper than the president knew at the time.

Long after the crowds began to disperse and darkness en-veloped the Washington Mall on that cold January day in 2009, what still hung in the air was a powerful sense of America's ability to reinvent itself, to allow its many peoples the time and the space to dream dreams of better days and to see them partly realised. What we had witnessed was nothing less than the ability of a nation to embrace the kind of change that never fails to astonish.

In his novel *The Invisible Man*, written in the 1950s, long before the dreams of Martin Luther King, Ralph Ellison squares up to the issue of racial injustice and put these words into the mouth of one of his main characters: 'America is woven of many strands . . . Our fate is to become one and yet many – this is not prophecy but description.'

The new president could not have put it better.

But politics is the oddest of addictions. It never moves in a straight line. It turns in unpredictable ways and has a way of stopping journalists in their tracks.

Although no longer regularly assigned to the country as a reporter I've been back to the United States frequently enough to observe the glory of Obama's inauguration eclipsed by the harsher realities of American political life.

The birth of the right-wing Tea Party so intimidated Republican members of the House of Representatives and the Senate that they decided to adopt a policy of outright opposition to any and everything Obama said or did, to any legislative measure proposed by his administration. Republicans were prepared to paralyse Capitol Hill and effectively shut down the Federal government rather than strike a compromise with the new president – about anything. I became convinced that Republican attitudes went beyond politics.

What was surprising was how shamelessly open the rage at Obama's election became. The Republican leader in the Senate said it was his party's intention to make sure that Obama became a one-term president. And in an unprecedented outburst at one point during the president's State of the Union address to Congress one member shouted at him, 'You lie!' The legislature had seen nothing like it in its history. It shrieked naked hatred.

Following these events on the other side of the Atlantic, I became convinced that something else was at work. Some Republicans were unable to hide their disgust at the fact that a black man had been elected president and commander in chief. I am not alone in coming to this view.

A recent analysis by Alan I. Abramowitz, a political scientist from Emory University, discusses the factors likely to make a citizen a Tea Party supporter. He acknowledges that conservative ideology comes first. A close second, though, he concludes, is racial resentment and dislike of Obama. This is Abramowitz's phrasing of his assessment:

> These results clearly show that the rise of the Tea Party movement was a direct result of the growing racial and ideological polarisation of the American electorate. The Tea Party drew its support very disproportionately from Republican identifiers who were white, conservative, and very upset about the presence of a black man in the White House – a black man whose supporters looked very different from themselves.

When the noise of the carnival that greeted Obama's inauguration died away, those words, sadly, might be the last on the true significance of the election of the first black president of the United States. Something had changed in America but not in the way we thought on Inauguration Day. The very fact of a black president has led to a coarsening of the political discourse. The incendiary language employed by many of Obama's opponents needs no decoding.

In 2011, when the billionaire businessman Donald Trump thought of running for the presidency, he openly questioned whether Barack Obama was an American citizen. In one of his typical campaign rants Trump demanded that Obama produce his birth certificate for public inspection, this despite the fact that the document had been publicly available for years.

Trump knew precisely what he was doing. Quite simply, he could not resist finding a way to refer snidely to the president's race. He knew the code and knew that his listeners knew it, too. They understood precisely what he meant. Race baiting in

America has always had a language of its own.

It is tempting to dismiss any significance of this by saying it is what Donald Trump does. In one of his books about his life he says plainly: 'I play to people's fantasies.' A few years later, in 2015, he was doing the same thing in the way he spoke about immigration – playing to people's fantasies about murderous Mexican gangs polluting white America with their foul deeds. He went further. He talked about building a wall to keep Mexicans out and even more audaciously about charging the cost of its construction to the Mexicans themselves.

Today, as president, Donald Trump sticks to his anti-Obama theme. When he criticises the Affordable Health Care Act he calls it 'Obamacare', not to point out its failings but to emphasise his hatred for his predecessor's name. And when he alludes falsely to the size of the crowds at his inauguration he aims to make another cheap, mean-spirited attack on America's first black president. He now finds it impossible to disguise his disgust that Obama, too, once held the highest office in the land.

The basis of coded references to a black man in the White House could not be clearer. In January 2008, Obama won the South Carolina Democratic primary largely because of the high turnout of black American voters. American journalists immediately alighted on the political significance of the fact that a state in the Deep South known for its conservative views had given a black candidate a big push in his attempt to get to the White House. Very soon after the inauguration Obama's opponents began talking about 'taking our country back'.

That sentiment was not dissimilar to words attributed to the young lunatic Dylann Roof, who, on a day in late June 2015, sat quietly in the Emanuel African Methodist Episcopal Church in Charleston, South Carolina, before shooting and killing nine black churchgoers. According to one of the worshippers, Roof, who confessed to the murders, told one of those he eventually killed: 'You are raping our women and taking over the country. And you have to go.'

Republicans seeking their party's nomination in the 2016 presidential campaign also spoke about 'taking our country back'. It has assumed the status of the party's mantra. Trump's version of the same thought is 'making America great again'.

Jon Stewart, once host of *The Daily Show* on American television, famous for mixing his weekly digest of the news with a hefty slice of comedy, made the point that the church killings were another example of a 'a gaping racial wound' in American life 'that will not heal but we pretend doesn't exist'.

In a eulogy to church victims President Obama sang 'Amazing Grace' and talked about the growing racial divide in his country. He mentioned Republican attempts to introduce new voting rights that would make it more difficult for black Americans to vote. He talked about police brutality towards black communities. In the first seven months of 2015, according to figures published by the *Washington Post*, twenty-four unarmed black men were killed by police. In 2014, forty-three-year-old Eric Garner, an asthmatic, had been arrested in Staten Island for selling loose cigarettes. He had been held in an illegal chokehold and had repeatedly cried out to officers: 'I can't breathe.' Those words became a rallying cry of a nationwide protest movement against police killings. In a recent interview, the Reverend Jesse Jackson, who in 1984 and 1988 was a candidate for the Democratic Party's presidential nomination, long-time civil rights campaigner and close associate of Martin Luther King, told the *Guardian* newspaper: 'Black men, it's obvious, we are targeted more by police.' After the shootings in Ferguson, Baltimore, New York and Charleston, Jackson suggested that there had been no discernible upward curve in improving race relations since Barack Obama's inauguration. To the contrary, he concluded that America's first black president confronted the same challenges faced by Lyndon Johnson in the brutal days of the civil rights marches in Selma and Montgomery and by Abraham Lincoln in the bloody battle to abolish slavery in the American South.

President Obama has frequently talked about Martin Luther King's 'the arc of the moral universe' that bends inevitably towards freedom and justice. What he means, I believe, is that progress to end the most obvious and abusive forms of discrimination may not come in a discernibly straight line. There will be twists and turns and curves and bumps along the way. Putting to one side the philosophical root of that idea, it is depressing to see in America today evidence of the racism of the past.

In Southern states like North Carolina and Alabama, voting rights for black Americans are again under threat. They conceivably clouded the result of the presidential and congressional elections in 2016. Altogether seventeen states announced new rules which civil rights activists described as 'an all-out retrogressive attack on voting rights'. The states are doing nothing illegal. But they're up to their old tricks again. Voters must show one of several eligible photo IDs to cast a ballot. Offices where such identification could be presented are open infrequently, if at all.

This was not the future I envisaged when I walked among the crowds on Barack Obama's Inauguration Day. It was a sad end to a moment of the most hopeful promise.

Obama's election as president of the United States *did* make history. Perhaps it was not quite the history we imagined.

Martin Luther King talked about the 'tranquilizing drug of gradualism'. Perhaps in the end Obama's election to his country's highest office was much less of the dramatic change we considered and merely another step in the still gradual pace of real change. Such is the sorrow and the pity.

2

A Trinidad Apprentice

'To strive, to seek, to find and not to yield.'
          Alfred, Lord Tennyson, 'Ulysses'

Nothing in my early life suggested that I might one day find myself in Washington reporting on the inauguration of America's first black president.

The island on which I was born in 1939, and where I spent my early years, sits on the continental shelf of South America and lies at the end of a long curving chain of islet stepping stones which begin to sweep southward a few hundred miles from the jutting tip of North America. Cuba is a mere ninety miles away, and with Jamaica and the smaller Leeward and Windward Islands it begins to form a necklace hugging and enclosing the blue waters of the Caribbean.

This is how Columbus must have seen them in the late fifteenth century, as did Cromwell's expeditionary force 150 years later. Some islands appeared mountainous, others heavily forested and rugged, all palm-fringed and alluring with only the sound of the rolling waves crashing on spotlessly white beaches.

But geography can be deceptive.

By any measure of wealth, modernity or international prominence, these tiny outposts of the age of European expansionism had little in common with North America. The

Trinidad of my youth, with a population of just over a million souls, might just as well have been part of another universe, light years away from the United States.

It used to be said that we West Indians lived in America's 'backyard'. That was true, but it referred more to a doctrine of international politics and in reality it had little to do with our day-to-day lives. If it was ever supposed to imply conspicuous benevolence on the part of America we saw nothing of that. Washington's sole interest was that our governments did nothing to challenge its concept of regional security. Our islands were tiny specks in the giant shadow of a world superpower and were expected to behave accordingly.

Not too many Trinidadians are aware of the fact, for example, that when, in the 1990s, a few years after I left the island, a politically minded, aggressive Muslim group seized the Parliament building in Port of Spain and held the prime minister and members of his government hostage, the insurrection was brought to an end by the Americans. A crack team of fully armed security operatives flew in unannounced and demanded that their plane be allowed to land. The runways had been blocked but the Americans insisted on entry and, given the green light by a small group of government ministers, immediately assumed control. Within hours of their arrival the visitors intercepted all communications from the Muslim group and were able to listen to everything that transpired in the besieged Parliament building. At one point the Americans felt sufficiently confident to offer to 'take out' the hostage-takers. Local politicians demurred and the crack American team gradually wore the hostage-takers down. The crisis ended quickly and the Americans left as discreetly as they'd arrived, making no declarations and having scrubbed their hotel rooms clean. They left no trace of the fact that they'd been in Port of Spain or anywhere near the Trinidad Parliament building.

Ronald Reagan assumed the identical American posture

in 1983 when an elected government in Grenada, much too friendly with Cuba for Washington's liking and with a pronounced socialist agenda, spawned political unrest in the tiny country. On the pretext of protecting American medical students at a university in the capital, St George's, Reagan sent in the troops. Grenada had been a British colony and maintained its relations with Britain as a member of the Commonwealth, yet not even the British prime minister, Reagan's friend Margaret Thatcher, had been informed of the intended invasion.

So little did the troops know about Grenada that when they took the island's governor-general into their custody they were totally baffled and were forced to seek clarification from the Foreign Office in London about the status of a native Grenadian claiming to be the Queen's representative. He was Paul Scoon, and he had appeared in all his formal regalia.

I remember being in Washington at the time and managed to contact a former prime minister of Grenada who was living in exile in DC. My colleague Jon Snow and I had great fun listening to the charming but slightly out of touch Eric Gairy explain, with a politician's eye to the main chance, why he should be returned to his island home immediately to restore order and to end the crisis which had prompted Reagan to send in the Marines.

Fortunately, even under America's stern gaze, the horizons of small-island people extend beyond their physical boundaries and the perception of others. We islanders look outwards and our gaze takes us to points beyond the edge of our hemmed-in existence, beyond the parameters of our daily lives.

There's also something in the nature of small islanders that inhibits too much introspection. Perhaps there's probably not enough to be too introspective about. We are persistently driven by thoughts of self-advancement and live in hope that, from somewhere beyond our shores, something unexpected would turn up to spur us on to making it and making it big. People born in such distant corners of the world frequently allow themselves, in George Bernard Shaw's words, to 'dream things that never were' from somewhere out there.

That in part is the genesis of my story. And not only mine. It's an experience echoed down through the corridors of West Indian life and is heard in the voices of West Indian writers. In fiction and in poetry they summon memories of the warm shores by which they were born, if only as points of departure for journeys to far-flung towns and cities to begin new lives among new people in lands of biting winds, slanting rain and snow. That is the bittersweet rhapsody of Caribbean life. The luxuries of sun and sea and the charm of a tropical existence largely untroubled by vexing international issues are not the ideal they may at first appear. All too soon they come to be seen as a pattern of life that is easy but too unhooked from the real world and altogether too restricting. It lacks the attritional grit that nags away at the edges of the human spirit, challenging it to do better.

* * *

I was introduced to poetry at a very early age and loved it. We were made to learn poems by rote and to recite them, sometimes in their entirety. I fell under the spell because I revelled in the glory of the language. I thought poetry, as I was taught it, expressed the English language in its finest form. Even now I can recall those glorious lines in 'Ulysses' by Tennyson where the mythical hero talks about the end of his life and he says:

> Tho' much is taken, much abides; and tho'
> We are not now that strength which in old days
> Moved earth and heaven, that which we are, we are,
> One equal temper of heroic hearts,
> Made weak by time and fate, but strong in will
> To strive, to seek, to find, and not to yield.

Not all my schoolmates felt that this was a useful way to spend one's time, but I loved it. And it has always been a part of my life. I remember when I was terrified going into war zones in the Middle East and, for that matter, spending time in the early seventies in Northern Ireland. The one thing I always carried with me was a book of poems, and I would console myself by reading poetry when all the noise and violence was around us.

Almost everyone I knew in my childhood talked of breaking through the bonds of island life, of getting out and moving on. If someone in a regular circle of friends hadn't been seen for two or three weeks the first thought was that he or she had probably gone off to London, New York or Toronto. These places danced longingly in the imagination, dangling the promise of a better future. We weren't always sure what that future might be or precisely how it would be better, but we hoped that it might be one that fulfilled our dreams.

Thousands of my fellow West Indians moved among the islands in search of work. One destination in the early 1900s was Panama, where construction of the famous canal presented opportunities for thousands. Work on other capital projects in Latin and Central America encouraged West Indians to try their luck in other countries.

My father opted to stay in the Caribbean, but he, too, left his island home in Grenada to travel to Trinidad and work in the oil industry. Grenada's economy was built around small agricultural holdings. It was never sufficiently labour-intensive. A number of my father's contemporaries fixed their sights on more distant pastures. The very young and the very brilliant were encouraged in their late teens to seek admission to universities abroad. Every year two young Trinidadians were offered island scholarships to Oxbridge. Those who failed to scale those academic heights sought places at other British, American or Canadian institutions.

West Indian ambition was not limited to the groves of

academe. It led to the exploration of a variety of other avenues.

There were times when it seemed to me that everyone was anxious to prove that he or she could do better. The atmosphere crackled with aspiration. I so clearly remember being stopped on my walk to school on some mornings by a middle-aged road sweeper who was keen to impress me with his ability to spell difficult words. 'Give me a word, any word, and I will spell it correctly and quickly.'

After a while I thought I understood what the man was doing. He was in effect telling me that, since he could spell, he could do better than road-sweeping. I suppose it was his way of expressing the desire to do something else, to aspire to a better life.

Context first.

I was brought up to believe in the importance of success. That is crucial to any self-examination. It framed the approach to almost everything I did. I sought my version of success with passion, ambition and at times with barely concealed desperation.

Determined to be a success, I set off on the path to achieving it with uncompromising zeal. That created all sorts of problems and affected the lives of those close to me, not always for the better. This is an admission I make without qualification if for no other reason than that it would be useless to pretend otherwise. It would be equally useless to try to make excuses for that now.

Without wishing to saddle anyone with the responsibility or the blame for the way I pursued my career and lived my life, it's important to say this: it was drilled into me in the West Indies of my youth that striving ceaselessly to be very good at whatever you chose to do was not only the way to achieving a measure of social mobility but the equal of survival itself. I came to believe that blindly, profoundly. I was a willing convert to that belief.

Conversely, I was told, few options were left to those deemed to have failed. Quietly mocked or, even worse, conspicuously ignored for not having made it, they simply fell off the cliff face. There were no soft landings – no safety nets – and in the country in which I was born no system of state help to cushion the fall. Nor was there any obvious forgiveness for failing.

Admittedly, in practical terms, the West Indian tradition of the extended family was generally supportive. In a climate where the seasons were kind and there was no need to think of keeping warm during long, dismal winters, and in an age when the word 'community' still had real meaning, it was always possible to eke out a tropical existence of sorts.

But getting by, surviving only in the margins, carried the stigma of failure and the signs were unmistakable.

It may not have been easy to define success. The stench or even the suspicion of failure, on the other hand, could be detected a mile away. It hung in the air like the plague. Failure carried the mark of Cain. It was a curse stamped in bold letters on foreheads, visible to all and mocked by all. People you know struggled to avoid eye contact and walked by on the other side of the road.

The poet Philip Larkin muses somewhere about lives permanently haunted by fear of failure. He might have been writing about mine. I lived with a nagging fear that I might not make it, without ever defining in my own mind what making it was. At times it came close to self-administered torture. I am conscious that even when it is put that way I may be letting myself off too lightly. It would be no exaggeration to say that my life was almost crippled by insecurity. That feeling was permanent, and was from time to time eased only by constant striving and ceaseless work and by thoughts of ceaseless work.

I never did manage to wean myself off what appeared to be an uneasy tryst with destiny.

Today the one thing that never fails to astonish me is that, despite all that mental baggage, in some respects I survived professionally. It is even more astonishing when other professionals convince me that I have. I constantly brush aside the cobwebs of the past wondering if I could have done better. Could this all be attributable to the fact that I grew up in a quiet, dirt-poor backwater in the West Indies and then chose to live in the harsher, more unforgiving spotlight of metropolitan London? Possibly. What is indisputable is that dire warnings of the fate awaiting those who did not live up to popular notions of success followed and at times haunted me all my life.

The warnings came early.

They were the subjects of repeated, sternly delivered parental lectures. My mother by way of emphasis could point to significant failures by name, and frequently did. She was not alone, and she did not mean to be uncaring or unkind. I am as certain as I am of anything that it was done with nothing but love – tough love, tough working-class West Indian love. It was an expression of the way parents viewed the impossibly difficult world that lay beyond our distant island outpost. What parents of my generation of West Indians drummed into us represented their view of what their offspring needed to do to survive.

Looking back at it now it makes some sense.

I was born in Trinidad at the outbreak of the Second World War. The actions of a Nazi maniac were changing the world I had come into. War did not fade into history as we had been led to believe it would, and an entire continent was bathed in blood. Trinidadians, in true colonial spirit, were volunteering in droves to cross the Atlantic to fight for the mother country and for what Churchill called freedom and Britain's survival as a nation race. We felt connected to that fight and compelled to join it.

I have dim memories of young men, bound for the war in Europe, training in our village. Unless I am mistaken, I saw them patrolling around our backyards. My parents would have been acutely aware of the dangerous international waters in which their children would have to navigate their lives.

Every family in our neighbourhood could recite mournful tales of young people without ambition, who, having never applied themselves sufficiently well, tried to buck the system and ended up drifting through lives of aimless desperation, of finding themselves on the scrap heap, in many instances in and out of prison.

I grew up with frightening visions of a fate I knew I had to avoid at all costs. Work hard. Aim high. Shoot for the stars. Be the best that you can be. An infinite variety of those burdensome admonitions was ritually driven into my skull. They formed the drumbeat to my early life. They were meant to be encouraging and were in all probability the finest expressions of parental care. But they terrified me.

For long periods of my adolescence they were a source of pure terror and sent me spinning into spasms of scary introspection. But in the end, of course, I was duly admonished. I fell into line.

For a young Trinidadian in the late 1950s and early 1960s finding a position in radio journalism and later in the television industry, as I wanted to do above all else, was not the easiest proposition. For one thing it defied the more accepted route to success by training for the law or becoming a doctor. Engineering or accountancy were fine, too. Never for a moment did I contemplate any of those professions. From the age at which I consciously thought of doing anything as work I wanted to be a radio reporter. That was a long time before television came to Trinidad. We lived by radio news. I wanted to be a part of doing the news.

I don't know if the phenomenon was unique to Trinidad but when local radio stations became popular after the Second World War, Radio Trinidad was inundated with applications from people wishing to become announcers. Few thought about radio journalism. They just wanted to be on the radio. On some days the number of people waiting to be auditioned could be counted in the hundreds. In my mind's eye I can still summon up images of the scenes outside the offices of the radio station in Port of Spain, snaking lines of hopeful applicants mumbling impatiently, shuffling along in the acute discomfort of the mid-morning heat to be given the chance to prove themselves.

What awaited them once they sat in front of the microphone in the cool, unnerving silence of the studio was a test designed by a masochist with a mischievous sense of humour. They were confronted by rambling paragraphs, sprinkled with difficult names of famous composers, artists and foreign heads of state, devised to weed out mercilessly those unsuited to reading the news or anything else with the required conviction.

My compatriots were undeterred. Back they came time and time again to accept the challenge of intoning meaningless sentences wrapped around names like Beethoven and Berlioz, Goethe and Nietzsche and places like Ouagadougou. Everyone in Trinidad, it seemed, craved a position in what was felt to be the relatively easy and popular business of radio announcing. The competition appeared formidable if only by the weight of sheer numbers.

For me there was a more serious problem. The best jobs went to expatriates from the United Kingdom, Canada or Australia. They were imported into the islands in a steady flow. This was not an anti-West Indian conspiracy. Those countries were considerably larger than our tiny island, with a greater pool of experienced broadcasters and, of course, we were all part of the large family of Commonwealth nations. Why bother with training local broadcasters when there was already a large pool abroad, willing and able to spend a few years working in an island in the sun? To top it all, Radio Trinidad was owned by a British company with its headquarters in London. Game, set and match!

The people who came to work in Trinidad were almost without exception professionally competent and helpful to young, native broadcasters, but their presence in our fledging industry meant that fewer positions were open to locals and that in turn fuelled the perception that there was a colour bar to getting some jobs. It was in some cases more than mere perception.

That didn't sit too well with Trinidad's reputation as a place where peoples from widely different cultures – natives who had originally been brought from Africa or India as slaves or indentured servants, and British, Spanish, French, Portuguese, Chinese and Syrian expatriates among them – lived in settled harmony and where discrimination was a scourge suffered by countries less fortunate than our own. That boast, repeated ad nauseam especially to visitors of our island home, was never entirely true. In fact, in several respects it was glaringly untrue.

I have never forgotten one example of that aspect of Trinidadian life. It had nothing to do with finding a job in broadcasting but was nevertheless revealing about an enduring facet of Trinidadian life. There was, early in the 1960s, sometime after Trinidad had gained political independence from Britain and at a time when there was reason to think that the worst of colonial attitudes begun to subside, an incident at the Port of Spain Country Club.

Two Americans staying just around the corner at the Hilton Hotel were allowed to book a tennis court at the club over the telephone but on arrival were inexplicably turned away. They should have been allowed to play. The courts were not all being used. They were nevertheless given a cock and bull story and never got past reception.

The reason for the outrageous snub was quickly established. It had not occurred to the club employee who accepted the booking that visitors from the United States or tennis players with American accents were not all uniformly white! The Americans had been allowed to book the court but not to play because they were black.

News of the incident leaked and spread across Port of Spain like wildfire. It dealt a shattering blow to local pride, exposed

some social divisions which were well known but only infrequently remarked upon and embarrassed the Trinidad and
Tobago government into rushing through the Parliament
legislation to outlaw discrimination on the grounds of race or
colour.

The government reaction was commendable, but the cat
was out of the bag. Race relations and the view that Trinidad
was a place of good-natured harmony among its variety of
peoples were not as they were cracked up to be. And what was
extraordinary was that this had happened not in Mississippi or
in Alabama or in Georgia in the American Deep South, but
in the capital of a newly independent Caribbean island where
the majority of the population was black.

It exposed the casual acceptance of social divisions based on
perceived class, cultural origin or more decisively on colour.
For decades the country club had been an oasis of white
expatriate privilege. Local people knew this and accepted it
grudgingly. No one made too much of a fuss. Indeed, many
club members were Trinidadian – of the right colour, of course.

The country club had been allowed to exist and to thrive. It
was hugely popular among its own set. It took the experience
of two black Americans to put a stick of dynamite under its
unchallenged status.

Of greater consequence to me was the fact that the incident
shone a none-too-flattering light on a side of Trinidadian life
that went beyond not being allowed to hit tennis balls on the
clay courts of the country club. These same attitudes played
a part in the jobs people did and it was strongly hinted – perhaps much more than hinted – that these prejudices were
particularly evident when locals attempted to find jobs in the
media.

Many years later, in conversations with colleagues and
friends in London about race relations in Britain, I was in the
habit of making the point succinctly. The Trinidad in which
I grew up had a colour problem. There were no big protests

about it, no marches through the streets of the capital demanding fair treatment for all Trinidadians. My compatriots were not much given to such shows of frustration or anger. We had tamely allowed ourselves to slip into a benign acceptance of the way things were.

My parents, more aware of these entrenched prejudices years before they dawned on me, worried that I might never succeed in getting a job at either of the island's radio stations. Waving away their concerns as young people do, I ploughed on. It was what I wanted to do, and nothing was going to stand in my way. I suppose deep down in the flush of youthful ambition, I refused to bow to the notion that I could be prevented from doing a job I wanted to do in the country of my birth.

All that may have counted for little but for a stroke of luck.

The man who gave me my first job and who became my mentor was one of the few native Trinidadians at the time to have broken through barriers, real or perceived, to reach the top of the broadcasting ladder. Ken Gordon, my first boss at Radio Trinidad, took an interest in me and my work and gave me the benefit of his time and wisdom.

We had always had something in common. Years after I met him he told me that he too was told that he'd never succeed in getting a job at Radio Trinidad because of the colour of his skin.

I survived by applying what's required in any profession – persistence and hard work, aided by the faith and assistance of countless friends and colleagues and by the indulgence of my family.

One of the enduring memories of my early years is listening to groups of young Trinidadians who were either unemployed or who worked fitfully, sitting around on balmy evenings plotting to travel illegally to Venezuela. The plan, if it can be called that, was to make the journey by sea. It would not be easy. The first problem was that these hopeful adventurers – usually four or five in number – owned not a single serviceable vessel among them. They would have to steal one of the ramshackle fishing boats bobbing idly on the shoreline near our village, left unattended while their owners were asleep.

In my mind's eye I can still see the spreading trees under which the young men sat, and I still recall the drift of nervous conversations sprinkled with flecks of audacity about how the stolen boat would be cut from its moorings and silently hauled out to sea before anyone could sound the alarm. As someone whose natural caution borders on cowardice, and who equates stealing a boat at night with robbing a high-street bank in broad daylight, I saw the enterprise as reckless, fraught with all manner of danger and doomed to fail. I convinced myself that the less delusional among the planners must have felt the same.

And yet something drove these young hopefuls to believe that their half-baked schemes were worth the risk. They, too, were responding to the tug of ambition.

Venezuela, the country to which they were hoping to steal away, has the largest oil reserves in the Western world. In that one fact it appeared to offer the prospect of more jobs than these men could ever hope to find in Trinidad. If those who managed to get that far didn't like what they saw of the capital Caracas, they could pack their bags again and hitch a ride to some other city in some other country. Venezuela was part of the vast South American landmass and could be a jumping-off point to other places and to greater employment possibilities than there were on any Caribbean island.

At various times it came too easily to my immature mind to scoff at such far-fetched designs to leave our island home. On reflection, the men in my village who sat around planning an improbable future in a country about which they knew little were driven by the same quest, the same gleams of opportunity that have stirred the hearts of aspiring migrants in their millions throughout the ages.

In pursuit of one chance to make a fresh start in a larger country, young Trinidadians were willing to put a stake on unpredictable ocean currents and gamble with their lives. Not only was the crossing between Trinidad and Venezuela treacherous, my compatriots were to a man ill-equipped to take such a leap into the unknown. With comic tenacity they allowed themselves to be seduced by the notion that, should they ever make it to that friendly, foreign shore, they could, with native wit and cunning, talk their way past any inquisitive Venezuelan immigration official. And they would do it by employing a few elementary Spanish words and phrases – the sum total of their knowledge of the language of the country in which they were hoping to begin a new life.

In short, they were about to venture into a foreign country without proper documents, without permission and with no working knowledge of the language.

I was not around long enough to discover whether anyone actually made the crossing. I heard no reports of successful landings on the other side. Yet, laced with liberal libations of cheap local rum, the planning discussions, or 'old talk' as my mother dismissively described them, went on for hour after hour on long, lazy nights.

The hopeful adventurers had something else in common with a wider spectrum of Trinidadian life. Bluntly stated, generations of young West Indians had been educated for careers away from the Caribbean. They had been taught to think of Trinidad almost as a transit point to a wider, more progressive and more fulfilling world. Not much was ever made of this. It was never necessary to be put it into words. It was considered a natural consequence of the way we were brought up and of all we'd been taught.

Get up and get out to wherever you could. Head off to New York or Toronto. Go to Miami or Los Angeles. Go anywhere, but *go*. Be ambitious. Let your aspirations soar. The island cradle that nurtured you from birth was beautiful, its people were lovely and its appetite for throwing the best parties was legendary, but it had always been too small, and was always a remote part of something larger and something more internationally prominent.

Trinidad never promised to sustain you for life. The land of eternal sunshine was sadly not a land of boundless opportunity.

I do not remember the point during my teenage years at which I talked to school friends or to my parents about leaving Trinidad to try to build a new life abroad. No words were needed. There was an unspoken assumption that many of us would someday leave the nest.

The destination of choice for me was London. It was, after all, the metropolitan centre of Empire and its gravitational pull was as natural as it was irresistible. In my small village in the southern part of the island, to have a son or daughter or any other relative working or studying in London was regarded as a mark of distinction. It didn't matter what that relative did in England.

I remember how surprised I was when I learned that many Trinidadians were content to do quite menial jobs. The real point of significance was that he or she had managed to drop anchor abroad and to survive in a country we thought we knew well.

Trinidad had been British since the late eighteenth century. Britain was last in the line of seafaring adventurers in the era of European expansionism and we young natives were all taught as young English schoolboys had been for centuries. Our textbooks bore the imprimatur of the finest English educational institutions and we were schooled in what we understood to be a decidedly English way. Our social conduct and our sporting values were those of the mother country, or so we were told.

My parents, who had never been to England, and my earliest teachers, who probably had no hope of ever going there, insisted that I spoke 'the King's English'. Lapses into sloppy grammar incurred sharp rebukes. In the playground we were confirmed into the tradition of conducting ourselves as gentlemen, treating victory with magnanimity and accepting defeat with grace. We were told that we should never fail to 'Play up! play up! and play the game!', in the words of Newbolt's poem 'Vitaï Lampada', and that meant playing with stoicism and fairness.

One game stood out by virtue of its perceived cultural superiority and its origins shaped by English history and tradition. Playing cricket well was as close as one got to sporting nirvana. Trinidad's only national newspaper faithfully reported the results of matches played in the English County Championship and saluted the deeds of the finest batsmen and bowlers at Old Trafford and The Oval. Cricket books were regularly serialised in our local newspapers.

In no other game was individual brilliance praised in such glorious prose. We lapped it up. The batsman with immaculate timing was said to be capable of taking the ball 'between the wind and the water'. The action of the finest bowlers came in for equal praise. I knew Trinidadian sports fans who, with little urging, could recite flawlessly from memory the analysis of players' techniques by the celebrated writers Neville Cardus and John Arlott. How could we resist the charm of a game that inspired such flair for the language!

We never tried. We succumbed as meekly as lambs. It was impressed upon us that sport played in the proper spirit enriched the very art of the truly gracious life. Cheating was the most abominable of all the sins and in sport it came close to treason. It never occurred to us that, in the course of drinking in all this, we were being immersed in values not our own – values, in fact, of somebody else's country. With rare exceptions, we embraced them without malice or distrust of their imperialist origins.

Along the way we found some things uniquely Trinidadian to boast about and in which we could take genuine native pride – the ingenuity of the calypso and the inventiveness of the steel band – and we told ourselves and any and every non-Trinidadians who cared to listen that our bacchanalian carnival, around which many of my friends planned an entire year and to which they committed a decent share of their annual income, was unquestionably the best in the world. (I never managed to escape the idea of the lure of Trinidad's carnival. Years after I left Trinidad and was reporting regularly for ITN in various parts of the world, I would, without remembering the significance of the date, turn up at Heathrow. I would almost without fail run into a fellow Trinidadian traveller so pleased to think that I, too, was heading back to Port of Spain for carnival. When, as was usually the case, I disclosed that I was heading off to Beirut or Belfast, nothing much was said but there was a stunned look of consternation and, if I am honest, one of pity.)

In almost every other aspect of our lives, and certainly in our schools, we were taught to look beyond our shores. Island life was a stepping stone to achieving something of genuine worth – somewhere else.

C. L. R. James, the Trinidadian historian, political and cultural polemicist and cricket writer extraordinaire who was a pupil in Port of Spain in the early 1900s, described the effect this had on his education. In *Beyond a Boundary*, a West Indian classic, James reminisces about the time he devoted to the study of English literature: 'Dickens, George Eliot and a whole bunch of English novelists. Followed the poets in Matthew Arnold's selection, Shelley, Keats and Byron; Milton and Spencer.' Then he says he discovered criticism: Hazlitt, Lamb and Coleridge.

By the time he was fourteen, James had read Thackeray's *Vanity Fair* some twenty times and he would, he says, challenge his classmates to open the book at any point to prove that he could finish a paragraph if they gave him only the first few words. It should be said that James was exceptional among the majority of his fellow Trinidadian students and almost certainly better than his contemporaries in England, too! It is, however, a moving evocation of how deeply aspects of English life seeped into the very spirit of young West Indians. James makes no bones about the schizophrenia this promoted in him and perhaps to some degree in us all.

Here he is again writing not about English literature but about playing sport in the West Indies in the English way: 'The British tradition soaked deep into me was that when you entered the sporting arena you left behind you the sordid compromises of everyday existence. Yet for us to do so we would have had to divest ourselves of our skins.'

Whatever we had to divest ourselves of we were happy to do it.

Generations after C. L. R. James's years as a young boy, I was brought up in a similar way. I never came close to reading *Vanity Fair* twenty times, but I fell under the spell of the characters in Charles Dickens' *Great Expectations* and I could quite easily remember salient passages from *Julius Caesar*, *Hamlet*, *Macbeth*, *The Tempest* and *King Lear*. I was made to memorise stanzas from the poems of Milton, Byron, Tennyson, Kipling and Wordsworth and told uplifting stories about the exploits of Nelson, of the grand insouciance of Drake's game of bowls on Plymouth Hoe before setting off to harass the Spanish Armada, and about Raleigh's vain attempt to fill the coffers of the English Treasury with the gold of the fabled Caribbean El Dorado.

Much was made of what seemed the heaven-sent circumstances in which Trinidad became a British colony. Its Spanish occupiers, on sighting the approach of the gallant English fleet and sensing inevitable defeat, scuttled their ships and surrendered meekly. Such tales of conquest confirmed the pre-eminence of all things British. There was little need for us to be taught anything much about West Indian history.

If history is the memory of great deeds by great men and

women, we in the West Indies had little of either to be taught about. So I learned about the Tudors, the Elizabethans and the Victorians, about Clive of India, about the oratory of Burke in his impeachment of Warren Hastings and about Winston Churchill's nation-saving speeches during the Second World War in which he memorialised the spirit of the few who did so much for so many.

We sang 'God Save the Queen', 'Jerusalem' and 'Land of Hope and Glory', praising the ever-widening boundaries of the Empire even though by then its glory was fading. I have vivid memories of standing for hours in orderly lines and in full school uniform on the roadside near our secondary school to catch a fleeting glimpse of Princess Margaret or some other member of the British royal family passing by in an open-top car. I remember classmates falling flat on their faces in the acute discomfort of the mid-morning heat. The royal car whizzed by with a passing glance and a royal wave, those who had fainted were helped back to their feet and in a matter of seconds we trooped back to our classrooms in the same orderly lines. Nobody protested. We did it because we had been ordered to. Our schoolmasters and our parents saw it as part of our identification with life in the mother country.

Perhaps the single most important factor in my decision about the career I chose came from my devotion to the broadcasts from the BBC's World Service in London. Having persuaded my father to buy the first radio we ever owned, a quaint looking box fired into life by an industrial-size battery, I became a World Service addict from about the age of ten or eleven.

I grew to admire and envy the life and work of the BBC's roving correspondents who were sent to major capitals of the world to report on significant political events. Those correspondents travelled to East–West summit meetings in Moscow, Washington and Paris. They covered elections in the Indian subcontinent and outbreaks of civil unrest wherever they occurred; they interviewed the great and the good and their reports were informed by conversations with politicians, diplomats and academics.

Even in those early years I was convinced that the work of those correspondents was crucial to our understanding of international affairs and to the way voters made their choices about how they should be governed. For me the World Service helped to provide some context for the scraps of information of international events I might have picked up from Trinidad newspapers. It was an opening to my small window on the world.

I would be less than honest if I didn't add that I was much taken with the idea of travelling to famous world capitals at someone else's expense. Of course I understood a great deal of it involved hard work. From listening to the adventures of some correspondents I knew some assignments were difficult, even dangerous. But I suppose what attracted me most of all was also what I saw as the glamour of pursuing such a globe-trotting career.

It was everything I wanted to do, and I quickly surmised that it could only be done, it seemed to me, thousands of miles from the confines of my island home. And so to the dismay of my parents, who for admirable reasons had always marked out for me a career in the law or in medicine, I set my sights on roaming the unpredictable but fascinating fields of international political journalism.

My ambition to work in Britain was given an unexpected boost when my first employers at Radio Trinidad sent me to London to report on Trinidad's Independence Conference in 1962. I was not yet twenty-four; I had never been out of the Caribbean and I had been preferred for the assignment over a former politician turned journalist and commentator. The reports I was expected to send from London were to be sponsored by a large Port of Spain firm which favoured the more experienced commentator for the London conference.

There was apparently quite a row about the decision to give me the London assignment and I learned all about it just before I left Trinidad. I had joined Radio Trinidad only a short time before and though of course I was excited, I was disheartened that my first big assignment had occasioned such controversy. I left Trinidad terrified that I might not do the job sufficiently well.

A long English winter, arguably the worst of the century, had done its usual trick of staying well beyond its time and lingering on into late spring. Well wrapped up, I reluctantly left the comfort of my Russell Square hotel room to stand with a clutch of other reporters in the chilly forecourt of Marlborough House at the bottom of Pall Mall. We watched the conference delegations go in, saying nothing, and we were back later in the day to watch them emerge when their deliberations had ended, saying as little as they had when they went in.

The conference press officer, an urbane, pipe-smoking civil servant with a brisk, courteous manner, did his best to assure me that I would miss little or nothing at all if on some days I decided not to turn up at all. I was a little shocked to be told that, although I had begun to form in my own mind a similarly dispiriting view.

I ventured out of London and filed a report on the 1962 Epsom Derby one evening and spent the rest of my time seeking out members of the Trinidad and Tobago delegation at their hotels, in restaurants and in bars, trying to pick up any snippets of information about what went on behind closed doors at Marlborough House. I was about to learn that good reporting requires persistence but thrives on luck.

My luck was in finding one delegate, Sir Learie (later Lord) Constantine, who was willing to share with me on a non-attributable basis what was being discussed at the conference between the representatives from Trinidad and Tobago and those of the British Foreign and Commonwealth Office.

Constantine was perhaps the most famous of my compatriots. He had been a cricket all-rounder of dazzling brilliance. He'd played for Nelson, a club in the Lancashire League, for Trinidad and for the West Indies. He had qualified as a lawyer, was a member of the Trinidad and Tobago legislature and, when Trinidad gained its political independence, would become its high commissioner in London. Constantine was also one of the people to whom my parents continually drew my attention as a way of impressing on me the heights to which Trinidadians from humble origins could ascend. To add a touch of gold to my good fortune Constantine, dignified and charming, was generous to a fault. A routine was agreed between us.

At the end of each conference day we retired to his Mayfair hotel suite where for forty minutes or so he would give me as much information as he thought he could. He was very circumspect about what he could tell me because he was above all a faithful government servant and wary about volunteering too much, but he corrected any misapprehensions I had about how the conference was going and responded frankly to pointed enquiries.

The exercise worked. The great man of the world had taken pity on a cub reporter clearly struggling on his first major assignment.

I had been assigned to prepare a ten-minute nightly radio report (it had been sold to a sponsor and heavily trailed), although the only official information came from a maddeningly terse three- or four-line daily communiqué. Constantine's off-the-record chats filled in some of the spaces and saved my bacon.

The five-hour time difference between London and Port of Spain worked to my advantage, too. My Constantine-assisted evening reports were easily ahead of whatever the next day's Trinidad newspapers said about the Marlborough House meeting and gave my radio station record audiences. Radio was a powerful medium in those days and Trinidadians were keen to follow the course of a London conference called to determine the political future of their small island.

I got a small hint that my conference reports on Radio Trinidad may have hit the mark. At an end-of-conference party at the Mayfair Hotel in London, Dr Eric Williams, a leading Trinidadian academic and politician, asked about the substance of the reports I had been sending back to Trinidad. Not wanting in any way to implicate my source, I mumbled something about how difficult it had been to determine with any accuracy what had gone on behind closed doors at Marlborough House over two weeks. Williams, puffing on his pipe, was having none of it. He said, 'My brother who is a journalist tells me the whole island is glued to what you have to say every night.' I accepted the compliment and hurried off to find another drink.

That conference gave me the taste for reporting big set-piece international events. In its margins I was also given an invaluable lesson about the relationship between big British companies operating in the West Indies and governments in the region. Well before the Trinidad independence deliberations were due to begin, I was asked to present myself at an office in Lower Regent Street to meet Lord Buckhurst, the then chairman of Rediffusion Limited, Radio Trinidad's parent company. I kept the appointment on the agreed day only to find that the chairman had been detained at an earlier engagement and would be late. I sat outside his office for as long as I could, but he never showed up.

By a happy coincidence, on leaving, the cab I hailed in the street outside was the one from which the noble lord alighted. In the freezing rain I introduced myself and we had the briefest of conversations. Lord Buckhurst went straight to the point. 'Look,' he said, 'we in this company think this chap Williams is a good man. He'll certainly be the first prime minister of an independent Trinidad and Tobago when this conference ends, and we don't want to do anything to offend him. So I'm sure you'll remember that in your reports.' With that he was off, as was I into the warmth of the cab.

This was new to me. I'd never before been instructed to ensure that my reports caused no offence, but the chairman's message was clear and made good business sense. Radio Trinidad was a profitable commercial enterprise, part of a family of companies in other islands of the Caribbean and beyond. Its owners – a British company with its headquarters in London – were keen to do nothing to jeopardise their prospects of future profits. My radio station had, to all intents and purposes, been run from the city in which I now found myself. But times were changing. Trinidad was about to become an independent country with its own views about the role of overseas companies and how they should be run. Lord Buckhurst was anxious to ensure that we at Radio Trinidad did nothing to displease the new independent government or its prime minister and I should be aware of that.

It was an introduction to what I was to learn over many years and in much greater detail about the perpetual tension between the owners of media organisations and governments the world over. It was not a difficult instruction to follow. There was, in reality, nothing I could say in my reports to hurt Radio Trinidad's business prospects or harm its relations with the government. I could only report what went on at the conference and what I had been told by my trusted source, Learie Constantine.

But my card had been marked. Lord Buckhurst was taking no chances with his company's profits.

The man Buckhurst referred to in our brief conversation was Eric Williams, the brilliant if somewhat prickly Trinidad historian who had distinguished himself at Oxford. His doctoral dissertation on the abolition of the slave trade attacked the view that moral and humanitarian motives were the key factors in the work of British abolitionists. Williams wrote about the massive contribution the slave trade had made to the British economy in general and in particular to the great Industrial Revolution in Britain and theorised that the trade ended when it was no longer useful to the capitalist enterprise.

In a remarkably short time after his return to Port of Spain in 1956 he had formed a new political party, the People's National Movement. It challenged existing political orthodoxies. Williams brought new faces into his new party, initiated a successful campaign to force the Americans to hand back a naval base they had acquired as part of a Second World War deal with Britain and spearheaded the drive to political independence from the mother country.

From a podium in Woodford Square in the capital, Port of Spain, he explained the independence movement in the context of British colonial history. Plain Woodford Square was rechristened 'The University of Woodford Square'. Williams was not a gifted speaker. His voice was deep, and his tone was flat. His accent was clipped and his manner didactic. But he played the crowds with all the skill of an accomplished politician. He understood Trinidadian passions. At one point he linked the desire for independence from Britain with the historic success of the visiting West Indies cricket team to England in 1950. Almost at a stroke, that transformed a rather scholarly recluse into a man of the people.

No West Indian alive needed to be reminded that their team had beaten England in a Test series for the first time and at Lord's, the spiritual home of cricket. The game in the West Indies was played with religious dedication and success against the mother country was as close as you get to a heavenly blessing. In 1950 the batting deeds of Worrell, Weekes and Walcott and the bowling of Ramadhin and Valentine were celebrated in calypso. Williams translated those deeds into the language of raw politics. To wild cheering he told his Woodford Square admirers: 'On previous tours of England, we went to learn. Now we go to teach. If we can beat England at cricket, we have the ability to govern ourselves.' Did that stretch the point a little? Perhaps. But that's the nature of politics and more to the point it worked for Williams. He had also managed in the run-up to the general election to lift the level of political debate.

In a heady time of change and self-assurance in Trinidad, rival election candidates, accustomed to talking about the price of bread and the availability of running water in tiny country villages, debated the comparative merits of the philosophical schools of Aristotle and Plato. That was the Williams effect. He was after all 'an Oxford man'. Living up to his reputation he would occasionally throw out a Latin phrase or two to a crowd of rural farmers who would rise up from their haunches as one and applaud as appreciatively as if Latin was their mother tongue!

No other Caribbean radio journalists had been sent to London to report the change to Trinidad's political status and Williams, who was generally quite snooty about the local media, was positively happy to speak into my tape recorder when the conference ended to confirm that after 165 years the island was breaking free of its colonial bond. Williams would, as predicted, become Trinidad's first prime minister.

That afternoon in a small room in Marlborough House, he and I had a minor disagreement about how long he should take to make the triumphant declaration of independence, but the final conference session had gone on longer than expected and time was pressing on me. I stood my ground, and Williams climbed down and stuck to the limit I had imposed. Then, with tape recorder under my arm and leads trailing, I rushed out of Marlborough House into Pall Mall and hailed the first taxi to speed me to the London studio for my final radio hook-up to Trinidad.

Back home, the broadcast was received with celebration parties, calypsos and rivers of rum.

The fact that I had been preferred for the London assignment ahead of more experienced colleagues was a boost to my career. Working at a radio station in a small island allowed me the freedom to turn my hand to anything. I excelled at nothing in particular, but I read the news, played records (I was never sufficiently accomplished at this to be called a disc jockey) and I was given the chance to be a sports commentator covering cricket, football, tennis, horse racing and water polo. Never quite certain whether I'd be good at any one thing, I resolved to try doing as many different jobs as I could. It turned out to be the perfect training ground for a young journalist.

I still cringe a little at the memory of having to read death announcements at the end of the news. These were a source of revenue to our company and one senior member of our newsroom staff was assigned the task of making sure that these notices were done to the highest professional standard. We had to be particularly careful about the pronunciation of difficult names and they invariably were difficult. John Smiths seemed immortal. Mispronunciations of more unusual names carried terrible consequences.

A significant feature of the announcements, meant to be delivered in sombre tones and given a kind of faux gravity by the stately lament of Handel's 'Largo' playing in the background, was references to the number of the deceased's relatives who had emigrated to London, New York or Toronto. It was as if a gracious passage into the afterlife was greatly enhanced by the very public boast of having relatives abroad.

The gist of my brief conversation with Lord Buckhurst during the Marlborough House independence deliberations came back to me many months later when I attended an Eric Williams news conference at the prime minister's office in Port of Spain. These were not news conferences in the accepted sense. They were more like prime ministerial lectures to the nation and were recorded for broadcast. There were few opportunities for close questioning. Reporters knew the rules and the prime minister's monologues were rarely interrupted.

New to the game, I had been given the assignment that

afternoon only because our senior news editor was unavailable that day. At a pause in the prime minister's monologue, I challenged him about an apparent contradiction in what he had said that afternoon and what had been stated earlier as government policy. For the life of me I cannot remember what the issue was, but my question posed as a challenge to a previous prime ministerial statement was frowned upon. It was simply not done. It was regarded as bad form. I can still recall my discomfort as an embarrassing hush swept the room. Other journalists avoided eye contact with me and gazed intently at their notebooks. The prime minister himself said nothing, suggesting that my cocky intervention was unworthy of comment.

Later that afternoon I was told in confidence that all the members of Radio Trinidad's local board had descended on our offices and were taken into a small editing suite to listen critically to my exchange with the prime minister. Nobody said a word to me. I was given no formal reprimand, but I was never again assigned to a prime ministerial news conference.

I had no reason to believe that the prime minister had been offended by my lack of deference; Radio Trinidad's owners were just being very cautious. The prime minister had to be kept on side for the good of the company's interests exactly as Lord Buckhurst had intimated.

More to my taste was the radio station's airport beat. It gave me the chance to meet and to interview every political leader, US senator, ambassador, sports star or entertainer who came to Trinidad or who was merely on a brief stopover. The airport VIP room became my Studio B and part of my reporting life.

I cherish the warmest memories of the people who found the time to talk to me, sometimes very late at night after tiring flights and frequently in the uncertain hours of early morning. One of them was Adlai Stevenson, a former governor of Illinois and one of my American political heroes. I had admired him because in the rough and tumble of American political campaigns he had time and time again refused to sacrifice his principles on the altar of expediency. Thoughtful and laconic, he told one election rally that as president he was not quite sure he would have had the answers to all his country's problems.

Honesty of that kind wins few votes in any country and is particularly frowned upon by political managers in the maelstrom of American politics. It didn't help Stevenson's presidential aspirations. Defeated by Eisenhower twice, when he lost the Democratic nomination to John F. Kennedy in 1960 he was banished by the administration to the political wilderness of the United Nations. But Stevenson was a good man and he surprised the Kennedys and the United Nations with a stunning attack on his Soviet counterpart, Ambassador Valerian Zorin, at a critical moment. He sharply demanded information on whether the Soviet Union had placed missiles in Cuba ninety miles off the North American coast. When Zorin hesitated in his reply, Stevenson seized the opening and launched his own verbal missile. 'Don't wait for the translation. Answer yes or no,' the American ambassador said. 'I'm prepared to wait for my answer until hell freezes over.'

A few weeks later there he was in the flesh restlessly pacing the tiny airport VIP room, explaining to me in his quiet, professorial manner how the world came within a hair's breadth of a nuclear catastrophe during the missile crisis. Nikita Khrushchev, the Soviet leader, knew from what had transpired at the United Nations and from the notes passed between Washington and Moscow that the Americans weren't bluffing about attacking Soviet ships heading for Cuba, and turned them round. The world was spared the possibility of a nuclear Armageddon.

I've never forgotten the thrill of meeting Adlai Stevenson. He wore his integrity like few contemporaries. I thought the airport beat was the best job in the media in Trinidad.

There were other memorable moments. Well past midnight on his arrival from London, Sir Grantley Adams, a towering figure in Caribbean politics, was bowed and close to tears as he discussed the failure of his visit to Britain to save the West Indies Federation. Adams was its first prime minister and the Federation had not quite been five years old when it collapsed in the roiling noise of inter-island acrimony. Looking directly at me as I shook his hand he said: 'Mac, what's to become of the West Indies cricket team?' even before I pressed him on why London had been unable to help in saving the Federation.

I remember, too, the then Guyanese opposition leader Cheddi Jagan, who kept a plane waiting on the tarmac and ignored several announcements asking him to board in order to conclude to our mutual satisfaction an interview he'd agreed to do.

The American singer Sam Cooke was incredulous when in the course of our conversation I told him about a concert sold in his name by a Trinidadian fraudster – a concert about which the singer knew nothing. Johnny Mathis and Johnny Nash were generous with their time. The Platters, then the group singing sensation, allowed me to take them to a Port of Spain nightclub, and Sammy Davis Jr, more diminutive in real life than he appeared on-screen, was hustled into an uncomfortably crowded room but with stoic patience stayed to talk about his Rat Pack days with Frank Sinatra and Dean Martin.

T. S. Eliot suggests that the use of memory is 'for liberation' and he describes thoughts that trigger deep reflection in later life:

> . . . the conscious impotence of rage
> At human folly, and the laceration
> Of laughter at what ceases to amuse.

And he goes on to say:

> At last, the rending pain of re-enactment
> Of all that you have done, and been.

That rending pain of re-enactment of all that I have done and been is always with me. Warmer memories are more simply expressed. In the curious trade of reporting we survive by the grace and kindness of others and by their willingness to take visitors into their communities, their homes and into their confidence. That is how countless number of people, many of whom I had met only briefly, became part of my story and a part of my life.

Radio Trinidad's limited resources forced us to make good use of the output of the BBC's World Service. The BBC approved and its London representatives were frequent visitors to Port of Spain to encourage us to use even more. I told them all that my ambition was to work in London.

My entreaties, which must have been tedious if only in their repetition, unexpectedly bore fruit when I was telephoned in Trinidad by Christopher Bell, the assistant head of the Overseas Regional Service at Bush House in the Strand, and offered a job as producer in one of the current affairs departments. I've always hoped I was not too embarrassingly effusive in my acceptance. The BBC even agreed to bear the cost of transporting my modest collection of books from Port of Spain to London.

Here was my point of departure. I began the painful process of self-consciously cutting myself off from my roots and left the West Indies in Tennyson's exhortation 'to seek a newer world'. I was surprised to discover many years later that what I had done was in no way out of the ordinary. A survey for a popular internet site in 2012, a long time after I left the island, found that more than half of all Trinidadian families have at least one member living abroad. My decision to leave the West Indies may have been momentous to me. The fact was I had simply joined the throng.

Despite that, a few West Indian colleagues were surprised that I had decided to live and work in London. It was generally felt that I had been doing well in my job in the media at home. I struggled to explain something so deeply personal until, after I'd been living in England for many years, I came across lines by Saul Bellow. Bellow, who won the Nobel Prize for Literature in 1976, once paid a touching tribute to Chicago, the city in which he grew up and loved but from which he felt the urge to escape. He did so, he said, because 'of narrowness of life together with a strong intimation of scope, a simultaneous expansion and constriction in the soul, a clumsy sense of inadequacy, poverty of means, desperate limitation, and, at the same time a craving for more, which demanded that "impractical" measures be taken'.

It is perhaps immodest of me to steal someone else's words to express my emotions on making the major decision to leave the West Indies. But Bellow put it perfectly. He said what I felt.

I will always be a part of the land that gave me breath, the island that nurtured and cared for me and watched me grow. Tiny Trinidad allowed me to dream of things that never were; it inspired me; it gave me visions of a wider world. It encouraged ambition; it gave me a strong intimation of scope and never restricted my craving for more.

3

Between Two Worlds

'. . . how choose
Between this Africa and the English tongue I love?'
                    Derek Walcott, 'A Far Cry from Africa'

The great wave of West Indian emigration to London crested in the 1950s. People from the islands had been making the journey for generations before that, but a manpower shortage after the Second World War compelled the British government to seek more workers from the Caribbean. They came by invitation and were offered incentives to fill yawning gaps in the still relatively new National Health Service and in what remained of the British transport system after the German bombers had done their worst.

My decision to try my luck in journalism in England was reached in a different way.

I have said in this book that young Trinidadians growing up in the time I did were in a sense primed in their education for a life outside the West Indies. My parents must have been aware of that and yet my decision to accept a job in London came as a surprise and distressed them greatly. They were pleased at what we all hoped might mean better prospects of a decent career, but they suspected that they were losing me to another country for good. That was painful for them and I felt it keenly.

I was the oldest child and I had benefited most from the care and devotion my parents gave to their offspring. There were four of us. My father boasted of a certain symmetry in our family: two boys and two girls. I was the first. My brother JC came after me and then there were the two girls: Lynette, my elder sister, and Eunice, who still lives in Trinidad and until her retirement worked as a lawyer in the government service. We were a very close-knit family and as children we played a lot together. We had to make up many of our own games. We were never able to be taken on expensive (or inexpensive) holidays anywhere. In any event, since we were living in the Caribbean, where the sun more or less always shone, we didn't need holidays, so we were left very much to our own devices. Generally we got on extremely well. I remember no great rows as children.

Much later on, my brother, who now lives in Canada, tried to tell me about my father having a greater relationship with him than he had with me, and also a greater relationship with my elder sister, Lynette, who tragically died in a car crash many years ago, than he did with the rest of us. I never discerned that at the time. I thought my parents showed a great deal of skill in bringing us up equally as siblings. We were a happy band of people. As we grew older and geographically apart, perhaps my brother felt that, as the first-born, I got the better of any deals that were going. I think to some extent that was true. The first-born child in the West Indies, especially if a boy, is often thought of as the one who would be given the best opportunites, and I suppose my brother did in the end feel that.

Throughout his working life my father took on an improbable variety of jobs – mending shoes, keeping pigs and growing vegetables on plots near our house and on others he managed to lease, to supplement his main income as an employee in the oil industry. One of my enduring memories is the zeal with which he latched on to any chance to earn a little more money. There was always some new idea running through his mind. Would becoming a part-time insurance salesman be worth the effort? Could such a job be done part-time? His appetite for doing odd jobs seemed insatiable.

With the exception of the pitifully small amount of drinking money he allowed himself weekly, he ploughed everything he earned into the running of our household. When money was really short at the end of a particularly difficult month, I would follow my father as he collected his pay packet before he clocked on at the Texaco oil refinery. He would hand over to me a small brown envelope with almost every penny he'd been paid by Texaco, to be taken home to my mother.

My father lavished on me by far the greater share of his paternal attention. He took me to my first school on my first day and he was there to meet a slightly bewildered schoolboy when that long day ended. For many years he ambushed any teacher who had the misfortune to pass near our house to enquire how I was doing. Anything less than a fulsome report – and I don't recall many of those – condemned me to extra lessons, sometimes on a Saturday when I was desperate to be allowed to play cricket.

Of course, extra lessons placed an additional burden on the family purse. My father saw it as part of his duty. The only time he came close to breaking down was the day I came home with the list of books I was required to purchase on my entry to secondary school. My father was shocked by the cost of the books and unthinkingly and quite unreasonably I turned down every offer to buy some of them second-hand from older boys. I still find that a painful memory.

Nor have I forgotten my father's horror at my suggestion that I should, as a few of my school friends did, take on part-time work to try to boost our family finances.

My father later found time to go with me, some twenty miles by taxi, very early one morning, to my first day's work at Radio Trinidad. He exhibited pride in what I did, encouraged ambitions he never understood and was a willing listener to my doubts and fears. He was by any measure the finest and most generous-spirited man I have ever known, respected by all who knew him and quietly adored by his family.

The real organisation of our family life was left to the genius of my mother. She counted the pennies with the skill of a trained accountant, divided up what was to be spent on food, clothes and school books and managed to deflect our thoughtless demands for non-essentials with a gentle firmness against which there could be no appeal.

We survived without anything that might be classed as luxuries. Raw, native pride prevented us from ever describing ourselves as poor but we were always short of money. We never went without food but our choices were limited.

For almost all the time I was at home we lived in over-crowded rented houses. That was never ideal. There were frequent demarcation disputes with quarrelsome landlords. The pettiness of some rows was humiliating and tested my parents' patience to the limit. It was an affront to their dignity. Were we children, for example, entitled to some of the fruit from the trees in the garden of our rented house? That row was never satisfactorily resolved. (My brother and I found a way of helping ourselves to most of the oranges and mangoes anyway, leaving no incriminating traces and with the unspoken approval of our parents.)

We walked two or three miles a day to our primary schools and cherished the memory of those rain-soaked mornings when, drenched to the bone, we would be given a ride part of the way by a driver who took pity on us but also because he knew our father. Shoes were a recurring problem. We nursed them into repeated use even when their days of natural usefulness had gone. It should in all fairness be admitted that part of the problem was that we invariably wore the same pair of shoes for walking to school, playing cricket, football or going to the cinema.

Local shops allowed us food and household essentials on credit and when the first supermarkets came to Trinidad my job was to join the Saturday queues in the sweltering mid-morning heat, hoping to buy cheap off-cuts of meat, the shavings of what was left of expensive joints we could not afford.

I always did pretty well at this unpredictable exercise, but I do remember the morning I fainted and fell heavily on the pavement in a longer than usual line of shoppers. Nothing but my pride was hurt but I was terribly embarrassed and despite my half-hearted protests I was allowed to move to the head of the queue and given stern lectures by matronly women I didn't know about the importance of having a proper break-fast before queuing in the heat to buy meat or anything else.

On some mornings my mother sent me down to the stretch of beach not too far from our house where the fishing boats came in after a night at sea. I devised what I thought was a clever ruse to make sure I didn't go home empty-handed. At the first sight of a little boat nearing the shore, I took off my shoes and waded into the water to help the fisherman haul his vessel on to dry ground. Bookish, nervous and lacking self-assurance, I had never been seen as a particularly helpful child but on those mornings at the beach I excelled, and having made such a conspicuous effort at coming to the aid of a tired old fisherman who had probably spent most of the night without sleep, I was assured of preferential treatment when catches proved smaller than the number of people waiting to buy fresh mullet, kingfish and grouper.

I hated the inconvenience of having to take off my shoes and getting soaked wading into the water, sometimes up to my waist, but I couldn't bear the thought of disappointing my mother. My little ploy always worked. I never went home without a few pounds of fresh fish.

None of these chores was seriously burdensome and al-though they sometimes got in the way of our sport, none made us feel deprived as children. On the contrary, we ignored the sacrifices and the compromises we were forced to make and convinced ourselves that we were fortunate to share the joys of life on a lush, tropical island.

We lived by the rules of a tight-knit village community of no more than a few hundred – respectful to our elders, always acknowledging neighbours and family friends if we passed them in the street. If ever I failed to do that, walking along absentmindedly, lost in the wilderness of zany childhood dreams, or just concocting an excuse for not having done my homework, I was told off by my parents.

Village life had its downsides. Petty robbery was common and simmering feuds about unpaid debts or landownership could drag on for years. Fights were the most common cause of trouble and they occurred mostly at weekends when the owners of rum shops, filled to capacity and brimming with noise, tried to call time on drunks who had stayed longer than they should have done. It was easy then for trivial arguments to turn into full-blown rows and spill out on to the streets.

If things got really bad, knives and cutlasses were the weapons of choice. Gun crime was not unknown but it was rare.

I say this with some caution, but to the best of my knowledge our lives were until then untainted by the scourge of drugs and the bloody drug wars that have in recent years spawned a riot of menacing no-go areas and threaten to destroy much of what's left of civilised, contemporary West Indian life.

It was recently drawn to my attention that a sign above the emergency wing of the Mount Hope Hospital, just outside the capital Port of Spain, reads: GUNSHOT AND CHOP WOUNDS THIS WAY. 'Chop' is Trinidad-speak for the aggressive use of machetes or knives meant to kill or to maim for life.

Smoking marijuana was quite common in my teenage years but not by anyone I knew. The authorities saw it as a semi-serious social problem and surprise police attempts to destroy acres of the plant growing luxuriantly in the countryside were as much a cause of mirth as an example of principled law enforcement.

On my most recent visits to the Caribbean almost everyone I met had a tale about once popular areas where it is no longer safe to be seen, especially after dark, and about the circumstances in which people were gunned down in broad daylight in drug-related killings. Walking around a part of Port of Spain where carnival revellers gathered I was amused to see a sign outside a small shop which read: NO DRUGS SOLD HERE. I was sorely tempted to ask its owner whether he could point me to a place where drugs were available. Better wisdom prevailed.

Way back in the Trinidad I knew, we spent our spare time, mostly at weekends, playing sport, taking on the names and pretending to imitate the feats of famous sportsmen, mainly cricketers. Our streets were full of Clyde Walcotts, Everton Weekeses and Frank Worrells.

Our obsession with cricket was that it gave us, as almost nothing else, pride in being West Indian. When we got on to the cricket field, we were equal to anybody else in the world. That was not so in any other sphere of life. So, we could play Australia. We could play a huge continent like India. And, of course, we could play and beat the mother country at cricket. That gave us a pride in ourselves which was unequalled in any other sphere of life. That, at its base, was why we loved cricket so much. It was also great fun and it was something that we could play ourselves. We could dig up our own patch of ground or take over a bit of the roadway, much to the discomfort of people who were trying to drive their cars by, and make our own games.

And we spent all our time, all our weekends, doing just that. The sound of a cricket bat hitting what was mainly tennis balls in those days was perpetual. I have a clear memory of playing very late into a Sunday afternoon and the dreadful sight of my two sisters being dispatched by my mother to drag us off the cricket field to come home and do homework because it was getting too late. I have never forgotten my sisters, Lynette and Eunice, summoning us off the cricket field.

The rest of our lives was cricket-oriented. We took on the names of great cricketers. Somebody would call himself Gary Sobers and somebody would call himself the great Frank Worrell or Clyde Walcott or Everton Weekes.

Much later in my career, I wrote biographies of Clive Lloyd and Vivian Richards, probably the outstanding cricketers of their generation. I had the wonderful opportunity of getting to know both of them well. One of the perks of my job as a television reporter was that I knew who they were, of course, but after a while they began to know who *I* was and we gravitated towards one another.

After that, it was natural that I would want to write about these two great men and I asked them and they agreed. I spent wonderful hours with Clive and Viv. I remember my first exposure to the great obsession that is cricket in India was when I went to finish the Viv Richards book in Mumbai, and I did so at a Test match in which he was playing. It was such a great time for me, because at the end of the day I would go back to my hotel room and work on my typewriter, as it was then, and start trying to hammer out a few pages. My telephone would ring and Wes Hall, that doyen of pace bowlers in the sixties, who was the West Indies manager, would call me up and say, 'We are all at the next hotel and in room 505 and are wondering where you are?' He would invite me over, and I would spend the rest of the evening not doing too much work on the book, but in the convivial company of people like Wes Hall and Viv and some of the other great players, such as Gordon Greenidge, Malcolm Marshall and Deryck Murray. I still know no better way of spending a day.

So nothing came close in the West Indies to our interest in cricket. We had no great scientists. There were, I'm sure, many

West Indian intellectuals, but that was a rather distant concept for a child. I'm sure there were great doctors and lawyers and so on, but nothing brought people in contact with everyday life as cricket did.

One of the things that heads of industry and bosses of large companies learned was that when the West Indies played England in England everybody sprouted earphones and no work was done in offices that day. Everyone listened to the cricket. And not only listened; we adopted the poetry of cricket. There are West Indians alive today who will remember John Arlott's words when Weekes and Walcott or Worrell and Weekes were taking the English bowling apart in the 1950s: 'This is not cricket,' he said. 'It's civilised murder.' And there are West Indians today who would, at the drop of a hat, remember exactly at which point of the game he uttered those words.

On potholed roads not ideal for the purpose we raced self-assembled go-carts and scooters. We played cricket with home-made bats and tennis balls on the beach and on rough pitches carved out of vacant plots of common land. We played football on quieter streets, unfazed by the appearance of the odd passing car. In the late afternoon shade from the dying sun we caught crayfish in near-stagnant stretches of lazy streams coursing through the fields near our village.

Ours was the exquisite delight of simple pleasures.

We were as adept at mischief-making as young boys the world over. We disrupted the activities of gamblers by pretending to be policemen and shining torches in the bushes where they assembled at night and then cut off their means of escape by burying their bicycles in mounds of builders' gravel and sand. And we operated a small self-serving protection system.

Our main accomplishment was that we eventually banished from our village the man who came around once a week selling whale and shark oil. We blamed our parents. My father and mother, perhaps conscious of the fact that we might not always be fed to the highest nutritional standards, acquired an annoying faith in inexpensive dietary supplements and were in the habit of buying whatever came their way. The whale and shark oils sold by this man were decidedly unappetising. Even as children we could see that they were viscous, thick with all manner of impurities and with a sickening odour to match. By shouting and threatening youthful menace every time his nasal tones signalled an approach in the vicinity of our house, we persuaded more than one hapless salesman to abruptly change course and seek out customers for his ghastly dietary supplements in some other streets.

I had a strange regret at tearing myself away from such a part of our family history and of the world in which I had been brought up. I was also troubled by the fact that I was about to move four thousand miles away from my ageing parents. My father accepted my decision to work in London with his customary equanimity. He said little. That was his way of dealing with things, especially when he didn't understand why I had set my heart on a particular course of action.

My father lived long enough to hear that I was having modest success as a television journalist in Britain. News of how West Indians were faring in England, whether good or bad, travelled back to the islands at lightning speed and clothed in hyperbole. My father had hard evidence, too, that I was surviving. On his first and only visit to London, I took him on a sightseeing tour. Nearing the end of a sparkling summer's day we stood looking down the Thames from one of the bridges at that proud and uplifting view of the Houses of Parliament bathed in golden sunshine.

A coachload of schoolchildren stopped very close to where we stood. As they stumbled out, one of them recognised me and, because of the way young people of a certain age blindly follow what everyone else is doing, I found myself at the centre of a buzz of small boys and girls requesting autographs. In no phase of his life in the Caribbean would my father have encountered the undoubtedly strange phenomenon of asking someone you knew only by sight to sign his name in a book.

My dad took a few steps away to take it all in and when I looked back over my shoulder he was beaming with pleasure. Although it was something he didn't understand I know that he never tired of telling the story to his friends when he got back to Trinidad. He said nothing to me as we continued our tour and I never found the words to explain to him what he had just witnessed. I felt he knew that I was perhaps doing well enough to be noticed at least by people in the street.

Whenever I went back to Trinidad I indulged my father's love of good whisky. Trinidad's fame as a producer of fine rum has never eclipsed its reverence for Scotland's best. To this day I believe whisky is still regarded in the West Indies as the tipple of the discerning drinker. It soon became clear to me that the speed at which my duty-free gifts were consumed alarmed and distressed my mother. Very weakly, I pretended not to notice. The simple truth was that I could not bring myself to deny the odd bottle to the man who had given me so much and to whom in his declining years the occasional glass of expensive whisky provided great comfort.

It tickled me to discover that my mother found her own way of controlling perhaps only a small part of my father's love of booze. Before I returned to London she invariably presented me with a neatly wrapped fruit cake. Alcohol is a vital ingredient in all Trinidadians cakes and my mother's treats appeared to include more than most. I thought to myself she had found a highly plausible way of cutting back on my father's supply.

On those visits home my father would insist on making it clear to people walking past our house that his son who lived and worked in London was back in town. He would stand on the veranda of our small house and loudly invite anyone who happened to pass to come in and talk to me. Only then did it occur to me that I was expected in the presence of his friends, many of whom he surmised I'd remembered, though in many instances I had not, to rattle off a string of tall tales about the far-off places I had been to and the people I had met in the course of my work as an ITN journalist. My father enjoyed showing me off. Deep down I felt he knew that he'd played no small part in helping to make me what I'd become and wanted to share that fact with friends. He had the strongest sense that he was ultimately responsible for what his children had made of their lives.

Whenever I went back to my parents' home, regardless of the time of day my father would insist on taking me to the local rum shop, a place of gloomy ordinariness where, with a sweeping gesture on our arrival, he would announce that I had come to buy a round of drinks for everyone who happened to be there. To this day I pray that my embarrassment was not too obvious. I'm afraid I shrank at those expressions of paternal pride. As a consequence I was not as communicative as I might have been. I regret that. I failed to live up the billing of 'local boy returns in triumph'. It was not how I saw myself. It was, though, I know now, a poor excuse for my half-hearted reminiscences and my long silences. I should have done a better job of storytelling even if it meant embellishing the facts.

I am pleased to say, however, that I never failed my father or his friends at the bar!

His lasting bequest to me was that throughout my early life he encouraged me to read. In fact, encouraged is not the word. I was pressured relentlessly to read by someone, who as far as I know, had never read a work of fiction. He was never very discriminating about what I read. At one stage of his life when he did odd jobs for a Scottish doctor who lived in a smart oil-industry compound, he brought home discarded copies of the medical profession's trade journal, *The Lancet*. I feigned an interest in medicine and to keep my father off my back pretended to read it. To this day I shudder involuntarily when there is some vague reference to the journal in the news.

Beyond the importance of reading widely, my father impressed upon me that a lowly birth in itself placed no limits on ambition. His abiding philosophy was that with determination and ambition you could become whatever you wanted to be. Like all West Indian parents of my generation he stressed the importance of education. It was the magic word, the key to anything resembling social mobility. That much was obvious. None of us had been born into socially prominent families and none of us expected to be the recipient of a large family bequest.

My mother, the anchor of our family life, never got used to the career path I had chosen. She was too loving and too gentle to reproach me. Years after I left Trinidad and found myself on assignments in Belfast or Beirut, and snippets of news about bombs and bullets were flying imprecisely around the world, I would telephone her to play down the significance of any reports she might have heard and to assure her that I was perfectly safe. She was always delighted to hear my voice. We never discussed at any length what I was doing in those places. If I said I was reporting on warring factions in the Middle East, she stopped me in my tracks with the simple question: '*But why?*'

Mother instilled in us the loftiest of human values. I remember protesting at her insistence that I should take food to neighbours who had fallen on bad times or who were worse off than we were. Naive to a point of cruelty, I wondered aloud why people who couldn't afford them had so many mouths to feed. My mother slapped me down, insisting that I did as I was told.

I still smile at her injunction that we should be especially generous to strangers to make sure that we never missed 'the glorious chance of entertaining angels'. In my later life I tracked down the origins of most of her sayings. I've never pinned down that one. It has, it seems to me, a distinctly biblical ring. My mother exuded an abundance of Christian grace.

Although she never understood why I had forsaken the

tranquillity of Trinidadian life to work in places fraught with such peril, my mother, too, knew that I was enjoying modest success. She was overjoyed to be invited to London to see me the subject of the popular television programme *This Is Your Life* and took great pride in the fact that on a visit to south Trinidad the then Archbishop of Canterbury, Dr Robert Runcie, had begun a speech by saying how pleased he was to be visiting near the town 'where Trevor McDonald was born'. No vindication of the career path I had chosen could have been sweeter.

Her friends were told and retold the story until they must have been heartily sick of it.

I didn't talk about it a great deal, but I was always unsure about the thread of decision-making that occasionally landed me in Northern Ireland or in Lebanon. All emigration is difficult. Moving from one country to another is never an easy proposition. I worried constantly about whether I had done the right thing. I was haunted as ever by the fear of failure. Of course, we all looked to London as the great metropolitan centre of Empire and our countries were closely bound by colonial history. At times that seemed merely an abstraction, as much as the belief that the knowledge we had absorbed from all the books we had read about England equipped us fully to live in London, Birmingham or Manchester. But the link between our countries had its limitations. Some things had a deeper resonance.

Our forefathers had come not from England but from Africa and India. They had been uprooted and in the case of those who came from Africa lured from their villages by unscrupulous middlemen and tribal chiefs and taken in chains across the seas to work as slaves on West Indian colonial plantations. Tens of thousands did not survive the grotesque horror of those Atlantic crossings.

We, the descendants of those who had grown up with only a historical whiff of the stink of slavery, became in due course children of Empire. We were largely uninformed about who we really were, knowing only what we had become through acts of war or aggressive occupation.

None of it could be wished away. In my own case our very name McDonald must have been that of a plantation owner. In all probability those who toiled in some now forgotten field from dawn to dusk cultivating coffee, tobacco or sugar cane came to be known by the name of its owner. One of my antecedents would in that way come to be known as one of McDonald's boys. It was not a name of choice. It came with a reminder of the age of European expansionism and with the baggage of an explanation.

The issue of who we West Indians really are is sharply observed by the St Lucian poet and Nobel Laureate Derek Walcott:

> I who am poisoned with the blood of both,
> Where shall I turn, divided to the vein?
> I who have cursed
> The drunken officer of British rule, how choose
> Between this Africa and the British tongue I love?

My blood runs cold whenever I am reminded of Walcott's devastating phrase 'divided to the vein'. If I ever tried to make light of it, I told myself that I had turned my back on the land of my birth with all the history it held about my antecedents, and come to London to do a job making use of the 'British tongue I love'.

No one who leaves the West Indies to work in broadcast journalism could have a softer landing than at Bush House on the Aldwych just off the Strand in central London – the home of the BBC World Service from 1941 to 2012. In the hectic bustle of London life and in the late sixties when I arrived, and in the still-simmering tensions about immigration control and the state of race relations in Britain, Bush House was an oasis of easy internationalism. It looked out to the world beyond. I was in awe of the BBC's brilliance. Its reputation for balanced reporting is still the envy of the broadcasting world. For me it opened up vistas of a universe I was desperate to be part of.

I have never forgotten the thrill of walking through the doors of Bush House for the first time in 1969. To me it was the closest thing to being a member of the General Assembly of the United Nations. I was captivated. I immediately fell under its spell. Everywhere you looked there were highly regarded journalists and radio producers from every part of the world. We talked international politics in the corridors, at our desks and in the bustling bars. It has been said that the tone of conversations in the Bush House canteen were the equal of any discussion at an Oxbridge tutorial. I was learning a lot about life in countries I thought I'd never get the chance to visit. Professors from the London School of Economics nearby were regular contributors to the Bush House output. I interviewed them and sat at their feet.

The ethos of reporting accurately and fairly informed everything we did and has shaped my view of my duty as a journalist ever since. Today when I listen to debates about modern journalism – the rise of social media and its obsession with the cult of celebrity, the blogosphere, the undisguised attempts to shock and to antagonise, the tendency to state blatant falsehoods as fact and the Twitter feeds that pass for news – I still think of Bush House and the World Service as having set the gold standard for journalism.

The BBC's overseas broadcasts maintained that standard even in the face of Nazi propaganda during the Second World War. A recent search through the BBC Written Archives Centre reveals this from work done by Dr Vike Martina Plock of Exeter University: offering impartial news was vital even if it meant broadcasting information about Britain's military setbacks. Accurate information was the bait to draw in German listeners. It gave distinction to the BBC's work.

In some respects modern journalism has lost its way. The need for speed has damaged the culture of thoughtful reporting. And we have sadly confused the lofty concept of balance with equivalence. Put simply, we place too much importance on giving equal time to contrasting views without any consideration of whether either of the views merits the time allocated.

Thus, if someone argues *for* a proposition, the need for balance suggests that another person must be found to put the opposite case. That may well be a worthy concept. A problem may arise if the opposing view is badly argued and without merit. It has become the curse of our modern political discourse. The reader or viewer is frequently left with no idea which version may have come closer to the truth. And we seem to have forgotten the degree to which people in high political office are prepared to tell lies to further their own narrow interests. And to do so without the slightest hint of shame.

Reporting which is accurate, fair and balanced has to do with much more than the presentation of competing points of view. To think of balanced reporting only in that context does great disservice to journalism. In the method of reporting I dislike most, the interviewer seeking out opinions of passers-by on a busy London street considers the job done as soon as two contrasting views have been expressed. That tells the listener or the viewer nothing and is all too often a waste of precious television or radio broadcast time.

When I went to Bush House, Britain was in the first flush of its embrace of what at the time was known as the European Common Market. The Labour MP and minister Douglas Jay was one of those who fought doggedly to ensure that British membership did not permanently damage the status of agricultural exports from the Commonwealth. He was always willing to see me and frequently at short notice. He paid me the compliment of saying that he would always respond to any message from me left 'behind the Speaker's chair'.

I remember many of my Bush House interviews for purely sentimental reasons. In the 1960s the Trinidad-born pianist Winifred Atwell became a household name in Britain. For years she had a weekly programme on prime-time radio. She was, of course, regarded as one of my island's most famous exports to the world of entertainment. I was delighted when Miss Atwell agreed to talk to me for the World Service about her life. Nervous at meeting such a star I arrived at her Mayfair flat indecently early.

She ushered me in and invited me, while she changed, to help myself to a glass of bourbon. I had never tasted bourbon before and certainly not at that time of day. In the circumstances I felt it impolite to refuse. Miss Atwell talked engagingly about her early life in Trinidad, about how she rose to prominence in England and about touring the world. At the end of our interview she presented me with a pair of gold cufflinks stamped with the motif of a piano keyboard. I wear them with great pride to this day.

There were exceptional examples of the high regard in which BBC World Service broadcasts were held. One week I produced a fifteen-minute programme about the state of Ghana's economy. Sometime over the next few days I received a note from the economics minister in Accra requesting a transcript of the broadcast. I was terrified. In my experience such a request would almost inevitably be followed by a stinging rebuke about how bad or biased the programme was. Nervously I consulted my editor. He explained that such requests from World Service audiences were routine and that I should comply with the minister's request at my earliest convenience. Weeks later we received a letter thanking us for the transcript and explaining that the minister had missed the programme when it was first broadcast because he had been at a meeting with the prime minister.

I never got over the thrill of working for a broadcasting service so well regarded.

I remember being told a story about one of the Russian journalists at Bush House, Anatol Goldberg. I knew him slightly. He was one of our in-house experts on Soviet Union policy and I had interviewed him frequently. Bespectacled and sternly unsmiling, he always carried a stopwatch and, on being asked to explain a particular point of Moscow politics, would demand to know how much time his interviewer required, set his watch and deliver his answer in the time allotted, correct to the second. He was a producer's dream.

The crusty dinosaurs in the upper echelons of the Soviet Union did not approve of Goldberg's trenchant criticism of Soviet Communist Party policies. But his work found a devoted audience behind the Iron Curtain. I met Goldberg at a time when dissidents like the novelist Alexander Solzhenitsyn were regarded as preaching sedition and packed off to remote gulags to serve long sentences. Sometime after Solzhenitsyn was released he appeared at his first press conference in the West. He had not been seen or heard for years and was bombarded by questions from a noisy gaggle of reporters.

Solzhenitsyn recognised one voice.

'Ah, Mr Goldberg, we meet at last.'

The clear, uncompromising voice of Anatol Goldberg and the BBC World Service had penetrated the darkest recesses of a Soviet labour camp. The Soviet Union had for a time found a way to silence its dissidents. It had failed to silence the voice of the BBC World Service.

The most wonderful thing about the BBC World Service as far as I was concerned was the fact that it gave me the chance to do a great variety of things. As a producer I could commission interviews to be done by others. But I enjoyed doing them myself and so from time to time I would ignore the tried and tested procedure of employing freelance reporters and commission myself to do the interviews. This was not the way the 'BBC system' worked and was not always popular with my editors. I overcame their objections by persistently ignoring them.

I especially enjoyed working on a show called *Profile*. A longer than usual conversation with a person of international repute would be edited into a fifteen-minute programme. In the course of doing many of these interviews I met people like Lord Caradon, who as Hugh Foot was a member of a remarkable British political dynasty.

The Foot family had produced writers, journalists and leading lights in the service of their country abroad. Caradon had been governor of Jamaica and Cyprus and Britain's representative at the United Nations. We talked a great deal about his appointment to Kingston and to Nicosia at a time when Britain was being pressed into giving up her colonial territories. In one of his books Lord Caradon had described himself as 'a colonial governor running out of colonies to govern'.

Bishop Trevor Huddleston gave me tea at his church offices in the East End of London and talked with quiet humanity about his courageous and dignified stand against the evils of the apartheid system in South Africa. I left Bishop Huddleston with a burning determination to learn first-hand how a political system had managed for so long to deprive the majority of its citizens the most basic human rights.

The Reverend David Sheppard was a name I had remembered because of his feats with the bat against a touring West Indies cricket team in the 1950s. We talked at length about that and about his decision to give up cricket while still in his prime to follow his Christian calling. David Sheppard was the personification of charm.

I have the fondest memories of reporting the 1970 Commonwealth Games in Edinburgh for the Overseas Regional Service of the BBC. How is this for name-dropping and sheer good fortune? My fellow commentator was the world-famous Trinidad-born athlete E. McDonald Bailey and one of the people with whom we shared the commentary box was none other than Harold Abrahams whose performance in the Paris Olympics in 1924 inspired the film *Chariots of Fire*. I have always regretted that I never found the courage to talk to him about his career and about the pride he brought to Britain. In my mind's eye I still have these images of him in his country-brown suit, stopwatch in hand and standing quietly at the back of our commentary box. He was invariably smiling and his eyes sparkled with good-natured generosity in reply to any question about the performance of British athletes at the Edinburgh Games.

When many years later I saw the film about his life I kicked myself for missing the chance to try at least to get to know him better. I was too new in my job and too scared to approach a man of such distinction.

I was happy at Bush House. To a large extent it had responded with abundant grace to my risky decision to leave Trinidad to find work in Britain. Even so, I never imagined that I would spend an entire career in one place. Bush House was wonderful but much too comfortable. In the end it was as simple as that. All too frequently I ran into colleagues who seemed to have become part of the furniture, Bush House habitués too content to spend their working lives in the cuddly embrace of 'Auntie', as the BBC is affectionately known.

There were odd periods when I was almost at the point of convincing myself that I could easily slip into the gentle, lilting pace of life at Bush House, the unfailingly good company, the leisurely lunches, the sparkling conversations in the canteen and the almost mandatory whisky or two in the friendly bar just after six. The more restless side to my personality has always made me suspicious of the thought of too much ease.

The glory of life cannot be separated from harsh reality of life's inevitable challenges. And I remembered Tennyson: 'How dull it is to pause.'

In more practical terms I wondered whether a Bush House current affairs producer was as far as I could go or whether sterner tests of my ability as a journalist were beckoning just around the corner. I felt the need to do more and to learn more.

My leaving came in a manner I could not have anticipated.

I was perhaps guilty of talking a little too much to my BBC colleagues about the work I had done at Trinidad and Tobago Television in Port of Spain before coming to London. I had presented the nightly news and I had anchored a weekly discussion programme, *Dialogue*, which I had helped to devise. It was not particularly brilliant, but it attracted critical attention perhaps because it was prepared to tackle in lively discussions some of the more controversial issues of the time. No other radio or television programme in Trinidad did that.

There is a slice of Trinidadian life that turns its face away from controversy. It thrives on the pretence that there is an inherent virtue in imagined tranquillity and that those who disagree have a narrow, personal interest in encouraging dissent and disharmony in what is in effect one big happy family of reasonably contented Trinidadians. My guests on *Dialogue* did not subscribe to that view and said so openly.

In small islands like ours those in power find it relatively easy to keep fairly tight control on the output of the media. I was always surprised at how efficiently it was done. There was no harsh censorship, nor to my knowledge were there edicts or direct orders about what could and could not be done. There was no need. We censored ourselves. There seemed to be a general understanding of what should or should not be said or done. Very rarely did governments actively interfere. They had no reason to.

I still smile when I recall the rhetorical dance I was obliged to perform each week as we prepared for the Friday-night broadcasts of *Dialogue*.

I was asked to present myself to the station manager in his office to tell him who would be appearing that night and the issues to be discussed. Our guests were never, as I far as

I can remember, politicians opposed to the government. We tended not to invite them. Instead I would have senior figures in public service or in the commercial world, lecturers from the University of the West Indies and visiting political commentators, many of whom may have held unconventional but interesting views.

The poor station manager was invariably a nervous wreck at these meetings, occasionally muttering to himself how terribly unwise he'd been in allowing me to come up with the idea of such a show in the first place. Our unedifying two-step ended after he'd worked himself up into a state of undisguised anxiety and after he sought my assurance, almost in a childlike plea, that nothing the programme did would 'cause trouble'. His parting line was always the same: 'If your show does cause a stink, I will lose my job. Remember my neck is in the noose.'

I am happy to report that although *Dialogue* caused some controversy and rated well, the station manager kept his job. He was hugely relieved when I told him one afternoon that I was leaving Trinidad to work in London.

I was proud at having launched *Dialogue* on Trinidad and Tobago Television without causing too many political insurrections. So much so, in fact, that when I got a telephone call at Bush House one evening from the head of one of the BBC's television channels and was asked to go to his office in southwest London, I convinced myself that news of my television work in Trinidad had somehow found its way to London and that I was about to be interviewed for a television job at the BBC. I hugged myself at what appeared to be a moment of extraordinary good fortune.

I was getting ahead of myself.

Over glasses of excellent white wine and delicately cut smoked salmon sandwiches, the BBC executive explained that the Corporation had been coming under increasing pressure from the newly constituted Race Relations Board to find more black reporters and presenters. He wondered whether I would like an attachment to BBC Television to see if I might make the grade. He proceeded to explain how an attachment would work and talked about the conditions that came with the offer.

I swallowed another large glass of wine to hide the fact that the words Race Relations Board had sent a jolt like an electric shock through my body. My spirits sank. I had nothing against the Race Relations Board. On the contrary, I was proud of its admirable work. I believed that its existence was a sign of progress in British society and one that was absolutely necessary. Moreover, I felt that the BBC, the recipient of a vast sum of money through the state-imposed licence fee, was duty-bound to be transparently inclusive in its employment policies to reflect more clearly the changing face of Britain.

I was also pleased to learn that the BBC was taking that responsibility seriously. I have always believed that in some circumstances this kind of 'positive discrimination' could be a virtue – if only a qualified one. These were decidedly not the circumstances in which I wanted to be offered a position with BBC Television. Put more plainly, I did not want to be offered a job because the BBC was on the trawl for a black candidate or, in fact, for any black candidate.

It can never be pleasant or healthy for an employee to be aware that he or she has been given a position not on merit but because of the colour of his or her skin. I am aware that in some cases that kind of discrimination is essential in the cause of political and social reform. South Africa after the end of apartheid is a good example. But I have never believed that positive discrimination should be the guiding principle of employment policy. In some circumstances it may be necessary. In the guise in which it was presented to me that day, I wanted no part of it.

The BBC executive had been warm and courteous throughout our conversation and I took care to phrase my response in similar terms. As diplomatically as I could I said it was not for me. I might even have apologised for wasting his time.

After twenty minutes or so the wine had done its job and I summoned up the courage to enquire whether he had been aware of the television work I had done in the West Indies. The question carried more than a whiff of desperation. Had it been answered in the affirmative I might have been tempted for a few seconds to reconsider my position. As it turned out the man had never heard of Trinidad and Tobago Television and knew nothing of *Dialogue* or any other aspect of my work there.

I gave up on BBC Television and made my way back to Bush House suitably chastened. If I were ever again offered a job in the media in London, I would be on my guard.

I might well have banished from my mind all thoughts of working in television in Britain had it not been for that encounter with the BBC executive in his Shepherd's Bush office. He had reawakened my interest. I was finding it difficult to put out of my mind the television work I had done back at home for about three years. I couldn't be sure that I would make it in London. There was a vast gap between the work I had once done and the high standard of what I saw on television screens in London. Still, the appetite was there and I wanted to be able to tell myself that I had tried. I would have hated myself for not having done that at least.

Having spent three happy years at Bush House, and at the urging of a few close associates who had perhaps had their fill of hearing me talk about reading the news on Trinidad television, I applied to Independent Television News, ITN, for a job as a reporter. In a short time ITN had won great accolades for its news service. In the foreword to Richard Lindley's book *And Finally*, about the birth and early history of the channel, the distinguished BBC journalist and presenter Andrew Marr wrote: 'For those of us at the BBC it may be a hard truth to acknowledge, but ITN virtually invented the modern news broadcast as it is understood. When it first arrived in September 1955 this little platoon ruthlessly exposed the BBC's stuffy and picture-scared traditionalism. They did it again when *News at Ten* launched in 1967, with American-style newscasters and a half-hour bulletin.'

ITN was indeed the talk of television news in Britain when I arrived in London in 1969 and I was taken aback when my letter to ITN's editor, Nigel Ryan, requesting an interview for a job as a reporter, was answered promptly.

Just after lunch one early November afternoon in 1972 I presented myself at the ITN office in Wells Street in London's West End. Certain that I would be kept waiting before seeing anyone in authority, I took the precaution of buying a paperback on the way to the interview to pass the time. I had not opened my new book before I was ushered into the editor's office.

My meeting with Nigel Ryan did not begin well.

I was nervous. He seemed a little unsure of what to make of me. Quite unexpectedly he asked me what I thought about one of the biggest news stories at the time, the decision by President Idi Amin to expel Ugandan Asians from his country. I made an offbeat remark that in a way went to the core of what I've always believed about social interaction. It was, however, not the conventional view of what was happening in Uganda. Amin's appearances on television had ensured that the focus stayed on him.

The ITN editor expressed some surprise at my comments. I thought we had got off on the wrong foot and that I had blown my chances of a job. After what seemed an age our conversation turned less controversially to the television work I had done in Trinidad and to what I had been doing at Bush House as a producer of current affairs. At the end of a discursive romp through my career in Trinidad and in London, I was asked to do an audition.

My delight was mixed with terror. I had not been anywhere near a television camera for years and was sure that would become very obvious very quickly. And so it was. My ITN

audition a few days later was not my finest moment in television. It might have been even worse had it not been for the
fact that I was greatly helped by the ITN crew. They coaxed
me out of my nervousness.

Even so, the most generous thing that could be said about
my performance that day was that it might have suggested the
slightest hint of promise. Two weeks later I went back to see
the editor at ITN and at the end of another interview I was
offered a job as a general reporter. Ryan told me some time
later that he thought I had a reasonable voice.

I wanted the job but the ITN offer came as a surprise. From
somewhere I summoned up the audacity to say I wanted time
to consider. If Nigel Ryan was taken aback he was much too
gracious a man to let on. He suggested that I might like to talk
to people who had recently joined the firm. A few had made
the change from Fleet Street, where the majority of British
newspapers were based. 'Talk to some of those who have
recently come to ITN,' he told me and then rattled off a few
names. 'Let them tell you what they think of our journalism
and the kind of company we are.'

When I got back to Bush House and reported to my friends
the gist of my ITN visit, they were flabbergasted. I was told
bluntly that I had been a fool not to accept the editor's offer
on the spot and that pleading for time to think it over was the
action of an idiot. I was told I should telephone ITN forthwith
and accept the offer of a job immediately.

Partly to save face I contemplated my folly with nagging
anxiety for no more than forty-eight hours, then did as my
friends had suggested.

I was shocked to discover that news about the ITN job was
of interest to the national press. I was even more discombobu-
lated when newspaper photographers rushed round to Bush
House to see me. I was unprepared for the fuss, and more than
a little embarrassed at seeing my picture and news about my
new job in the papers. Despite my encounter with the BBC

executive at his Shepherd's Bush office, I had naively seen ITN and British television simply as another place to work, another step in my career, another way of surviving in my adopted country. That view quickly crashed to the ground around me.

The newspaper pictures told the story about which I had perhaps deliberately closed my eyes. I had become the first black reporter on national television and that was deemed newsworthy. I understand that so clearly now. I didn't at the time. My new ITN job made no difference to the way I saw myself, but the tag was there in pictures and in bold print.

The attention of the newspapers, mildly irritating though it was, gave me the opening to make an important point to my new employers. Tactfully but in unmistakable terms I explained that I had not joined the firm to be forever labelled 'ITN's black reporter'. I was determined not to become part of the second division of the reporting team. I had no intention of being a specialist in stories about the problems of so-called immigrants in Brixton or Bradford. I made it clear that I wanted to be assigned to stories on the same basis as other reporters were at home and abroad. With not a moment's pause I was given that assurance.

Years later in my time at Independent Television News I was told that in those first uncertain weeks in the job there were a few howls of protest from viewers about a black man appearing on their screens in an unfamiliar role. I was never told about those protests at the time and I am grateful that, so far as I know, they were given no encouragement.

Surveying all the evidence over many years I am as certain as I can be that ITN hired me in good faith. The editor and his colleagues could not have failed to notice that I am a black West Indian. I am sure it was not their intention to relegate me to a minor league of reporting assignments. If anything, the opposite is true. I was given every opportunity to do almost everything to which a television journalist can aspire. The job and the latitude I was allowed and the diversity of things I did exceeded my own expectations by a considerable margin.

Whenever I didn't perform well ITN was not to blame. I could never have had greater support, encouragement and assistance from the company and from my more-than-generous colleagues. Never in my wildest dreams could I have written a script of the turn my life had taken.

I plunged into it with gusto.

I sought and found diversions on the bleakest assignments. I convinced myself I needed them to survive.

One of the biggest and longest-running stories when I joined Independent Television News in 1973 was Northern Ireland and its Troubles. That was the euphemism employed for that unending catalogue of bloody incidents bred by sectarian bigotry and bitterly divided communities; evident in nightly riots and far-from-peaceful parades, in the frequent explosion of bombs aimed at devastating towns and cities and maiming the unsuspecting, and in countless cases of cold-blooded murder.

At the height of the Troubles I played cricket next to a makeshift shelter which served as the ITN office and editing suite, on the roof of Ulster Television in Belfast. The size of our pitch made anything vaguely resembling a proper game a bit of a problem. But we devised our own rules and did our best to be true to the spirit of the great sport. We used hurling sticks as bats and bowled underarm with discarded tennis balls. Shots had to be played along the ground. Decisions favoured those who appealed the loudest. Our frequent cries of 'Howzat?' reverberated incongruously around one of the quieter streets of the Northern Ireland capital. I've often wondered what passers-by made of the strange noises floating down from our rooftop playing field.

There were sad epilogues to our escapist games of make-believe. Out on the roof, with a sweeping view of part of the Belfast city centre, we could clearly hear the roar of explosions and from the belching flames and smoke rising in the distance we could roughly guess where the bombs had gone off. We were therefore able to scramble our camera crews well ahead of any official news of an incident from the security forces.

Belfast, the place to which I was so anxious to be assigned, was a city of guns and bombs and of rampaging mobs spewing hatred. Those convulsions, interspersed with ritual calls for civility, peace and harmony, became part of the daily diet of British television news and framed the early years of my career.

They got me noticed. With no effort on my part I stood out as a black reporter in the grim and sullen ghettos of the Falls Road and Andersonstown.

The news that I had become a journalist on national television in Britain and was reporting regularly on street clashes and gun battles in a part of the United Kingdom predictably found its way to Trinidad. One of my former colleagues at Radio Trinidad sent me a typical West Indian message of congratulation. 'I'd heard on the grapevine you'd gone to London,' it said. 'Now I read that you've arrived.'

More than ever I reflected on the unexpected turn my life had taken. Over time and after a career marked by the unexpected and the adventurous, I remembered the memorable truth of the last lines in Robert Frost's poem 'The Road Not Taken':

> Two roads diverged in a wood, and I –
> I took the one less traveled by,
> And that has made all the difference.

4

The Arch of Experience

'Yet all experience is an arch wherethro'
Gleams that untravell'd world whose margin fades
For ever and forever when I move.'

Alfred, Lord Tennyson, 'Ulysses'

The ITN building in Wells Street off Oxford Circus in the heart of central London was a grey and black hulk at the end of an uneven line of offices and an assortment of flats which had seen better days, one branch of a high-street bank, a magistrates' court, clothes shops, cafés, restaurants, wine bars and pubs.

I joined ITN at a time when eating well and drinking copious amounts seemed as essential to the life of a journalist as breathing. I am told those days are largely gone. I am genuinely surprised that they lasted so long. Back then, few of us went without a good lunch and dry ones were rare. I remember with awe the colleague who rarely went without a cocktail of brandy and Benedictine at lunchtime (he invariably insisted on mixing the drink himself) and performed his duties flawlessly if called upon to do so later in the afternoon.

The location of our office was one of those happy accidents of London geography, blessed by the gods of commerce. Our constant demand encouraged the unfailing desire to supply. Eating out was part of the routine of the working day. We contributed over-generously to the commercial survival of the restaurants, wine bars and pubs, and their owners rewarded us with gushing familiarity dressed up as high regard.

Before the advent of the mobile phone, the most well-thumbed section of any news editor's contacts book listed the telephone numbers of all the nearby places reporters patronised. From any of them we could be summoned back to work in the event of a breaking story. Every waiter and publican knew the importance of passing on messages from the ITN news desk. The news desk knew most of them by name. I never lost the surprise of hearing my name shouted out from behind some bar or in some restaurant, followed by the words in a distinct Italian accent: 'Mr McDonald – the news desk wants you.'

We were a convivial though odd assortment of competitive spirits. Time spent in each other's company was invariably good fun, but that was not the whole story. It was also the acknowledged method of keeping track of what colleagues were up to and who was being given the choice assignments.

Our actual offices – our place of work – were as understated as the entrance to them on the ground floor of the building. There were none of the multiplex screens that are such a feature of media offices of today, no repeats of the company's greatest hits and thankfully no swirling chords of tuneless music. Tacked on to one wall was a modest montage of photographs of reporters on location at major news-making events.

A lone receptionist sat behind a desk on which, if I remember correctly, there was a single telephone. With its curtain of faded off-white plastic strips, the ITN reception seemed much too calm for the entrance to an enterprise which was supposedly keeping its finger on the pulse of domestic and international crises.

The reception area only came to life just after 10.30 at night in the banter and friendly jostling for taxis to take us home.

The newsroom one floor up was no less ordinary. Off to one

side was a row of offices for editorial managers, two or three of them, each just large enough to host a meeting of half a dozen people. If attendance suddenly went up, latecomers sat on the floor. There was a room for senior political and industrial correspondents. On busy days it was noticeably too small.

The rest of the newsroom might have been considered spacious were it not for the number of bodies – editors of home and foreign desks and their assistants, programme editors and their assistants, production assistants and a pool of secretaries and typists. It was not particularly well lit. It appeared businesslike but my first impression was that the place might struggle to be described in the unforgiving language of our age as a reasonable working environment.

With a casual bearing – cultivated over time to conceal any latent urge to spring into action should a domestic or international crisis arise – reporters sat around a staid arrangement of untidy desks overrun by half-read, half-discarded newspapers and piles of newspaper cuttings, dog-eared magazines, notebooks and coffee cups. There was barely enough space for two outstretched arms.

It was obvious to me that we weren't all meant to be there at the same time. There was sound logic to that. It was not unreasonable for our managers to assume that on any given day reporters should be out reporting, not sitting in an overcrowded newsroom competing for space and hoping to catch the news editor's eye. With more bodies than seats, colleagues on early morning shifts teased those of us on a later roster that we could, in exchange for a small fee or a couple glasses of wine, be allowed to rent a chair and a temporary place at a desk with a telephone.

Breezy banter apart, I thought it unusually quiet for a working newsroom. It was for most of the time bathed in civility. Some voices did from time to time rise to break the barrier of low-level murmur – reporters on telephones speaking with such controlled excitement that anyone close by might conclude that ITN was about to land a scoop; and news editors talking to reporters in distant fields, who, if one were to judge by what could be overheard, appeared unresponsive to the most reasonable requests.

And there were the cries of anguish from the logistics manager whose look of permanent persecution would have convinced any jury that camera crews he'd dispatched in good faith to all points of the compass only a few hours before had mutated into specialists in human torture and were taking a perverse delight in making his life a misery. Our amusement at his episodic rages bordered on the blatantly unkind.

The most welcome sounds were the calls twice a day of the tea trolleys. The cheerful ladies who wheeled them in were among the most popular people in the building. Their arrival set off a minor stampede and a babble of splintered conversations.

The new kid on the block had been subsidised by commercial television which, at its inception in the 1950s, was thought by well-heeled doom-mongers to presage the end of civilisation as we know it. ITN had taken on the might and the formidable reputation of the BBC and was in many cases beating 'Auntie' at her own game. Indeed, the success of the ITN news became a story in itself, if not as notable as those we reported from the United States, the Middle East and Southern Africa.

Our flagship programme *News at Ten* was always close to the top of the television ratings. Its regular presenters – Reginald Bosanquet, Andrew Gardner, Sandy Gall and later Alastair Burnet and Anna Ford – became household names. A rookie staff reporter starting off in a newsroom so proud of its journalism, and in which there was an unspoken but obvious pecking order, was expected to spend a few weeks cooling his heels, observing the routine and getting accustomed to the rhythm of this new universe. I managed by a stroke of luck to avoid most of that.

I joined ITN on 1 January 1973.

These days the first day of the new year is a bank holiday but it wasn't then, and although my letter of appointment named it as my start day there was mild surprise that I turned up promptly just after nine that morning. It quickly occurred to me that had I decided to take the day off no one would have noticed.

The half-empty newsroom was shrouded in a blanket of post-Christmas somnolence. The streets through which I walked to the office, usually bustling thoroughfares with crowded pavements, were as quiet as country lanes. All London seemed to be recovering from the New Year's Eve hangover.

Public holidays like 1 January have always been considered 'slow' news days and from where I was sitting nothing much was happening to change that view. My first day in British television crept from slow to comatose.

Then it all changed.

The mood was unexpectedly broken.

Rising from his chair and scanning the room with a querulous gaze, the duty news editor bellowed to no one in particular that there was an interview to be done in the ITN green room, one floor down, almost immediately. At that precise moment I was the only reporter within shouting distance and the assignment fell to me. It was not the biggest story of the day and would probably be totally be forgotten now by anyone but me. I think it had something to do with the Queen's New Year Honours list and would have caused not a flicker of interest on 2 or 3 January.

Its interest to me was the fact that the interviewee was Sir Ronald Bell, Member of Parliament for a Buckinghamshire constituency and a leading light in the Conservative Party's far-right pressure group, the Monday Club.

Some Monday Club members were senior Tories whose influence never counted for much. They grabbed the occasional newspaper headline only on account of their controversial political views. Monday Club members praised the benevolence of white rule in South Africa and Rhodesia, had little time for talk of self-determination for indigenous colonials, voted against the British Race Relations Act of 1965, claiming that it sought to promote unwarranted equality, and urged an immediate halt to immigration to Britain coupled with an effective repatriation scheme. Mildly ironic, then, that Sir Ronald should be greeted in the ITN green room by the first black reporter on national television in Britain.

In very few other situations would we have found ourselves in each other's company. Among those of my friends who followed my first day at ITN my encounter with a member of the Monday Club was the cause of great hilarity. Who on earth could have planned it, they joked. If the MP was surprised at his interviewer he gave no hint.

I attached no significance to the meeting and in fact there was none, but the following morning at the main editorial meeting of the day I was congratulated by Nigel Ryan for having broken my duck. My interview made it on to the late evening news on 1 January and I gained the distinction of getting 'on air' on my first day in the job. Now that I had gained the editor's public commendation, news editors felt no constraint about sending me out on jobs. I had managed to skip most of what should have been my induction to the firm. In one fortuitous leap I had become part of the team.

Assignments were not always as easy to come by. I learned very quickly that it was possible to sit around for days without ever contributing a story to the main evening news bulletin.

When assignments began to flow I revelled in the variety of jobs on which I was sent, although at times variety was the only thing to commend them.

An ITN reporter, especially one new to the job, was a troubleshooter and a dogsbody, a jack-of-all-trades and a humble factory-floor worker sculpting into hopefully watchable reports anything and everything remotely newsworthy

– a sudden change in the weather (I've always struggled to understand why a sudden snowfall in winter on a group of islands in the North Atlantic could cause such consternation), a disastrous fire, a student protest, mass demonstrations, riots, strikes, train crashes, road accidents, political speeches and campaigns, an unbelievable range of human-interest stories, criminal trials at the Old Bailey or complicated legal tussles at the High Court in the Strand. They all came my way in the frenetic tumble of my first months.

General news reporters were expected to cope with the unexpected. I have enduring memories of the overnight editor who seemed to relish calling me at four o'clock in the morning so that, in his words, 'I'd be given enough time to compose myself'. After a suitable pause to make sure I was fully conscious, I would be informed that a taxi had been ordered to pick me up at five to take me to the airport so that I could make the 7.30 flight to Dublin or to Belfast.

There were times when it was obviously important to get to one or other of those destinations at an ungodly hour. In several instances a later flight would have done just as well. In kindness, it could be said that the overnight editor was taking no chances and that he was exercising the caution demanded by his job. I would be less than honest if I didn't say that he exhibited a more than passing fondness for the overdramatic. That's only to be expected, I suppose. The news business thrives on an overdeveloped sense of frantic urgency – the 'hold the front page' syndrome so popular in American movies.

Some assignments came my way in the luxurious ease of mid-morning. Soon after I joined ITN I was sent to report on one of the many Churchill anniversaries (although by then the great man had long gone) at the Banqueting House in Whitehall.

Lady Clementine Churchill was the celebrant-in-chief. She sat with a smile of warm approval of all that was going on. An impressive protocol of ambassadors to Britain took their places in what seemed a never-ending line to pay their respects. Scores of senior political figures, civic leaders and veterans of the Second World War floated around in the spirit of heroic deeds remembered and on a sea of Pol Roger champagne. (Even in his declining years the Pol Roger family ensured that the Churchill cellar was always well stocked.) I could hardly believe my luck as I took my third surreptitious sip of bubbly.

Alas, my new life in television was not always drenched in fine wine, and I acquired pet hates.

I disliked what is probably one of the most common of reporting jobs – standing outside some great office of state, some important building or institution, usually in the cold, waiting to be fed scraps of information of dubious worth by someone in authority or more often than not waiting only to be conspicuously ignored. Stake-outs, as they are known in the trade, tested my patience to its limits and I detested anything vaguely resembling too much of an interest in someone's private life, even when the subjects were the not so private members of the royal family.

I was sent to report on horse shows at various bucolic locations in the home counties to watch for any sign that Princess Anne had begun a widely rumoured romantic relationship with fellow competitor Captain Mark Phillips.

We duly observed the skill of horses and riders clearing high fences, but that was not why we'd been sent. If it had been I would have been pretty useless as a reporter because I know nothing about the sport. That didn't matter. We were there to keep our cameras trained on who went in and out of large horseboxes and to be on the lookout for any sign that the princess and the captain might even barely acknowledge each other's presence. As far as I can recall we saw nothing of the kind.

I would love to think that I never did put my name to too many stories like that. Looking back at it dispassionately, it was probably wrong of me to be so uninterested and uncaring

about something on which millions of our viewers were fixated. I cannot change that now, but neither am I consumed
by guilt. My attitude to stories of that kind remains resolutely
the same.

Years after those unobserved horse-show trysts I reported
on Princess Anne's work as an ambassador for the charity Save
the Children. I was able to explain how the charity was improving the lives of young people in Mozambique, in Uganda
and, unforgettably, in Peshawar on the North-West Frontier
in Pakistan. The Russian invasion of Afghanistan had driven
thousands of people across the border and into Pakistan and
one scene in particular stays with me. The princess was asked
to meet some refugees. Sixty or seventy of them, all male as
I remember, squatted on their haunches on a hillside on the
edge of the city. They were all heavily bearded and wore large
turbans. In the bright morning sunshine it was an image I will
always remember.

Those assignments were more to my liking and conformed
more closely to my view of how television news can enlight-
en those who watched us about critical issues in the lives of
others.

Although I was learning the basic elements of the trade of
television reporting, it didn't take me very long to appreciate
the power of the medium and its ability to influence how
people behaved when facing a camera and a microphone. I
observed the reaction of those who were mesmerised by the
magic of the lens and by the thought of appearing on the
box. I was always worried whether a man or woman in the
street or an interviewee picked at random was performing for
the camera or telling you what he or she actually believed.
I felt that in the main the majority of street-side interviews
testing popular opinion lacked merit. I think that is the case
even more so today when pointing a camera at someone in
the street has become virtually indistinguishable from reality
television entertainment.

I felt that even when interviews were freely given, people needed the protection of journalists and editors.

I was once dispatched to the home of the popular television personality Bruce Forsyth to persuade him to talk candidly about his life away from the small screen. I was pretty sure he could be persuaded to have a short conversation with me on camera. He was flattered by the attention, although I also sensed that he was not entirely convinced it would be the proper thing to do. I decided that it was wrong in the circumstances to apply pressure on him to talk and more pointedly, as tactfully as I could, encouraged his reluctance.

It was probably wrong of me to do that, wrong to take it upon myself to make that decision. But I felt queasy about digging into someone's private life, especially as there was nothing significant or life-enhancing about such a quotidian tale. To me it seemed too close to the kind of mindless gossip I've always detested, and warranted no place on a tightly edited fifteen- or thirty-minute television news broadcast. I understood, of course, that a newspaper faced with the daily challenge of filling forty of fifty pages might react differently to such stories. That is their right and such news items would fall squarely on their turf.

Given the limited time we were allowed in the television schedule, I never felt they were worthy of ours. I believed then as I do now that television news should set the bar at a higher level. That is not to suggest that we think of ourselves as better than the written press. We initiate a deal when we ask people to watch our reports at fixed times every day and I thought we should take care to win their trust and avoid testing their patience with trivia.

At almost every turn I discovered how wrong I could be about judging the strength of such stories. It proved impossible at times even to be given the chance to encourage other subjects to hold their tongue. One incident burned itself into my memory.

Late one afternoon, returning from an assignment in the
north of England, we were asked as a crew to make a detour to
a small mining village on the Welsh border. The early edition
of a London evening paper had carried an item about a young
miner who had gone to America, had been employed as a
gardener by a wealthy and politically prominent family and
in the course of his work had struck up what was described
coyly as a strong friendship with a maiden aunt almost three
times his age. I was not only appalled that we were thinking of
following up such a tacky tale, but I confess at the same time
that I was peeved that we were following up a competitor's
lead and that we were late. How's that for double standards!

I was sure that by the time we got to the village every
regional newspaper reporter within a hundred miles would
be picking the story to bits and dragging its entrails through
the dirt. Apparently one fascinating aspect of the report was
the possibility that said maiden aunt, forsaking the comfort of
her American life, might be persuaded to live part of the year
at the young man's modest abode in the not-so-prosperous
mining village. This bore all the hallmarks of the completely
nonsensical and I remember saying so many times on the journey and in much stronger language.

I persuaded my equally reluctant camera crew to make the
detour by convincing them that, on arriving at the house, we
would be summarily asked to leave, and we'd be able in short
order to resume our journey to London. I was wrong.

We grumbled our way to the village and eventually found
the house. The young man of the story answered my knock
on his door, took one look at me, beamed with satisfaction
and then, making sure he was overheard by the five or six
reporters already camping out in an untidy sprawl in his small
living room, exclaimed: 'Trevor McDonald, *News at Ten* . . .
what kept you?'

I hope he never registered my dismay as he ushered us into
the house. Pleased with the attention, the young man offered

us coffee, confirmed details of the story in a half-hearted way, hedged his bets a little about the lady in question living in Wales for part of the year and smiled contentedly throughout the interview.

I am ashamed to say I didn't have the stomach to follow the progress of that transatlantic relationship or its breakdown. But I had been taught a lesson in how mistaken I could be in anticipating the reaction of would-be interviewees. I was perhaps wrong, too, in attempting to judge what might or might not be of interest to our news audiences. I am as unsure of that now as I was all those years ago.

The ITN I joined in 1973 was envied for the reputation of its heavyweight political and industrial correspondents. On any given day those two departments between them were capable of taking over every story in the news. It was a heady time for politics at Westminster; relations between trade unions and large companies were being stretched to breaking point and the industrial landscape was dominated by the demands of striking workers and the threat of industrial action.

ITN had also made a name for itself by its aggressive pursuit of major foreign stories. It pioneered a new and dashing style. When Turkey invaded Cyprus in July 1974, Michael Nicholson, not content to watch the arrival of paratroopers from a safe distance, went out to greet them as they fell out of the sky and into a field with the words: 'I'm Michael Nicholson from ITN in London. Welcome to Cyprus.' Such daring and journalistic enterprise had not been seen on television news before. ITN was the talk of the town.

The Middle East was forever on the brink of conflict. The interminable war in Vietnam was proving too costly in the loss of young lives. It was bleeding American commitment and dividing the country into ferociously antagonistic camps. And always close to the top of any news agenda at home was Northern Ireland and the Troubles. This meant that on any given day there were three, four or five general reporters chasing any other story with a fighting chance of making the news. This was serious competition.

One area seemed to me fertile with possibilities . . . sport. ITN had always found place in its news bulletins for the biggest sports stories and two camera teams with whom I worked were terribly proud of having devised a method of shooting an entire day's Test cricket on rolls of film, missing none of the critical moments in the game but doing it in such a way that a reporter and a film editor could later easily condense what they were given into a watchable two-minute report. Other games were equally well reported.

I was pleased to discover that very few of my colleagues were sports fanatics. In fact, the majority had little or no interest in sport at all and could never have been persuaded to spend a day at Lord's or at The Oval watching England play Australia. There were one or two rugby fans (for a great deal of my time at ITN the editor was a Welshman, David Nicholas) but in a country hooked on the popularity of football, I recall no diehard enthusiasts.

Along with three million other West Indians I was, on the other hand, mad about sport. Even so, I had no desire to become a full-time sports correspondent for ITN or for any other news outlet. I did not want to spend a lifetime in journalism reporting on something I enjoyed mainly for its entertainment value. Newspapers devote entire sections to sport, quite separate from the front-page headlines. Sport stories were rarely the main items of news on television.

The important point for me was that I had set my sights on cultivating a broader range of interests.

I did myself no favours, though, by talking a little too glibly about my contact with the sporting world and was happy to be assigned to major events. Three years before joining ITN I had, as mentioned earlier, been sent by the Overseas Regional Service of the BBC at Bush House to report on the Commonwealth Games in Edinburgh. Back home in the West

Indies I had been a commentator on cricket, tennis, football and horse racing. There were three racecourses in Trinidad and one in the sister island Tobago. Calling the horses was one of the more challenging jobs I ever did and I have fond memories of trying to name all twelve runners in a five-furlong sprint which was over in no longer than sixty seconds. None of my colleagues on the reporters' desk at ITN could boast of even a passing association with the sport of kings. A number of us played tennis but with no real competition to speak of. I was assigned to cover tennis at Wimbledon.

Sometime in 1977 I was summoned to the office of David Nicholas. It felt nothing more than routine, because members of the ITN management team were collegiate, always access-ible and never overbearing about status. While it was obvious that senior editorial roles carried great responsibility, we were all encouraged to feel that we were part of a team. We were all on first-name terms. ITN was a small place, compact in its organisational structure and at some time or other every week we all ate at the same restaurants and drank at the same pubs. Very conveniently there was a bar on the top floor of our building in Wells Street and a wine bar only yards across the street from our office. But of course David Nicholas was the editor and our boss.

He explained that he had a problem and needed my help. He wanted to assign me to cover sport. A problem had arisen, he explained, because our parent company ITV felt they were getting too little assistance from its ITN news arm in com-peting against the BBC in the coverage of sport. BBC sports programmes were well established even before ITV had come into existence and BBC news had easily accessible sources. ITV was determined to catch up, or at least to be seen to com-pete with the BBC, and required the support of ITN news.

It all made perfect sense. I understood ITV's point imme-diately. The ITN news was more than a successful match for news on the BBC, consistently ahead of it in the ratings, but the same could not be said about our sports coverage. When ITN did report major sports stories it do so brilliantly. I had worked with a number of ITN camera crews who made sport something of a speciality. But as a news service our sports coverage was at best erratic. The BBC reported sport stories more regularly than we did, and ITV now required us to sharpen our act.

When the editor called to see me, ITN did not have a designated sports reporter and ITV's suggestion that we appointed one would at least be seen as a start. It would demonstrate commitment and a willingness to give our sports reporting a more muscular and dedicated look.

In attempting to convince me to do the job, my editor unknowingly faced a problem as big as the one he had with ITV. I had no wish solely to be a sports correspondent and I said so respectfully but firmly. In truth I was somewhat conflicted because paradoxically I am close to being a sports addict. I have frequently joked that addiction to sport is something of a West Indian disease for which, I have usually added, there is no known antidote. For years after I came to London, I constantly chastised myself about the absurdly long hours I spent watching sport of every kind on television and at cricket and football grounds around the country and in other parts of the world. This, however, has never been anything more than an indulgence and a deliciously lazy way of whiling away long passages of precious time. But I had no desire to translate my love of sport into a career. I admired the work of the finest sports writers in their distinguished newspaper columns and I read them avidly, but I thought it much too narrow a field of interest and much too limiting in television news.

I say this now with modesty and trepidation, but I saw my position as non-negotiable.

It was not, by a long stretch, what I came into television journalism to do. In addition, if I ever wished to find a practical reason why I never wanted to be tied to sports reporting at

ITN, there was an obvious one. The reporting of sport at ITN had already been allocated its place in our editorial judgement. It was a second-class citizen. Snippets of news about football, cricket, rugby and tennis, while not entirely ignored, were invariably relegated, quite properly in my view, to the very last items on the news after all the day's important events had been given their due prominence.

Covering politics and industrial relations at home, wars in the Middle East, summit meetings in Moscow or Washington, European elections and political developments around the world had given ITN its mark of distinction. Reporting those big important events were the journalistic heights to which I aspired. I was already doing as broad a range of top-of-the-bulletin stories as I wished on all ITN news programmes and that was a position I wanted to retain.

Having stated my view as clearly as I could, and given that the editor was under pressure to placate our masters at ITV, I felt it difficult to refuse outright. I also thought it would be to my advantage to suggest a compromise. What about my becoming ITN sports correspondent on the clear understanding that it would be for a strictly limited period of about two years? It did occur to me as I made the offer that there was a football World Cup coming up in Argentina, where I had never been, and there was always the luxurious prospect of covering cricket in Australia and, if I was lucky, back in the West Indies, too. A little self-serving, certainly, but I felt a short stint covering sport would be fun and would do me no permanent harm.

Relieved at my suggestion, the editor agreed. He was able to tell ITV he had appointed a sports correspondent and I was able to show that I could shift a little on what I maintained was a matter of principle. I could also burnish my credentials as a team player. It is possible that David Nicholas felt that his sports-reporting problem had been permanently solved. He may have believed that I would become so engrossed in the job that I would in time forget the terms on which I accepted it.

I did not, never for a moment. Covering sport was to me a transit point and I was passing through.

When my two years came to an end I went back to the editor to say that I had fulfilled my part of the deal and, as agreed, I wished to resume my general reporting and news-reading career. It was not an easy conversation, but I had given the matter serious thought and steeled myself into having the meeting. Today I look back at my decision to stick to my guns, limiting my time as sports correspondent, with relief and some pride at the self-assertion and confidence I had demonstrated.

Today I am a member of the All England Lawn Tennis and Croquet Club – to give that hallowed institution its proper name – and whenever I drive through its front gates I have oc-casional flashbacks to my first visit there as an ITN journalist. I was taken to meet the official who managed press relations and I was assured that she would do everything in her power to help me gain access to players after significant matches. It was a pleasant encounter sealed with cups of tea. I had no idea of the maze of difficulties I had walked into.

Tennis at Wimbledon, one of the jewels in the British sport-ing calendar, is still at the time of writing a BBC event. For would-be interlopers the implications of that are profound. In the 1970s ITN had no rights even to be seen too prominent-ly around the place. A lone reporter could probably escape attention and the enforcement of strict tournament rules, but not one accompanied by a three-man television crew. I was allowed to request interviews through the press relations official, but only after a player had completed a full roster of them – first for newspapers, national and international, then for two BBC television channels – separately, two BBC radio outlets – one at a time, and one for a Canadian radio station.

I was permitted to position myself at the end of that line of player commitments to request yet another interview. By that point I could read the signs of exhaustion, if not of total exasperation, creasing the player's features. Then at the slightest hint of acquiescence I dropped the bombshell. The player would be required to accompany me to a camera position adjacent to a car park *outside* the precincts and some distance beyond the main tournament arena. That was the condition on which ITN had been granted news access to a BBC event. It meant a walk of about a hundred yards and it was, not surprisingly, the point at which the most genuine desire on the part of a player to be helpful slowly drained away.

I gained the highest regard for one of the greatest names in tennis – the American Billie Jean King. She was always willing to be led out of the main tournament area to record a short interview for the ITN news. But there were several interviewless days when I held my head in my hands, distraught and almost tearful at a succession of what were, under the circumstances, understandable refusals.

I was much luckier reporting cricket. It took me back to the West Indies, gave me an introduction to Australia and a front seat at one of the biggest events in the history of the modern game – the start of World Series Cricket, commonly described as the Kerry Packer cricket revolution.

Packer, a tycoon with interests in television and in publishing, was wealthy, influential and brash. He was also a gambler. For some years in the mid-1970s he'd been in dispute with the Australian authorities over the rights to broadcast cricket on his television station, Channel 9. For decades those rights had been awarded to the state broadcaster, the Australian Broadcasting Company, the ABC. To Packer that arrangement bore all the signs of a backroom deal stitched up by an old boy network. He was determined to change that and to have cricket matches shown on *his* television channel. He offered to outbid the ABC and when that failed Packer took on the might of the international cricket establishment and won a significant battle in the High Court in London.

I followed Packer's experiment from its unpromising start at the inappropriate trotting park in Perth, just across the way from the famous WACA – Western Australia Cricket Association ground. In Melbourne, Packer was not allowed to use Melbourne Cricket Ground and was forced to stage his matches at the VFL Park. It was not a known cricket venue and those early matches were watched by no more than a few hundred spectators.

But cricket's authorities had made the costly error of under-estimating Packer. They had either ignored or been unaware of the growing mood for change. Packer had pushed an open door. Player sentiment had run ahead of the establishment view. With consummate ease and several fists full of Australian dollars he recruited the support of many of the finest players in the world. For years they had felt unloved and undervalued and were only too happy to play for higher stakes.

There comes a point in all revolutions when the estab-lished order can outwit its opponents by acknowledging their strengths and stealing their ideas. But they never do. They re-treat to the laager, cower behind the barricades and hope the winds of revolution will blow themselves out. Faced with the credible threat posed by Kerry Packer's World Series Cricket, the game's governing bodies committed the sin of choosing confrontation in the High Court in London. Packer was bril-liantly represented. The cricket authorities lost.

Controversy persists about whether the Packer interven-tion did terminal harm to the sport. The man himself had his detractors and was loathed by the establishment. It was recognised that his initial interest in cricket was tied to its commercial possibilities, but there is much more to the story of his intervention.

Kerry Packer saw a popular game stuck in a traditional rut. He spotted an opening in the market to spread the game's appeal to a wider following. He saw the chance to give cricket what he once described to me as a twentieth-century look.

Above the heads of the game's international authorities and in the teeth of their fierce opposition, it had to be agreed that the brash Australian businessman had a point, had the law on his side and had gained the support of the players. The authorities conceded and were forced into making structural changes. Today players are better paid; the way the game is presented on television is a vast improvement to the way we watched cricket before Packer.

There are downsides, too. Perhaps most significantly the game has been pushed into making commercial compromises, the implications of which are only now becoming clear. Cricket-playing nations – be they India, the West Indies, Australia, South Africa or England – admit that schedules and formats are dictated by the demands of the broadcasters who pay millions to have matches shown on their networks. Some non-televised county and state cricket struggles to survive.

In India a new league pays star players from around the world to be part of matches designed primarily as television entertainment. There is now more cricket than ever before and in places like the West Indies traditional fans have lost interest. It is a shock to see Test cricket in some countries played in empty grounds. The broadcasters do their best to disguise that fact, and commentators say little about it, but the number of matches and the frequency of tours are decided largely by the game's television paymasters.

While the process of change continues it is probably pointless to argue whether the new compromises will work for the good of the game or to its detriment. What is unquestionable is that a game so deeply rooted in tradition has been dragged, or to put it more mildly, lured by commercial considerations into a new age. That is the nature of change. What comes in its wake is frequently unpredictable.

My visit to Argentina to cover the 1978 football World Cup taught me something else.

Scotland had qualified for the tournament and England had

not. The enthusiasm of the Scots was high but the performance of the players was a disappointment. Scotland didn't survive the shock of losing their first match to a team of Peruvian 'no-hopers' and the mood in the Scottish camp turned sour. The Scotland team manager Ally MacLeod, normally talkative and friendly, became defensive, tetchy and withdrawn. Faced with a barrage of hostile questions from the press he was unable to explain why his team had failed.

Then came a public relations disaster. A cocktail party organised to celebrate Scotland's participation in the competition coincided with the news that one of the team's star players, Willie Johnston, had failed a drugs test and was about to be sent home. I turned up at the party, camera team in tow, to follow up the story. I was on the point of confronting Johnston when, from across the room, MacLeod saw me and stormed over in our direction shouting and screaming that we should leave the room. He was in no position to make us do that, but he kept insisting.

The sad thing was that prior to covering the World Cup I had been on good terms with the Scotland manager and had even spent time at his home. He had been accommodating and generous. Now, in the aftermath of the Peru result and faced with shocking news about one of his players, he saw my arrival at the party as unwelcome and perhaps even as a betrayal of our relationship.

That was nonsense. A player about to be sent home from an international competition at which Scotland's hopes of success had all but disappeared was a news story of considerable interest and I was there to do my job. MacLeod didn't see it that way. Nor did he seem concerned that his anger was getting the better of him in the full view of dozens of people. What the Scotland manager could not possibly have known was that his audience was at that moment about to become much bigger than those in the immediate vicinity. His reaction was about to go viral.

As he got closer to me and to the ITN crew, arms waving and rage in full flow, he demanded that our lights be turned off. By that time, embarrassed at being the centre of such attention, we complied almost immediately, but my colleague, the highly experienced Peter Wilkinson, unfazed by the plunge into sudden darkness, kept his camera running. MacLeod shouted louder with no clue that his words were being recorded.

Within hours the sound of the outburst had been broadcast on the late ITN news in London and picked up by radio and television stations in Europe and around the world. Thousands of miles from Argentina, commentators concluded that the Scotland team had lost its way and its manager his mind. It was a gloomy end to Scotland's hopeful journey to South America.

MacLeod's career as a top-class football manager never recovered and I always felt a little uneasy when that Argentina World Cup incident was referred to in later years.

Spectacular failures make big news. Improbable though victory was for Scotland in 1978, we had all gone to Argentina with, as the Liverpool football anthem goes, hope in our hearts.

Of greater interest to me than the story of Scotland's demise was the fact that the tournament was taking place in a country run by a military dictatorship since 1976. It had become notorious for its brutality. The regime ran a navy school in Buenos Aires at which thousands of political prisoners were detained with no hope of release. Women who were pregnant when they were imprisoned were kept alive until they gave birth. Their babies were given to those the regime considered to be good military families.

The military strongman in charge during the 1978 World Cup was Jorge Videla. He had judged perfectly what Argentina needed to do to paper over its atrocious reputation. He did everything in his power to keep the focus on the wonderfully riotous festival that is football's World Cup and he prepared his country well.

In television advertisements and in public statements Videla ordered his people to be hospitable. No effort was to be spared in pandering to the wishes of visitors to the country. Much to their astonishment, Scotland fans who had not arranged hotel accommodation and who were seen wandering the streets late at night, in some cases having had more than the odd drink, were taken in by families who had never met them, housed and fed.

I found it an interesting political lesson. Only powerful dictatorships can so order their people. Argentines duly did as they were commanded. Many were naturally helpful, gracious and proud that their country was host to an international sporting pageant. Others were too terrified to disobey.

Many years later, in 2012, the heavy-handed Communist Party in China, acknowledging concern about Beijing's polluted air, simply told people to stay out of the city and watch the Olympic opening ceremony on television. They, too, did as they were told.

Argentina didn't quite get away with it in 1978. No government order and no show of genuine native hospitality could hide the country's darker side. It certainly couldn't be entirely hidden from visiting journalists, even those preoccupied with football. Every Friday, around noon, a group of mothers paraded around the main square in the capital Buenos Aires. As far as I can remember the group was never more than twenty or thirty in number. Dressed in black and bent with the cares of advancing years, they marched in solemn silence. They convened without drawing too much attention to themselves because the security authorities showed a distinct distaste for such demonstrations. We journalists were also expected to be discreet in expressing any interest in why the women had assembled in the square.

One afternoon, having watched the small, dignified parade,

I talked to one mother about why she had come to the square in defiance of the police. What she said was deeply moving. Speaking very slowly and with her eyes fixed directly at me she said in a voice soft but clear: 'Every mother has a right to know what has been done to her son.'

I've never forgotten those words. In their stark simplicity they were a powerful denunciation of the dirty war the government had been conducting against its opponents. Thousands had disappeared, never to be heard of again. Videla claimed that the state was putting down an anti-government guerrilla campaign. How often have we heard that? Had he been referring to them today he might have called them terrorists. Many of those arrested, tortured and executed without trial were political activists, intellectuals and students.

In the end the glory and the razzmatazz of staging the World Cup could not cover up memories of the bloody repression of Argentina's military junta.

Perhaps by the time the competition came to an end the regime thought it had achieved a victory of sorts. A charismatic Argentina football team, with players who were soon to become international stars, won the 1978 World Cup in dashing style and hundreds of thousands of people danced in the streets of Buenos Aires as loudspeakers blared out Queen's 'We Are the Champions'. Celebrations of sporting victories in South America are like no other.

Long before I had succumbed to the glamour of Wimbledon, cricket in Australia and World Cup football in Argentina I had become part of the rolling roster of reporters covering Northern Ireland.

It turned out to be the most challenging assignment I'd undertaken as a television reporter.

5

Under Fire

'Our religion is made so as to wipe out our vices; it covers them up, nourishes them and incites them.'

Michel de Montaigne, *Essais*

Just after four o'clock on the afternoon of Sunday 30 January 1972 a march through Londonderry was fired on by British soldiers. Twenty-eight unarmed civilians were shot. Fourteen were killed; seven were teenagers. Five of the wounded had been shot in the back and it all happened in the presence of the world's press.

Marches in Northern Ireland were steeped in controversy. They frequently ended in clashes between Protestant Loyalists and Catholic Republicans. At various times throughout the late 1960s they caused such widespread disorder that they were banned and declared 'illegal'. The one that day had been allowed on the understanding that marchers kept to the mainly Catholic areas of the city.

Such agreements, usually hammered out in times of great tension, were susceptible to differing interpretations and were in most cases worthless. The one relating to 30 January was no exception. That it began peacefully is perhaps the only point on which everyone agrees. Nearing its end, stones were thrown and it is alleged that in the ensuing confusion the marchers decided to go back on what had been agreed and changed the route. If they did, it was a fateful decision. What is not disputed is that British paratroopers then opened fire. One BBC journalist used the word 'massacre' in describing what happened that day.

The protest had been organised by the Northern Ireland Civil Rights Association, formed to press the general case for the fairer treatment of the province's Catholic minority. Catholic grievances covered every aspect of the way Northern Ireland was administered – mainly by the Unionist Party at Stormont and by politicians in Whitehall. Catholics had protested for years against the discrimination they faced in employment and in housing policies, and equally in the way gerrymandering of electoral boundaries deprived them of fairer political representation. The sense of discrimination ran so deeply that one politician from a decidedly moderate wing of the Republican movement was moved to say in 1971: 'Of course we can reach an accommodation with the Unionists, and we will. Once the Unionist understands that he has to take his foot off the Catholic's neck.'

By 1972 Republicans, especially in Londonderry, had mobilised a clutch of loosely based protest groups in a concerted effort to make the case for civil rights. They went as far as claiming inspiration from the epic marches for black equality in the American South. The march that Sunday was against the policy of internment without trial introduced by the British government at Westminster five months earlier. That detail was lost in the ensuing turbulence.

In a country where history is alive and where nothing is consigned to a forgotten past, the events of that Sunday poured salt into open wounds and poisoned political debate. It led inevitably to new waves of violence. Every roadside assembly, every gathering of fifteen or twenty people turned into a riot and riots became the accepted way of taunting and hurling abuse at the British Army. The noise of explosions reverberated through towns and villages. British soldiers, shouldering guns at the ready, kept anxious vigil in now openly hostile neighbourhoods and armoured personnel vehicles rumbled through the streets recreating images of Europe at war. The soldiers couldn't stop the mayhem.

The IRA repeatedly breached the security cordon thrown around Belfast city centre, planted bombs in broad daylight and killed and maimed hundreds on the mainland, too. The devastation did what it was intended to. It struck at the commercial heart of Northern Ireland and turned a busy shopping district into a bombed-out, bloodstained dystopia.

Public buildings – symbols of authority – were reduced to piles of twisted metal and shattered glass. In places like South Armagh, near the border with the Irish republic and described as 'bandit country', gunmen prowled in the dead of night and murdered at will. The British Army sent in three years earlier to keep the peace between Catholic Republicans who wanted to see Ireland – north and south – united, and Loyalist Protestants who held sacred the union with the Crown, had for a time been regarded as neutral. They soon came to be seen as an occupying force.

On the worst days Belfast, with its streets aglow from burning buildings and bombings, assumed the guise of a fearsome cradle of evil. Night after night the province's Troubles blazed into the headlines.

When I joined ITN in January 1973 I desperately wanted to be a part of the reporting of the Northern Ireland story. It was the lead item on the news on most nights and I was anxious to prove that I was being given the same assignments as every other reporter. It had been one of the conditions on which I joined ITN.

Eighteen months after what came to be known as Bloody Sunday, I was sent to Belfast for the first time as a television journalist. My friends, fellow West Indians and newer acquaintances in London surmised that I had probably taken leave of my senses. I know that my parents, back in the relative calm of the islands, were certain that I had.

I took comfort in the thought that I knew what I was getting into and that it was decidedly what I wanted to do. One drawback was that I'd never been close to anything resembling a war zone. And from everything I seen on television and read about in the newspapers, that is how Northern Ireland looked to me.

If I had any misgivings about finally being sent there, I told myself that at least I understood the broad outlines of the story. Two communities with sharply contrasting visions of the province's future were locked in mortal combat and each was prepared to do whatever was deemed necessary to ensure the vindication of its point of view.

I'd spent a few days in Belfast when I worked for the BBC's Overseas Service at Bush House. During that visit I'd heard the Reverend Ian Paisley, a Protestant minister and Unionist politician, deliver one of his thundering Sunday sermons. More significantly, I'd met and done an interview with William Craig, a former minister for home affairs who once declared he was prepared to make the ultimate sacrifice to keep Northern Ireland a part of the United Kingdom.

I had tackled Craig about one of the more persistent complaints of the province's Roman Catholic minority. For years they believed that they had been denied jobs in public sectors like the police service. The Royal Ulster Constabulary – the RUC – was regarded not only as overwhelmingly Protestant but also as anti-Catholic. Craig's response had surprised me. He'd embarked on a rambling discourse about the size of many Catholic families and how young men from such families didn't always meet the basic requirements for service in the police force. Our meeting had been so cordial, and Craig had been so generous with his time that I felt I could tell him in plain language that such an excuse was hardly likely impress a black West Indian who knew what discrimination looked like when he saw it.

I thought what Craig said was nevertheless interesting. It was to me one example of how prejudices casually expressed and just as casually allowed to take hold in public consciousness can become ossified into unquestioned fact.

Although I was aware of the divisions between Catholic and Protestant communities in Northern Ireland, first-hand experience of those divisions was a shock. Sectarian bigotry had its own diction and its own rituals. When rabbles from both sides of the divide confronted each other across the barricades they traded expressions of naked hate. Opposing gunmen traded bullets.

On my earliest visits to Belfast for ITN it took me some time to get used to the basic facts of everyday existence. There were Catholic and Protestant streets and enclaves known to everyone and observed by all. It was possible to determine a person's religion simply by asking where he or she lived, worked and, most important of all, where a person went to school.

Colleagues at Ulster Television with whom I came into regular contact did their best to convince me that the complexities of the issues in Northern Ireland went far beyond the question of religion. Frequent references were made to the historian and political thinker Liam de Paor, who described the Northern Ireland problem essentially as a colonial one. Read in the light of his work, the province's Catholics could be seen as blacks who happened to have white skins. De Paor concluded that since Catholics and Protestants had no burning desire to convert the other to the one true faith, the Northern Ireland problem should properly be seen as one where a 'racial' distinction between colonists and natives was expressed in terms of religion. It was a brilliant exegesis and over time I came to understand de Paor's view. There was, for example, the perennial question of political power-sharing. By the time I went to Northern Ireland for ITN two attempts at sharing power had failed.

My mother and father,
Geraldine and Lawson.

Beginning in Trinidad. At the local radio station I was newsreader, continuity announcer, disc jockey, and later sports commentator.

I joined ITN on 1 January 1973. Nowadays the first day of the year is a Bank Holiday, although it wasn't then. There was mild surprise when I turned up promptly just after 9 o'clock that morning.

I was at Scotland's ill-fated World Cup campaign in Argentina in 1978.

The poignant scene of the Bloody Sunday civil rights march in 1965, when armed police beat up demonstrators. The Edmund Pettus bridge was the site of the conflict and it is now a national historic landmark.

Smartly suited, confident and smiling, Saddam Hussein exuded total command. I was as nervous as I can ever remember.

With President George W. Bush in the West Wing before the invasion of Iraq in 2003.

Announcing the momentous news of 9/11.

For eight years between 1999 and 2007 I presented ITV's current affairs programme *Tonight*, and interviewed many major political figures of the day, including the Prime Minister, Tony Blair.

Even so, I could never get past the point of seeing the religious divide as a crucial one. The strongest evidence of that, it seemed to me, was the fact that religion had shaped the education system. Young Catholic and Protestant boys and girls went to different schools. On its own, that put an undesirable distance between communities living within a mile or two from each other in roughly the same part of town. It established a pattern of neighbours heading off in different directions from infancy through to adolescence and continuing into adulthood, fostering a separatism that inevitably became a defining force for life.

Religious lines were hardly ever crossed. Many Protestant teenagers progressed into adulthood and into their working lives without any but the most cursory contact with their Catholic contemporaries. Some childhood friendships did cross the religious divide, but they became remarked upon mainly because they were exceptions to the rule.

I remember my surprise at being asked to do television reports about small groups of ten- or twelve-year-old boys and girls, Catholic and Protestant, who were taken on trips to London by an interfaith charity, simply to be able to meet, to talk and to try to get to know each other on uncontested ground. The assumption, or rather the fact, was that such meetings would have been impossible in Belfast or Londonderry.

I'm not sure I ever got over the shock of that.

In the cosmopolitanism of our time it seems insane. I can only hope now that the tone of what I said in my earliest reports did not betray too much incredulity.

It is said that first impressions about Northern Ireland rarely stand the test of time. With greater exposure to life in the province, the theory goes, what had seemed obvious and easy to understand or to unpick would eventually be lost in a forest of complexity. Not entirely true in my case. I saw religion as a sharply dividing factor and I've never wavered in that belief.

When it was announced that Pope John Paul II planned to

visit Ireland in 1979 Ian Paisley felt it necessary to make sure His Holiness stayed south of the border. He said: 'This visit is not on – full stop. The Pope is the antichrist, the man of sin in the Church.' Such brutal language from a man of God about a man of God.

Paisley was not alone in expressing his view about the Roman Catholic minority in Northern Ireland. In 1969, shortly after he resigned as prime minister, Terence O'Neill said this: 'It is frightfully hard to explain to Protestants that if you give Roman Catholics a good job and a good house, they will live like Protestants because they will see neighbours with cars and television sets. They will refuse to have eighteen children; but if a Roman Catholic is jobless and lives in the most ghastly hovel, he will rear eighteen children on national assistance. If you treat Roman Catholics with due consideration and kindness, they will live like Protestants in spite of the authoritative nature of their Church.'

It was just about possible to understand why old political hands seasoned in the rabid, undisguised bigotry of their time could be so condescending. Of much greater concern was that there appeared to be no way of disabusing young people from cultivating and espousing similar views. The school system was no help. The fact that there were almost no integrated schools stood out a mile. It was the fissure along which communities were split. It played a huge part in creating the ground for feelings of separateness, distrust and eventually of hate.

I found it chilling to observe the actions of people who learn to hate when they are still very young.

Years after I stopped going there on regular working visits I discussed the schools issue with Brian Mawhinney, a former minister of state for Northern Ireland. He told me he had always considered the drive for integrated schools one of his most important policy initiatives. There had been progress, he said, but the pace of change had been slow. Personal experience had taught me that the minister's initiative would always have had nothing but a rough ride in Northern Ireland and for that matter south of the border in the Irish Republic, too. I had examples to prove it.

Nearing the end of a brilliant summer's day I stood in a cemetery on the edge of Dublin watching processions of mourners filing in to bury their dead. On the Saturday before, with no warning three bombs had ripped through Dublin city centre. Less than an hour later an explosion shattered the rural tranquillity of the town of Monaghan. In all, thirty-three people were killed; three hundred were injured.

Earlier in the day I had attended the service in the city's main cathedral and seen pallbearers struggle with austere dignity to hide the fact that the tiny caskets contained very little of what was left of the deceased. I followed on to the cemetery where a priest was officiating at several burials. He was a pleasant man and we conversed easily. In between times at different gravesides we talked in generalities of his country's troubled history and about how appalling it was that so many lives had been cut short by one act of insanity. Up to that point the officiating priest and I were in total agreement.

I then launched into my spiel about divided communities and the need for a greater emphasis on integration, especially in schools in Ireland north and south of the border. The Dublin priest was having none of that. He thought that a step too far. His belief, overriding the trauma of massive explosions and multiple deaths, was that Catholic children should be sent to Catholic-run schools.

After that I just about gave up expounding my theory about the importance of integrated schools. I discovered, too, that it was still possible to be surprised at random examples of how divisions in Northern Irish society were perceived by people who lived in the province.

I've often recalled with amusement that I once charged into a casual discussion in a Belfast hotel about mixed marriages. Convinced that I was on safe ground I said at one point that mine was a mixed marriage. 'Is your wife a Catholic then?' enquired one of the participants. It simply never occurred to them that I might have been referring to the colour of her skin.

The stories which consumed the greater part of a reporter's time in Northern Ireland were the incidents of violence day after day, night after night – attacks on British soldiers, sectarian bombings and ghastly murders. The disorder spawned a criminal underworld, ideal for robberies, protection rackets and for the settling of old scores. Getting hold of weapons was not a problem. The place was awash with rifles and sub-machine guns. The perpetrators of crime roamed city streets and country villages with near impunity.

The focus of security was on the campaigns of the Irish Republican Army – the IRA – a paramilitary organisation fighting to unite Ireland, and the Ulster Defence Association and its offshoots, formed to confront the nationalist community and to preserve the union with the United Kingdom. Under the banner of these two groups thousands died.

Many families were allowed to bury their dead. The sight of funeral processions and the silent tread of mourners became a Belfast staple. But scores of other victims bundled away from their homes at gunpoint disappeared into a void, never to be seen or heard of again. Today, after decades of pain, families know the bitter truth. Their brothers, fathers or uncles will not be coming back. Nor is anyone prepared to say how they were killed or to which stretch of barren wasteland their bodies had been consigned.

I was sickened by the violence I saw. To this day, and at times without warning, fragments of dreadful events still flash across the mind.

Late one afternoon I travelled with an ITN crew to a house on the outskirts of the city to investigate reports of a double murder. I found out much more when I got to the house. A gunman had knocked at a kitchen door and had forced his way in. People in the house ran for cover. The gunman followed two of them and opened fire. Shot and wounded, they tried unavailingly to drag themselves out of harm's way. They were cornered near the front door of the house and killed as they cowered in terror.

My colleagues and I had reported on similar incidents over the years and our ITN team that afternoon discussed, as discreetly as we could in the circumstances, whether the story was worthy of the telling. We decided that tracing the gunman's deathly trail and hearing from an eyewitness, who for some reason had escaped the killer's attention, might provide a riveting account for the news later that evening and we set about reconstructing what had occurred.

The cameraman had no difficulty following the gunman's path through the house. It was marked by splashes of blood. Blood was everywhere – in a sink, on the walls and in a tiny pool on the carpet. A relative of the two who died was recounting to me the horror of the incident when a girl of about nine or ten appeared to correct him on a point of detail. Only then did it hit me that the child had seen it all.

I've spent years trying to imagine how someone so young deals with the memory of something so horrible. I'm not sure whether it was ever obvious to those who survived the gunman's wrath or whether it was ever adequately explained to me why *that* house and the people in it had been targeted *that* afternoon. There must have been an explanation of sorts however complicated and counter-intuitive; there always was in Northern Ireland. A police report of the time would probably have listed it in a column marked: SECTARIAN. It would almost certainly have been put down as another incident in a blood-stained catalogue.

To me the horror defied reason. There were times when Northern Ireland itself defied all reason.

For visiting journalists and television crews the Belfast hotel of choice was the Europa. It was comfortable, close to the city centre, within walking distance of the Belfast to Dublin railway station and not very far from flashpoints like the Catholic and Protestant strongholds – the Falls Road and Andersonstown. It was also only a short car ride away from most city disturbances and explosions.

The hotel itself was bombed repeatedly. Partly because so many of us stayed there those incidents were always well reported. It gave the bombers the publicity they sought. As far as I know, journalists were never the targets of attacks on the hotel. We were probably considered useful; our presence had become an adjunct to their plan. There were usually warnings and we were given time to get out. We would then watch from a safe distance while the place went up in the smoke and fire either from a controlled explosion or as the bomber's timing device dictated.

For a time the hotel experimented with manned security gates. It was a token gesture undertaken perhaps to satisfy insurers, assuming that there were still companies willing to take on the risk. The gates and their keepers did nothing to deter the bombers. At the approach of any determined intruder, security guards made no pretence of standing on ceremony. They asked no questions, hastily abandoned their stations and ran for their lives.

It says a great deal about the temper of those times that we learned to look on attacks on our hotel with mannered equanimity, although every bomb blast sounded like the first. The pavements trembled beneath our feet. In my own case a bolt of sickening fear thudded into the pit of my stomach and for reasons I've never been able to explain I found it impossible to stop myself taking off in the opposite direction at full tilt, running away from something programmed to happen. When the rumbling noise died in clouds of dust we regained our war-weary composure and took bets on how quickly the glaziers would arrive to begin the well-practised job of the temporary refit. Glaziers did profitable business in Northern Ireland. To pass the time before we were allowed back into the building we resorted to gallows humour, as though the horror of what we had witnessed could be dissipated by bad jokes.

In reality the bombings induced a climate of fear.

One evening I thought I was being followed as I walked from Ulster Television to the hotel. I tried, without making it too obvious, to outpace my unseen pursuer and I did. Eventually shouting my name to be sure of getting my attention, the man, by this time terribly out of breath, explained that he simply wanted to tell me that a bomb had been planted at my hotel and that I should approach its vicinity with care. In the gloomy streets of Belfast, footsteps in the dark gave rise to suspicion. In that instance I had been trying to escape nothing more than a friendly warning.

We did our best to pretend that we could not be frightened away by the bombers. One afternoon an explosion destroyed the reception and blew out most of the glass on the first three floors of our hotel, exposing the restaurant on the first to the elements. My room, much further up, had been untouched but the manager demanded that we all sought alternative accommodation. The kitchen had been damaged and put out of use, he explained, in addition to which several members of staff had fled in terror. The hotel couldn't feed us.

I had arrived in Belfast only hours before the bomb. I had come directly from another assignment, hated the thought of having to pack my bags again and pleaded with the manager to be allowed to stay. I encouraged a few other journalists to do the same. It was eventually agreed that we could.

That evening, with little protection against the chill and with makeshift curtains billowing in the wind blowing fiercely through the restaurant, we were treated to as fine a dinner as I can remember during my time in Northern Ireland. I recall that its conviviality owed a great deal to the fact that during the course of the meal we had persuaded the hotel's manager to come up with a few choice bottles from his cellar.

Our Belfast hotel quickly acquired a reputation as the place for information trading. It centred on the Whip and Saddle bar – a noisy barn of a place on the hotel's ground floor. At lunchtime, on Saturdays especially, it was packed to the point of discomfort.

The air was thick with cigarette smoke and the high-decibel chatter of those who claimed to know the secrets and the hidden meanings of what was going on in the province. I'm sure that in the course of attempting to find out as much as we could about its tortuously complex politics and listening to contacts whose insight seemed to flow in direct proportion to the warmth of a reporter's hospitality, we were fed a diet of gossip dressed up as undisputed fact. That much is to be generally expected in difficult situations anywhere in the world.

In Northern Ireland it became an art. Its practitioners stalked the bars and restaurants like princes. Their appetites were insatiable. Their faces were masks of confidentiality and conspiracy and they developed a practised way of dropping juicy nuggets into otherwise discursive conversations. We were all ears. We never challenged the belief that only a few well-connected reporters had contacts at the highest levels in the political and paramilitary structures in Northern Ireland.

I would like to think that we treated what we were told with caution. I can't be sure that we always did. In Belfast even the truth could be complicated. One of the most persistent problems for reporters in Northern Ireland was deciding who and what to believe. In a very real sense the isle was full of discordant noises.

We kept in close touch with British Army press officers, and while soldiers' interpretations of events may have been partial at times, the army was usually a good source of basic facts. I was amused that army spokesmen always found a way of telling me, minutes after I'd settled into my hotel room, that my arrival in Belfast had been noted and that they knew where to find me.

That's why I was not entirely surprised to be awoken by a telephone call to my hotel room at about two o'clock one morning from a British Army contact. There had been an IRA attack on British soldiers in the small town of Belleek in Co. Fermanagh, near the border with the Irish Republic, and that there were fatalities. I convinced my ITN colleagues that we should set off from Belfast at five.

We arrived in Belleek at the break of dawn to a sight I shall never forget. Belleek is a pretty market town, proud of its ancient Celtic origins and surrounded by lush, rolling country-side. Earlier that day soldiers in a patrol vehicle were making their way back to base. As they crossed a small bridge over a tiny stream a bomb had exploded under their vehicle. It was a powerful device and had been detonated by remote control. The force of the explosion blew the vehicle several feet into the air and sent its shattered pieces tumbling around in a mess in the surrounding fields.

Six soldiers were killed. Before journalists and camera crews are allowed anywhere close to scene of an explosion army specialists are sent in to make a forensic assessment and generally to clean up. We got there early that morning before any other television crew and were allowed to record the specialists doing their work. Consumed by shock and by their ghastly task, they took no notice of us.

Dismembered parts of what were once living, breathing bodies hung loosely on gorse bushes. There was no blood. Occasionally I thought I could recognise a bit of an arm or a leg but I couldn't be sure. The soldiers went about their work with great care, placing what was left of their colleagues into plastic bags. Hardly a word was spoken. We covered the scene as best we could and left. The return journey to Belfast took place in almost total silence. As a compensation for having set out at the crack of dawn we had promised ourselves a full English breakfast. No one had the appetite.

Back at the ITN office on the roof of Ulster Television my

job was to prepare a report for the lunchtime news. There is an established convention on what pictures can be shown before what is called the evening 'watershed', meaning the time after which audiences can have no complaints and should in fact be prepared for the more hard-hitting images. The grimmest scenes are the most carefully edited. As conflicts around the world grow in number and become more accessible to cameras, we have become accustomed to nightly commentaries on the indiscriminate brutality of war. Even so, what is shown on television news must still conform to what's generally held to be 'in good taste'.

Appalled at what I'd seen in Belleek I had allowed my emotions to run ahead of my duty as a television journalist. I wanted to be as boldly descriptive as I could about what happens when a bomb rips through an army vehicle carrying six soldiers. I had perhaps been much too anxious to share my shock.

My report for the news that lunchtime contained images too graphic for the time of day and I was given a sharp reprimand by ITN. The British Army headquarters in Belfast took a different view. An army spokesman telephoned immediately after the broadcast to commend me on what he called my excellent work. He had an obvious interest in wanting the world to see the true nature of the army's battle with the IRA.

In the sturdier world of journalistic standards ITN was right and I was in the wrong. Guidelines about what we could show and when had been arrived at after serious thought. I should have followed them and I had not done so. If I were forced to make a half-hearted defence of what I did, I would say only this. Perhaps because we have become inured to reporting the most tragic events we slip, at times, too easily into the comfort and safety of understatement.

Journalists are bombarded by government-inspired lines and can be masters of understatement. I've always remembered that in his broadcast to the nation at the end of the Second

World War, Emperor Hirohito of Japan never once used the words 'defeat' or 'surrender'. He suggested instead that things had not worked out exactly as his country might have wished. That could have been a Whitehall department statement any day in 2019.

To a large extent government statements do their job. We repeat them over and over. Phrases like 'the war on terror' trip off the tongue with little thought of what the strategic aims of such a war might be or how it would be fought and whether, given its many front lines, it might ever end. And we once allowed into common use the euphemism 'extraordinary rendition'. Those words are unexceptional but referred to the practice of taking suspected terrorists who were either captured or brought to secret 'black sites' in Afghanistan, in the Middle East and in Europe to be tortured into revealing what they know, contrary to all military convention.

Some of the captured were terrorists involved in the planning and execution of acts of indiscriminate murder. Others had no terrorist connections. They were nonetheless bundled on to planes with hoods over their heads and faces, bound hands and feet to their seats and kept in prisons beyond the reach of the processes of international law.

As a television reporter and later as a news presenter I made it a habit of trying to weed out innocent sounding euphemisms whenever I spotted them in scripts. I hope that this partly explains my approach to reporting what I'd seen in that pretty market town in Co. Fermanagh that morning all those years ago.

As far as I can tell, journalists were never targeted by any group in Northern Ireland. I was always terrified to be in the vicinity of the noise of explosions or the crack of gunfire but violence was never directed at me.

A smartly dressed young woman once told me quite bluntly to get out of town.

I had gone with a camera crew to report on a Republican

rally in Londonderry. Nothing about it was unusual. A couple of thousand people had assembled in a small square to listen to rousing speeches relayed through an over-loud system. We stood at one corner of the square.

I saw the woman heading in our direction for some time before she arrived to our corner of the square. Picking her way through the crowd her eyes never left me. She came right up close and whispered in my ear: 'I don't like what you do,' she said. 'If you ever come back to this city you'll never leave alive.'

Having delivered her message she turned on her heels, walked back in the direction from which she'd come and was quickly swallowed up by the crowd.

Were such a thing to happen to me today, I would almost certainly demand some explanation. Perhaps I have become a little more confident even in the face of what might be called a threat. That afternoon in Londonderry I was so shaken that I never said a word.

I took the warning only half seriously. I was due to head back to London on the following day, reported the incident to my news desk and for a few weeks after my return to Northern Ireland I didn't go back to Londonderry.

On another occasion I was standing with a group of reporters in the dying moments of an attack on a police station and army barracks on the outskirts of the Belfast city centre. At the height of the disturbance I remember watching a bespectacled middle-aged man instructing five or six teenagers how paving slabs could be loosened, broken up into spiky pieces and used as missiles to be hurled at a company of soldiers from the Royal Green Jackets.

When the soldiers felt they had restored some semblance of order, a British army major approached us enquiring in quite a loud voice and in a distinctly clipped accent whether we reporters would like to be escorted up the hill to the police station to get the army's version of what had gone on. I was about to take one small step forward to do as the major suggested when I felt a hand on the back of my collar. Then there was a female voice. In tone and language which would in no circumstances be described as friendly, the voice said that if I had the slightest interest in surviving the afternoon, I should not move another inch. Without looking round or responding I did precisely as I was told and made no further attempt to move forward to hear the army's view of what had transpired that afternoon.

There were insults aplenty. They had become the stock-in-trade of Northern Ireland life and visiting journalists were frequently on the receiving end. I was standing in a Belfast street one afternoon delivering a few chosen words to the camera when someone shouted: 'Brits go home!' Momentarily confused that such a remark could be directed at me, I looked around and behind me to try to see who the unfriendly words had been aimed at. The cameraman and the soundman, both Northern Irish, collapsed to the ground in laughter. The insult had been meant for me.

In August 1976 Northern Ireland appeared to embrace the general spirit of a movement for peace in the province. It was born in the wake of a singular tragedy. A vehicle driven by a man believed to be a member of the IRA came under fire from British soldiers. The driver was fatally wounded. The vehicle careered out of control and ploughed on to a pavement, killing three children and seriously injuring their mother. One child was six weeks old; the others were aged two and a half and eight.

The children's aunt Mairead Corrigan and her friend Betty Williams issued an impassioned plea for peace in Northern Ireland. It touched a chord and the response was immediate. From across the sectarian divide, tens of thousands of people took to the streets to demand an end to the years of violence. The Peace People, as the founders and their supporters came to be known, aimed their message at all parties and all those in authority. They travelled to London to see politicians at Westminster and caught the attention of well-wishers in Europe.

The Peace People were never in a position to suggest or to help shape the mechanisms through which violence could be tamed, nor could they force those on opposing sides to a conference table. We knew that. We could see from very early on that there was a limit to how far one could go with a call for peace but without any power to make it happen.

But here was a Northern Ireland story that did not involve the usual sounds of violence. A mother's plea had become a campaign with a clarion call for change and we journalists were swept along with the tide. We followed Peace People marches, listened to the stirring speeches, delighted to report something refreshingly new.

It was inspiring to see Catholic and Protestant mothers join hands at rallies across the province. In those moments, all too brief, the peace movement provided glimpses of a world ordered by tolerance and civility. Its founders were feted internationally and awarded the Nobel Peace Prize.

I came to know Corrigan and Williams well and travelled to Oslo to see them receive the Prize. That night we celebrated with copious quantities of whisky, riotous laughter and lashings of hope. Hundreds of miles away from Belfast, we dared to believe that all things were possible, even in Northern Ireland. I remember we talked expansively about how the peace movement might evolve to shame the men of violence. I suspect even then we knew we had allowed ourselves to be caught up too much in what was for Northern Ireland an unusual moment of celebration.

In the sober light of day, and despite the glamour of the Nobel Prize, the problem was that call for peace in 1976 had no real transformative power beyond the fervent wish of decent, right-thinking people to deplore in unambiguous terms the senseless loss of three young lives.

It was in some respects something I had seen before. In

the midst of the sectarian strife and the killing in Northern Ireland, talk of peace was common currency. It came from every quarter and was part of the sorrowful riposte to every tragedy. It was not surprising that people living permanently in the shadow of violence have the need to give expression to hope, however faint, that the terror might eventually end. We all need dreams of survival. I heard those voiced by politicians, clergymen and by people in the street all through my time in Northern Ireland. They always seemed genuine. But whenever conversations turned to the tough compromises necessary to make lasting peace a possibility, the dreams revealed themselves to be what they were. Colliding with reality, like Prospero's spirits in *The Tempest*, they 'melted into air, into thin air'. And at that point the most reasonable sounding interlocutors re-treated to fixed positions behind their ideological barricades. No hearts and minds had been changed. The political reality was just the same. Everyone wanted peace on *his* terms. Real compromise was as ever in short supply. In many instances they were never possible.

I was always puzzled and saddened by the violence I saw in Northern Ireland, and no matter how often its roots were explained to me I never reached the point of totally under-standing how people who lived in such close proximity could turn on each other with such naked hate. Perhaps because it was my first big assignment for ITN I found myself talk-ing about Belfast and Londonderry in places as far away as Moscow and Beirut.

Today, after years of conferences and a succession of agree-ments, some concluded in elaborate ceremonies, Northern Ireland has taken many steps back from its darker past. Belfast has shrugged off its despondent, bedraggled look and now proudly shows off its prosperity as a centre of business enter-prise in elegant, shiny buildings. It invites tourists to admire its new face; the arts flourish. In 2010 Londonderry was awarded the accolade of UK City of Culture.

That is remarkable progress and a tribute to successive British prime ministers and to American presidents who have refused to let Northern Ireland languish in the political wilderness. It's a tribute, too, to political figures in Northern Ireland who have a sincere wish for peace. But just occasionally these days I am shocked into reminding myself why, from my first visits there, I thought some divisions in Northern Ireland might defy the process of healing for a good deal longer.

At the end of 2014, forty years later and a long time after I stopped reporting in Northern Ireland, a former American diplomat made several transatlantic journeys in increasingly desperate attempts to get the parties in the Assembly to agree on the still contentious issues of parades, the flying of flags and how to deal with the legacy of the long years of unconscionable violence.

There should, in effect, be no real problem about parades and the route they should take, save the fact that the two contending sides want to march through each other's areas. It's a determination to annoy and to humiliate. There appears to be a deep-seated yearning for confrontation. The same applies to the flying of flags. Their promoters seem eager to say: 'They are symbols of my political beliefs and I want you to see them, especially as I know how much they offend you.'

All this sits oddly with the progress the province has made in political and economic terms. I would never have foreseen a bitter dispute over the flying of flags. The historian and biographer Tim Pat Coogan, a scholarly observer of what he calls Ireland's ordeal and its search for peace, says that 'In Ireland, history repeats itself first as tragedy, and then as tragedy.'

I first went to Northern Ireland in the 1970s when the violence was at its worst, but once infected or once bitten you're never far away from the events there. Even today I never feel absent from what happens there.

Long after I ceased to be assigned to the province I would try to urge my colleagues in the newsroom to put Northern

Ireland at the top of the news agenda if I was doing *News at Ten* that evening. They would say to me, 'But Trevor, Northern Ireland has gone out of the news.' For me it never really did, and that is because I never saw an end to the fault lines in the society that for so many years had led to the problems there in the first place.

Over the years, people have made several attempts to heal the divisions in Northern Ireland and it occasionally succeeds when there's a tragic event. People in Northern Ireland are filled with emotion and vow that this must never happen again, but of course it does. I never thought I would live to see the Good Friday Agreement. I never thought I would live to see Martin McGuinness and the Reverend Ian Paisley sending a letter to the Irish cricket team congratulating them, signed jointly by them both. But eventually the divisions resurface, and that is what has happened today. The new devolved government in Northern Ireland has crashed and been suspended, because those fault lines have reappeared. And my great fear about Northern Ireland is that they eventually resurface and will always stymie any notion of political progress. I hope I'm wrong, but that's my great fear.

6

Foreign Correspondent

'The eye sees not itself, but by reflection.'

William Shakespeare, *Julius Caesar*

It took me the better part of five years to feel that I had survived my scary introduction to the world of British television journalism. I had done reasonably well as a general reporter, but the big change came when I began to be given regular shifts as an ITN newsreader. It turned out to be the defining phase of my career. It gave me name recognition and enhanced my standing as a reporter. Even better than that, I realised that it represented everything I wanted to do – to spend part of my time as a presenter, but to make sure that I didn't miss out on the opportunities to be sent abroad on big foreign stories.

In an industry like ours with very few structured opportunities for advancement, carving out a place as a presenter as well as that of travelling reporter was to me just about as good as it ever gets. Colleagues in our industry have different views about this, but I have always felt that time spent as a general reporter gives credibility to the job of presenting the news. It worked for me and looking back now I cannot imagine my career developing in any other way.

Way back in the afternoon when, nerves jangling and wracked by uncertainty, I made that tentative journey from the BBC World Service at Bush House in the Strand to the

ITN office in Wells Street for my first job interview, I could never have dreamed that such a work balance was possible.

The guiding principle of my working life remained a commitment to hard work. It had been a passion from my earliest days in Trinidad, an important element of the culture into which I had been brought up. Nothing came easily. Everything had to be fought for. Doggedly unrelenting in pursuing my goals, my work was now all-consuming. Almost every other aspect of my life was framed in the context of my work as a journalist.

I missed few opportunities to keep abreast of changes in the world of international politics. I read voraciously and I considered it part of my job to cultivate a broad range of contacts at home and abroad. I made a point of doing that. Foreign embassy press officers, ambassadors and other senior diplomats serving in London were almost without exception keen to represent their government's views on important issues. I found them accessible and they always found time to see me. Some became friends.

I regarded none of this as particularly burdensome, since a fair number of these contacts were cemented in frequent off-the-record conversations, at gossipy, informative lunches, cocktail parties and at convivial dinners.

I felt no great pressure and paid little attention to the fact that I continued to be labelled as Britain's first black national television reporter and newsreader, although subconsciously I knew that this was an important factor in the general assessment of who I was and how I did my job. I knew instinctively that I could not be seen to fail. I sensed it when people stopped me in the street to ask me how I came to be employed at ITN. Sometimes the questions hinted at a deeper enquiry. Some people simply wanted to wish me luck.

I gave great thought to every assignment. The medium of television can cast an unforgiving light on shoddy work. By its very nature, television affords few hiding places. The camera is unforgiving about sloppy work. I tried to remember that, especially when I was assigned to report on stories I didn't care too much about.

I quickly acquired the habit of never leaving home without a toothbrush and a passport. For the most part, this was done to show that I was as competitive as everyone else and expressed nothing more than hopeful optimism that I would be asked to rush off to Heathrow to be flown to some European city.

Whenever it amounted to anything more than that, it presented a nice line in conversational one-upmanship to be able to say that you began your morning in London but ended up doing the lead story for *News at Ten* that same evening in Geneva. I am not too sure anything like that happened more than a dozen times in my entire career.

I was on occasions assigned to places I knew little about and to countries where native customs and language were only the first of many barriers to professional analysis. The help of contacts on the ground – taxi drivers, local reporters, interpreters and academics – was invaluable. At times their advice was lifesaving.

Journalists who spend long periods far away from home to satisfy the demands of a career requiring dedication that borders on the psychotic know, whether they acknowledge it or not, that such a life is possible only with resolute family support. Mine has given me more than I can repay. I cannot make up for that now, committed as I was to working long hours in London on weekdays, weekends and on public holidays. Looking back, there were times when the number of tasks I agreed to undertake was thoughtless and absurd.

Such ceaseless striving to be successful, especially in an industry as highly visible as a career in television is, carries risks I never imagined or worked to avoid. It is, I think now, much too easy to become defined by what you do and not by who you are. I have often wondered if, over time, everything about you comes through images on a screen at the punitive expense of the loss of inner self.

When I was not working in town or in some other part of the United Kingdom, I spent weeks and months crossing international boundaries and time zones in pursuit of that elusive journalistic pot of gold. Some editorial pressure was exerted occasionally to remind reporters that we were supposed to be available to go anywhere at any time and frequently at a moment's notice. In truth no one pressed me too hard. I had willingly given up control of my time and a large chunk of my life to ITN.

I did on one occasion turn down an assignment to report on a siege at an OPEC meeting in Vienna a few days before Christmas. I had not wanted to be away. I remember now with mild amusement, how in that instance, for the best of personal reasons, I had made the wrong call. The siege ended in a matter of hours. I could have gone to Vienna, done the story and returned home for Christmas. As it was, I had needlessly incurred the mild displeasure of the ITN foreign desk by refusing to go.

Many years later, I refused on another occasion to go back to Iraq when I felt it was simply too hazardous. The country was in the grip of the unspeakable terror and bloodshed that followed the American invasion in 2003; Baghdad had become even more dangerous than it was during the war and certainly much more dangerous than in the worst days of Saddam Hussein.

The fact that I can so clearly remember those two incidents in a career spanning more than three decades is itself a comment on how infrequently I turned down assignments.

In the main I was happy to join the madding chase. At times what I did defied logic, save the dubious assertion that it was what the job required. There's a distinctly hollow ring to that now. The life of an international reporter is, of course, a peripatetic one, travelling to New York or Mumbai or Beijing one

day and being sent elsewhere the following day. I remember
one morning leaving home to play tennis and my bosses saying,
'Could you go back and change and get on to Concorde? I've
asked British Airways to hold it; to go to New York.' That life
can be very difficult for personal relationships.

Today, I cannot for the life of me recall what the story
was and why my journey across the Atlantic was deemed so
urgent. What I do recall is that on presenting my ticket at
the British Airways desk in New York to make the subsonic
hop to Washington, the attendant looked up from her com-
puter and said: 'Mr McDonald, I have a message here from
your wife: she says, "You were off to play tennis when I left
home this morning. What the hell are you doing in New
York?"'

Those are part of a pattern of painful memories. But it is
how I lived my life. I did things like that over and over for
years and I would be less than honest if I didn't admit that to
a large extent I found weird pleasure in that bizarre existence.

Throwing yourself half asleep in a disorderly flurry into the
back of a cab or rushing to the airport to get on a plane to
the next place to report on the next big event became the
equivalent of an adrenaline shot, a thrill, a drug. The craving
never died. Thus addicted, time spent on the move came to
be seen as evidence of success. There was always another story
to be done. The expanse of those waiting to be told was vast
and endless.

There was always another political or tribal leader to be
interviewed, another impossibly tangled tale to be explained.
If you are of a certain journalistic mind it was a world without
end.

T. S. Eliot writes in *The Love Song of J. Alfred Prufrock* about
measuring out life with coffee spoons. In a more prosaic vein
I came to measure mine by the number of assignments to
trouble spots and by totting up the number of countries and
cities – those where I actually worked and those glimpsed in

the comfort of a 747 through fleecy clouds from thirty thousand feet.

It is an odd way to pursue a career and an even odder method to judge its progress. But that is how I spent the greater part of my professional life and that is how many of my contemporaries felt as we competed to be top of the list to be dispatched to report the next bloodstained civil war or to be sent to the next impoverished backwater where children with flyblown faces, bulging eyes and distended stomachs were dying of malnutrition in full view of our cameras.

We rationalised our dependency on those assignments by convincing ourselves that there was virtue in getting the story and in shocking the world into an acknowledgement of the banality of evil and the murderous capacity of despots to inflict pain and distress on their fellow citizens. That, after all, is at the core of what responsible journalism does.

It must also be said, though, that to a large extent we ignored the thought that exposure to a succession of grim, tragic events can change one's view of the world and not always for the better. Perhaps we became too steeped in seeking out the political ghouls and the tragedies they rained with such casual wilfulness on their own people. Perhaps too readily we came to regard the ghastly and the appalling simply as mundane – recurring episodes in the sad, unending story of human misery. I do occasionally wonder whether we were sufficiently critical.

Over time the scars left by the memory of being close to such profane demonstrations of inhumanity dull the senses and perhaps bruise the soul.

For too long we judged disasters as the norm. We could hardly wait for the next tragic story to rear its ugly head. I see that so clearly now. Back then, completely immersed in the doing, I never gave it much thought.

I have one extenuating confession. I'd always felt a little queasy about the barely suppressed enthusiasm with which we prepared for the coverage of another senseless war. The newsroom went into overdrive. A jolt of frenetic energy coursed through the place. How soon could we get our people to the front? Could the Ministry of Defence assist? What about our contacts at the Foreign Office? The phones rang red-hot. Passports at the ready, we all soaked up the thrill of being put on high alert.

That much was to be expected in any newsroom worth the name. How strange it would be if it were not so. It is after all what journalists are supposed to do. What disheartened me and on one occasion moved me to tears was that too many of my colleagues couldn't wait to don the flak jacket and race to the front line. Wars were the biggest stories and were the most eagerly sought. Dodging bullets or watching others cut down by them was one step on the road to journalistic recognition and, who knows, to journalistic immortality.

I am not a pacifist but very early in my reporting career I acquired an interest in the possibility of peaceful solutions to disputes between peoples and nations. Quite often, as a consequence, I failed until the very last moment to see that peaceful settlements aren't always possible and that the drift to bloodletting is part of the thread that runs steadily through the sad, depressing history of our time.

When all else fails nation states pursue their interests and stake their claims, however unworthy, on the strength and in the ability of their fighting forces and the sophistication of their weapons. Diplomacy is frequently the last throw of the dice and seldom a sure-fire winner.

The pre-eminence of the role of the military-industrial complex in superpower politics is a twentieth-century phenomenon. We take immense if somewhat bizarre pride in the destructive power of modern weapons. And from the dawn of time war has been the ghastly spectre lurking in wings of international political discourse. It is always the ultimate threat. There is the feel of inevitability about it.

I learned to hate wars though, in the life I chose, I could hardly avoid them all.

There were times when my determination to be sent on the biggest stories on the television news agenda transcended my dislike of conflict and defied common sense.

I had joined ITN during what turned out to be the final phase of what came to be known as the Cod Wars. These were battles about fishing rights fought in acrimonious meetings in NATO and at the United Nations between Iceland on one side and Britain and a number of European countries on the other. The 'war' had been going on since the late 1950s.

Iceland, with an economy overly dependent on fishing, first set its territorial limits to twelve miles, extended it to fifty as fish stocks diminished and then in the mid-1970s unilaterally extended it further to 200 miles, telling all other fishing countries to keep out. Britain refused to accept that and sent Royal Navy frigates to do battle with Icelandic coastguard vessels in mountainous seas. Trawler nets were cut, and boats were rammed in daily episodes of maritime sound and fury.

No lives were lost in these confrontations, but the television images were dramatic and revived atavistic memories of the gloried history of Britannia's command of the ocean waves. As a consequence ITN reporters were regularly assigned to Royal Navy frigates for several days at a time.

One look at the forty-foot waves lashing over the sides of the competing vessels in freezing temperatures should have told me that it was rank insanity to think that I could have survived more than sixty seconds in those conditions. To say that I'm not a good sailor is an understatement. I'm put off at the mere thought of a breezy morning on the Thames. However, I signed up and was kitted out for my week in the North Atlantic with the Royal Navy. I wanted to be seen to be part of the drama. I was over-anxious to prove I was as good and as tough as any other ITN reporter. It was a prime assignment but, in my case, it was beyond stupidity.

Fortunately for me in this instance the gods were kind and I was spared the indignity of making an ass of myself in full public view. An agreement between the contending sides was reached just before I could leave London. It probably saved my life.

And yet, despite such examples of questionable judgement on my part, my life as a journalist has been a journey of discovery like no other, frustrating at times, occasionally with elements of danger, time-consuming inevitably, but always absorbing. In reviewing episodes in my travelling life I am reminded of the reaction of the Queen of Sheba on visiting King Solomon's court for the first time. Stunned by its magnificence she is said to have remarked: 'The half had not been told me.' I have a sense of what the Queen of Sheba meant.

Some experiences have to be lived. Descriptions by the keenest observers are at best a little more than half good. Nothing beats being there.

Along the way, with great good fortune I have had a privileged journalist's seat at some of the most memorable events in international politics. It was precisely what I dreamed of doing when in Trinidad all those years ago, on a clumsy, battery-powered radio I begged my father to buy, I listened to correspondents reporting for the BBC World Service from places I only knew as dots on a map of the world.

Back on the course I was beginning to set more clearly for myself, I resumed reporting on summit meetings in European capitals and following visits abroad by British foreign secretaries. I have vivid memories of Lord Carrington's visit to Israel in 1982. It turned out to be his last as foreign secretary.

Assistance on finding a solution to the Israel–Palestine conflict had for years been a stated priority of successive British governments. In fact, progress was patchy. There were talks, formal and informal, by British representatives but the reality was that the United States was regarded, quite properly, as the only country with the military and diplomatic power to push the competing interests to anything resembling a lasting agreement.

Anwar Sadat, the former president of Egypt, often said that the Americans hold '99 per cent of the cards in the Middle East'.

In my own time, buoyed by conspicuous bursts of optimism, there were hugely publicised summit meetings and uplifting images of enemies shaking hands at the White House and at the Camp David presidential retreat, and a huge effort by George H. W. Bush's secretary of state, James Baker, to get Israelis and Palestinians to agree on a framework for peace at a top-level meeting in Madrid.

Over the years, from the White House lawn and in European capitals, I watched processions of government ministers come and go, all coached into making carefully guarded statements about the possibility of a peaceful future for the Middle East. Words, thousands of them, filled with hope, devoured acres of newsprint and consumed hours of manpower, radio and television time.

Britain played its allotted supporting role in the search for peace in the Middle East and Lord Carrington's visit to Israel was an appropriately low-key affair. He had taken with him no new plans for a diplomatic breakthrough. That was also well-suited to the foreign secretary's quiet style. He was never boastful, and certainly not about what his visit could achieve.

It was nevertheless one of the pleasures of my reporting life to be part of the press corps travelling with the foreign secretary.

Sadly that visit to Israel was not one of those.

The first discordant notes were sounded when the foreign secretary was taken on a tour of the Yad Vashem Holocaust Museum in Jerusalem. For any important visitor to Israel it is a mandatory stop. It is impossible to be unmoved by exhibits seared with pain and unbearable suffering, in the historical sweep of the events that led to the unconscionable death of six million Jews.

Unsurprisingly, one section highlights Neville Chamberlain's pre-war visit to Munich and pictures of his infamous 'piece of paper' on his return to London, holding out the possibility of peace in our time. Stopping for a moment at the museum's exhibit, Lord Carrington seemed to be attempting to suggest, a little tentatively I must say, that it was perhaps possible to give too much political significance to that single event. Whatever the merits of the foreign secretary's point, that museum was almost certainly not the place to attempt to make it.

The museum's director's response was terse. He was having none of that. He cut off the foreign secretary abruptly. 'That is not the case,' he said, 'you made the same mistake with Hitler then that you're making with Yasser Arafat now.'

After that, everything went south.

Lord Carrington kept his appointment with Prime Minister Begin who lectured him for two hours, seldom allowing the foreign secretary to get a word in. To round off a baleful day, Lady Carrington was given similar treatment when she met Mrs Begin for tea.

Worse was to come.

Before his final press conference in Israel, word had begun filtering through from London that the Argentines had landed a small fleet of boats on the British Falkland Islands in the South Atlantic. Argentina had always disputed Britain's claim to the islands but had restricted its protests to angry words. Argentina's military leader General Galtieri had recklessly gone one step further. Landing boats on the Falklands was seen as too much of a provocation.

For the British foreign secretary, Argentina's action could not have come at a more inappropriate time. The diplomatic pace was being set in London. He was far away in Israel.

At his final meeting with the press he was bombarded with

questions about events in the South Atlantic, especially from those of us who had travelled with him from London. There were only a few routine enquiries about the Middle East and his discussions with Israeli Prime Minister Begin.

It was not the foreign secretary's finest moment. It was painful to watch and he knew it. There was not much he could say about a situation that had caught everyone in London by surprise. It was worse for him, since he was far from home. The press conference fizzled out in noisy disorder. It had satisfied no one.

Perhaps even then at the back of Lord Carrington's mind was the fact that the British government might have inadvertently encouraged Argentina's decision to invade the islands. Sometime before, Britain had withdrawn from the vicinity of the Falklands a number of protection vessels. Had they still been assigned to the South Atlantic their presence might have given the Argentines pause. Nobody could say for sure at the time, but Lord Carrington might have convinced himself that the withdrawal of the protection vessels might have been a major diplomatic blunder.

The foreign secretary knew the day had not gone well, and on the way back to London he asked us by implication what we had made of his performance at the press conference. We were only a small group, fewer than a dozen if I remember correctly, and not terribly anxious to tell Lord Carrington what he already knew. I replied a little hesitantly to say that he had not done particularly well, quickly adding that he had been put in an impossible position by the questions about events in the South Atlantic.

He didn't disagree but shrugged and asked me, not expecting a reply: 'Well, what was I supposed to say?' With that, he returned to his seat at the front of the plane.

They were the last words from the foreign secretary to those of us travelling back with him to London. Within a few days the invasion of the Falkland Islands had become a full-blown crisis and only a few days after that Peter Carrington resigned. Great efforts were made to persuade him to remain in post, but he resisted them all. Always a man of honour, he felt that the tragic turn of events in the South Atlantic, especially the withdrawal of the protection vessels, had occurred on his watch and that he should shoulder part of the blame. For a man of Carrington's character it was nothing more than the responsible, decent and honourable course. Few other politicians would have done the same then and fewer since have behaved with such conspicuous honour. In the lexicon of modern political practice such ministerial resignations are rare.

Carrington's departure from office was much regretted. I was at the Foreign Office the day his resignation was announced, and however well they tried, some civil servants could not hide their emotion and their tears. I had been given advance notice of the impending resignation and the Foreign Office's deep disappointment and shock were obvious when one officer attempted to stop me leaving the room before the full resignation statement had been made. I had been rushing out to confirm the news to my office. ITN had known it was coming.

In a very short time the War Cabinet was meeting daily, and a British task force was assembled. It embarked on a long journey south from Portsmouth on the hazardous mission to retake the Falkland Islands. The United Nations Security Council met in emergency session, and not long after that I was on my way to New York.

I should declare in all honesty that I thought the role of the United Nations would probably be conclusive and there would not be a shooting war in the South Atlantic.

The United Nations mesmerises journalists who are sent to report its deliberations. It certainly did that to me. The most fleeting glimpse of seasoned diplomats and leading politicians pacing its famous corridors, twisting the language of international politics to their liking, commands attention and respect and blurs impartial judgement.

Britain had won a significant diplomatic victory in the earliest stages of its dispute with Argentina over the Falkland Islands. It secured a Security Council resolution calling for the Argentines to leave the islands. Beyond that, my days reporting from the United Nations were dominated by nothing more significant than a few words from Secretary-General Javier Pérez de Cuéllar.

Every morning on his way into his office he would pause briefly and to a small group of us, anxious to hear anything he had to say, would answer a few shouted questions. The questions were obvious and invariably the secretary-general's replies were the same. How were the talks going? And how did he judge the prospects of a diplomatic solution? Pérez de Cuéllar answered by saying day after day: 'I think the talks are going well and I am very hopeful that there will be a peaceful solution.' And that view, expressed however cautiously by the secretary-general, provided the main thrust of my reports to London night after night. If you stand outside the United Nations to report on its deliberations, that's what you tend to get and it is then very difficult to ignore what its leading diplomat tells you.

That, however, was only one element of the fevered diplomacy involving London, Washington and New York. And as it turned out it was not the most significant.

My formidable and immensely supportive producer, Alexandra Henderson, was the daughter of Sir Nicholas Henderson, the British ambassador in Washington, and that connection gave me more access to the embassy than I might normally have had. The ambassador was the soul of discretion and on the odd occasions we met he would enquire how the talks at the UN in New York were going. He never pondered too long on my replies before saying, 'Well, keep them going.'

Other diplomats at the embassy were a little more

forthcoming, although it took me a long time to work out the significance of what they were trying to say to me.

Over chatty dinners in the Washington suburb of Georgetown, Robin Renwick, the de facto deputy ambassador, repeatedly pointed out to me that the outcome of the dispute with Argentina had in a sense been predetermined 'once the task force had sailed'. In other words, Pérez de Cuéllar's hopeful statements about the UN discussions were just his hopes and, in the broader sense, quite useless. Once the task force had sailed from Portsmouth on its way to the Falklands more than eight thousand miles away, there was going to be a battle. It could not abort its mission, turn tail and head back to Portsmouth.

It took me several days to grasp the importance of Renwick's warnings and it was not until another senior British diplomat in New York spelled it out to me one evening in unmistakeable terms that it really sunk in.

It had been raining heavily as we left a restaurant not a stone's throw from the UN, where we had eaten and drunk well. Almost as a parting word, the friendly British diplomat, rushing to his taxi, told us that the United Nations discussions had run their course and had become nothing more than a useful distraction until the British task force could arrive within shooting distance of the Falkland Islands and the invading Argentines.

Having night after night based my dispatches from New York on the secretary-general's optimism about the UN talks, I abruptly changed tone without going into any great detail about why I was doing so. On the following day on the ITN lunchtime news I reported that, despite the vague hopes the UN secretary-general had been peddling day after day, Argentina had not left the islands as the Security Council demanded. The decision had been taken in London and war between Britain and Argentina was now an absolute certainty and only a short time away.

ITN was taken aback by my sudden change of tack but showed faith in what I had reported. A nasty war in the South Atlantic duly followed.

I have often wondered over the years whether the secretary-general knew that the UN talks would not produce the desired solution. He must have known that time was the only factor once the British fleet had left Portsmouth. Even so, I am loath to suggest that he had been deliberately misleading in his morning soundbites.

More likely, I believe, is that Pérez de Cuéllar found himself so immersed in the tradition of United Nations diplomacy that he felt obliged to express hope in its power and its ability to bring about a peaceful solution, despite the odds.

I had managed to make the right journalistic call, but only in the nick of time. Sometime after the Falklands War ended I was told that one of the British Embassy's diplomatic coups was to convince the Reagan administration that Britain was serious in its determination to fight to retake the Falklands. The Americans had offered to replace our sole aircraft carrier heading to the South Atlantic, should it be disabled.

This had been a great credit to British diplomacy. For some time after the dispute arose, few people in America seemed to have heard of the Falkland Islands. Even more surprising to the Americans was that they were a British dependency. American television news commentators enjoyed themselves poking good-natured fun at Britain's expense by trying to pinpoint precisely where these tiny islands were on the map of the world.

My determined effort to interview the PLO chairman, Yasser Arafat, resulted in one of the strangest and most bizarre episodes in my time as a journalist. I'd always been envious and a little peeved at colleagues, mainly from international newspapers and American television, who boasted about having encountered Arafat apparently by accident in some unlikely location in the Middle East or in North Africa. I never had any such luck. Instead, I fell back on contacts I had with the PLO office in London. They were unfailingly helpful, but totally uninformed about airline schedules. So, they would call me late one afternoon to tell me that the chairman would be pleased to see me at nine o'clock the following morning in Morocco and I would patiently point out that there was no way I could get there in time.

These calls went on for a very long time as we both resolved to try again. Then, one morning, one of the PLO contacts called me to say that the chairman would be attending a meeting of the non-aligned nations in Harare for four days and that I could see him there. I booked the next flight to Harare. On my arrival, the Zimbabwean immigration officer demanded to know whether I had been accredited to report the meeting and when I said I had not he allowed me into the country on the strict understanding that I would go to the Ministry of Foreign Affairs the following day to be properly accredited. I agreed but had no intention of doing so, reckoning that I'd be in the country for less than twenty-four hours and that I'd be meeting Mr Arafat the next morning.

The next morning an Arafat aide arrived to take me to the conference hotel. On my arrival at the hotel, which was heavily ringed by what seemed to be every member of the Zimbabwe army and police force, the soldier at the door demanded to see my accreditation. I said I had only my passport. Looking at the Arafat aide, the soldier pointed out, referring to me as 'this man', that I could not possibly be allowed to enter the hotel without proper accreditation.

The Arafat aide was unimpressed. 'This man is a guest of the chairman and must be allowed in.' The soldier, becoming more than a little impatient by now, was even less impressed. 'He cannot go in,' he repeated, 'and if he takes one more step I will shoot him . . .', this time jamming his sub-machine gun into my ribs to make his point.

My Arafat companion was having none of it. 'You can't shoot him. He's a guest of the president.' At which point, with the weapon still poking into my stomach, I was pulled by the Arafat aide into the hotel lobby where, by then, I almost collapsed in a dead faint. Still shaking from my much-too-close encounter with the soldier's sub-machine gun, I was hustled into an elevator and through a maze of corridors to meet Chairman Arafat. I was overcome with relief.

Just as we were about to begin the interview, we were interrupted by a minor commotion in the clutch of offices headed by President Mugabe. Speaking in an audible whisper, Mr Mugabe explained to Mr Arafat that someone had failed to turn up to chair the next session of the conference and would Mr Arafat be so kind as to fill in for him for two hours or so. Mr Arafat agreed and my heart sank. Arafat apologised profusely and promptly left.

And this is how I came to be left at the heart of the delegates' lounge with no discernible right to be there. The next two hours were torture. We were constantly being asked by nervous security details to make ourselves as inconspicuous as possible. We were right in the path where delegates came and went, and they did. Occasionally one of them would stop, recognising me, to enquire what I was doing there. President Zia of Pakistan was one of those and his entourage swept by and then backtracked to enquire, 'Trevor, what are you doing here?' President Kaunda did the same. When I tried to explain to him how I came to be there, he hoped that I would succeed by the grace of God. The president of Zambia frequently invoked the grace of the Almighty in his greetings.

Then it suddenly got worse. We were asked if we could possibly blend ourselves into the walls to be even more inconspicuous because a few delegates wished to have a meeting a few feet from where we were standing. In no time at all they arrived: Fidel Castro, Samora Machel, Colonel Gaddafi and Thomas Sankara of Burkina Faso. They did their best to ignore us and we them. By this time I had no further embarrassment to hide.

My tortured two hours eventually ended. The delegates held their meeting and left and Arafat returned. All I remember about our encounter is that I remember asking him if after all those years as chairman of the PLO he had accomplished anything for the Palestinians. He told me that when the issue of the future of his people first came up at the United Nations the then secretary-general Trygve Lie said: 'Tell me how many they are and we will try to help them.' Arafat looked at me and said, 'Numbers. Numbers. That's what we were then. Today we are a cause.'

Back in London the television landscape was changing. A licence under a new charter had been given to a fourth terrestrial channel. BBC One and Two and ITV were to be joined by Channel 4. In winning a fierce contest to be the news provider for the new channel, ITN was about to enhance its place and its reputation in British television.

It never occurred to me that I would be involved in the new channel in any way, but that was only because I had given it no great thought. I was flushed with the experience of reporting a big set-piece diplomatic event at the United Nations in New York and was looking forward to other similar assignments.

I was slow to recognise the significance of the ITN victory in winning the contract to provide the news for the new channel. In all my years at ITN I proved hopeless at understanding the wider politics of commercial television. Perhaps I had spent too much time introspectively, trying simply to survive.

It was impossible, though, not to be aware that ITN had been devastated by its failure to secure the contract for breakfast television for ITV. We felt supremely confident that we were in pole position in the race and the champagne was on ice. The sense of loss was palpable and hung over the office as would a dark cloud. The ITN management was deeply upset and for a while no one in the senior ranks at ITN could bring themselves to talk of anything else.

The contract to supply the news for Channel 4 therefore became a commercial and reputational necessity. One problem was that Channel 4 advertised itself as the television service that would break the mould. It would uncompromisingly pursue a distinctive agenda and it was made clear that its news should do the same. As a way of emphasising this, a great deal was made of the proposition, for example, that there would be no 'royal stories' on *Channel 4 News*. This, of course, was a reference to what was regarded as one of the obsessions of British tabloid newspapers and some television news.

Put bluntly, the operators of the new channel insisted on a service that would have no resemblance to the ITN *News at Ten*. It would be conspicuously different. The new channel would devote a full hour to its news broadcast at seven every weekday evening and would insist on serious coverage of foreign news. The greatest importance was placed on that.

Branding was deemed important, too. The programme would openly advertise its distinctiveness. It would not be called *News at Seven*, a designation too close to what ITN did on its existing news programmes. That the service would immediately appear new and groundbreakingly distinctive was quickly established. The first editor of *Channel 4 News*, Derrik Mercer, came not from the television industry but from the *Sunday Times* newspaper.

Mercer spoke to me several times to encourage me to join *Channel 4 News*. Impressed as I was by the list of star journalists who had been recruited to the new service, I could not make up my mind. I did not apply to join.

Television journalism has, as I suggested earlier, a very narrow career structure; it is not always easy to see where you might end up, or to judge what avenues you should choose. I felt I was making steady progress where I was at ITN, and I was perhaps going through one of my frequent fears of change.

The matter was resolved in a manner I least expected. I was called in to see David Nicholas. He explained that a great deal was riding on the success of the *Channel 4 News* and he needed my help in getting it off the ground. It was not quite a command, but the manner in which it was put left me little choice. I could find no reason to refuse, and when I gave it some thought I did come to believe that the new channel would provide a new enterprise in which ITN could demonstrate its widely acknowledged professionalism. I should also say that I liked Derrik Mercer immediately.

On the day Channel 4 was officially launched at a ceremony in London's West End, it was intimated that David Nicholas could have been a little more forthcoming in trying to get me to be part of the new service. I was told that Channel 4 had made a special request about recruiting me.

The start of anything in the television world with such an obviously new agenda is never easy and the channel initially struggled to gain general acceptance. Not for long. Undeterred, *Channel 4 News* stuck to its remit to be innovative and never compromised. In time that policy paid dividends, and *Channel 4 News* embarked on the journey it still graces today as unquestionably the most informative and finest news hour on British television. Its respected anchors, reporters and its shelves bulging with awards are testimony to its continuing brilliance.

I have a sharp recall of morning editorial meetings in the heady atmosphere of the earliest days of *Channel 4 News*. Conversations about setting the day's news agenda were lengthy and high-minded. They had the feel of seminars on the complexity of world affairs. Everyone was an expert in his or her field. We were treated to brilliant analyses of the British political scene and the British economy, and learned disquisitions from colleagues on the real intent of Soviet diplomacy, the complicated role of tribal societies in the Middle East and differences between the various inflections of Communist Party thought in Albania.

Joining *Channel 4 News* gave me many of the most memorable assignments in my television career. I reported from India, Pakistan, Hong Kong, Egypt, Israel, Lebanon, Japan, South Africa, the Soviet Union and the USA.

Some assignments carried deep personal memories.

I remember being sent to Nicaragua where politics had become so enmeshed in America's support for right-wing dictatorships in the region. In 1979 the left-wing Sandinistas, led by Daniel Ortega, overthrew the Somoza regime. Sometime after, I had gone to the capital, Managua, to interview Ortega.

It was not easy to get to him. We met his wife Rosario Murillo, who talked about literature and her husband's plans for their country. The economy was in a dreadful state. I was surprised to see weeds flourishing in cracks in some of the main roads in the centre of Managua. Water was scarce even in the most popular hotels. The maid in my hotel always offered to keep my bath filled in the event of my needing a wash in the evening. I was amused to discover that Nicaragua produced decent cigars but for some reason lighting them up was a problem. Boxes of matches were scarce.

Word came suddenly one day that we were to meet Ortega and we drove in convoy off a main road and across miles of jungle tracks and dried-up riverbeds to a small clearing in the bush. We found Ortega hunting iguana near a small lake, unmarked on any of our maps, and surrounded by a small detachment of gun-toting protection officers. He talked about what his government intended to do to repair the damage done by the previous government, and invited us to lunch on what I had always thought of in my Trinidad days as repulsive green reptiles. Always the intrepid reporter, my worry after the interview and an inedible lunch was that we would never find our way out of the bush and back to civilisation.

One evening, to have a closer look at how the conflict

between the Sandinistas and their opponents was affecting the countryside, we were driven about 150 miles from the capital. That night we slept on a hillside under the stars. I was shaken awake from my sleeping bag in the middle of the night by our guardians to remind me that I should be careful not to roll too far down the hill in my sleep, for fear of coming within range of the guns of guerrillas who frequently patrolled the area.

The Sandinistas acquired as much of an international reputation as the anti-apartheid movement in South Africa and I remember meeting a number of young British volunteers who had made the trip to Nicaragua to help on coffee plantations. They worked for months, existing on very little food and equally little comfort in makeshift tents. One young woman, who had gone to Nicaragua without telling her parents, agreed to be interviewed but requested that her identity be hidden. We filmed her in profile, managing to hide her face. Sometime later in London she told me that, despite our efforts to conceal her identity, her father had nevertheless recognised her by her wristwatch. It had been a present to his daughter.

It is almost too distressing today to hear news about Nicaragua under the same hugely popular Ortega I met. He has become authoritarian, scornful of opposition and mercilessly tough on dissidents. Ever since a short-lived opposition takeover of the government, protests have been met with brute force, on one occasion by concussion bombs. Ortega has rigged elections, scrapped presidential term limits and has installed his wife as his deputy and given her day-to-day control of government affairs. Opposition forces have not been entirely silenced but hundreds have been killed and there has been a mass exodus from the country. It is a far cry from the promises of better times when Ortega took the reins of government, and it is chastening to learn that one of Ortega's staunchest supporters these days is Venezuela, a country struggling to feed its people.

Looking back at some reporting assignments in countries

where there was once such hope of progressive change is painful, and it poses grave questions about the people's will and about systems of government.

I spent several weeks in the Philippines reporting on the events that led to the fall of Ferdinand Marcos. The dictator and his wife ran the country as their personal fiefdom, although there were trappings of democracy. Marcos stole millions and Mrs Marcos was her country's unofficial cultural ambassador with a penchant for expensive shoes – lots of them. Thirty years after Ferdinand Marcos was chased out of the country Filipinos were still discovering parts of his collection of priceless French Impressionist art bought with the people's money.

One of my poignant memories is the fear the couple inspired among ordinary Filipinos.

One evening I made an appointment to see a doctor in my Manila hotel. He tactfully sounded me out on my views about the Marcos government, only to make sure that I would not report our conversation to anyone. He then locked his office door to whisper to me, almost in the manner of planning a conspiracy, that he was contemplating nothing more outrageous than a vote for Cory Aquino, the president's opponent in the election.

Trembling with fear, the doctor felt the need to stress that if news about what he planned to do got out he would lose his medical practice and would probably be killed. It was chilling to witness the mental torture suffered by one voter making a choice – that cornerstone of democracy.

Catholicism was the predominant religion in the Philippines, as it is today, and the most prominent religious leader in the country was the gloriously named Cardinal Sin, the archbishop. The Marcos government had allied itself closely to the Church, and even when the president's standing reached its lowest point the Church was wary about speaking out publicly against him. That position became untenable and the archbishop's office began in carefully worded comments to express the view that Marcos's long hold on office was coming to an end.

I once confronted Cardinal Sin about the Church's changing position about President Marcos. He stoutly denied it until I showed him an issue of the Church's own newspaper which had openly advocated support for the opposition's Cory Aquino. The archbishop looked at me, blinked several times, smiled sheepishly and said: 'I must have a word with Felix Batista, the editor, about this.'

With the president having so openly lost the support of the Church we suspected the game was up. Aquino won the election handsomely and the only question was: what would Ferdinand Marcos do?

One evening our quiet hotel in Manila burst into life with people running down the corridors, screaming, 'He's gone! He's gone!' The Americans, who had a large base in the Philippines, almost certainly urged the president to leave. Making sure he took several boxes of money and jewellery and precious works of art with him, Marcos boarded a helicopter and was secretly hustled into exile.

That night we made our way to the Presidential Palace where people were gathering, as if to make sure that Marcos really had left the country he had controlled with such tenacity. A remnant of palace guards, becoming used to life without their boss and protector, began firing sub-machine gun rounds at us. I cowered behind a tree as slender as my arm in a forlorn hope of safety.

Millions of Filipinos were left impoverished by the government of Ferdinand Marcos. It was common while I was there to watch people scratching through fetid rubbish dumps in search of anything vaguely useful.

One morning after the election I came upon a scene as distressing as I have ever witnessed. I saw people marking out lines in the ground near the shacks where they lived. On enquiring what they were doing I was told: 'Cory Aquino has promised us parcels of land, so we are just marking out the bits we would like to have.'

Do politicians know the effect of their glibly made promises on some sections of their electorate?

Cory Aquino's latest successor as president of the Philippines is the shamelessly violent Rodrigo Duterte. He boasts about his obsession to rid the country of drugs and drug lords, but the campaign is nothing more than a mask for illegality. In a trend that has become common in international politics he expresses pride in his most outrageous actions. He has been quoted as saying: 'my only sin is the extrajudicial killings.' He tells detained drug suspects that the only way they may avoid death is to hide behind bars in jail. He is ruthless with all perceived enemies, even if they hold high office, and the number of Filipinos who have needlessly lost their lives is put at more than ten thousand.

The hope of true democracy in the Philippines appears even further away than it was in the days of President Marcos. Cory Aquino's promise of political change all those years ago has been long forgotten. It has been replaced by a presidential shoot-to-kill policy.

* * *

It is relatively easy to recall countless tales of the exciting parts of a career as a television journalist. We thrive on the retelling of where we were, what we saw and what we did, frequently recalling everything in the most minute detail. In its own way that is almost a definition of what it means to be a journalist. Not quite as easy in my own case is to adequately describe or to come to any serious conclusions about how those incredible and exciting things happened to me. I am still puzzled that so many extraordinary events became part of my life.

If I ever possessed anything resembling a rock-hard conviction it was that I would eventually find work in the media.

That was as far as it ever got. My thoughts about working in British television were remote and sketchy. When I got over the surprise at being given a job at ITN, I kept working out what I wanted to do and where I wanted to end up. But it was all so remote from anything I might have expected, and I found it difficult to plan a career. There were glimpses of the paths I wished to follow. They held out the promise of enticing new points of departure, but they were bedevilled by my own uncertainty.

I was confident I could do some things well, but I never escaped the feeling that I had entered a world where there were absolutely no guarantees of success and we all needed large dollops of luck. What concerned me was that I had perhaps tested mine to the limit in the decision to leave my home in the West Indies to come to London, and then after a short time leave the comfort of Bush House to work in the more demanding atmosphere of ITN, a relatively new company already making waves in the television industry.

By the very nature of what we did, many of my colleagues at the World Service were like me. We shared something in common: we had all embarked on journeys to London from countries far away to seek new lives. ITN was not like that.

Given all that, nothing could have been further from my mind than the fact that after nearly twenty years I would be selected to be the first solo presenter of the ITN flagship *News at Ten*. I had by then seen enough of the place to know that in so many instances you did well simply by being in the right place to be assigned to the biggest running story. The *News at Ten* job was entirely different.

My colleagues and I had all received hints of the decision to change the format of the show, and I'm sure we all calculated what each of us would do if he or she was not chosen to do the new job. I say that without any hard evidence, because I remember few serious discussions about it. My fellow presenters must have given it as much thought as I had, but I suppose we all kept our counsel. In my case I was much too nervous to talk about it.

At my most anxious moments I fell back on the contemplation of failure. From that low bar I slipped easily into thinking whether there would be any place for me at ITN if I didn't get the job. It was as plain as that, and in my lowest moments I sank into a permanent fit of anxiety about work and life.

The arithmetic was simple. A two-presenter *News at Ten* required at least three people to satisfy the different combinations. If it went down to a single anchor, there was in reality just one job.

Deep in the gloom of thinking the worst I was too timid to ask any questions about the process of deciding who should get the job. Years later I discovered that ITN had decided to conduct a survey to guide its choice. I have never been sufficiently bold to ask too many details about the results. Then, after what seemed an unending interlude, I was told that the job was mine. I can recall the shock, the pride and the pleasure and the absolute, heart-stopping terror at taking on the responsibility of anchoring a news programme that had made ITN such a name in British television.

That was no surprise. The best of everything at ITN was directed into the production of *News at Ten*. Our resources were all aimed at making it the best. We were given the most qualified editors, the best producers and writers and reporters and they were left in no doubt that only their finest work would do. Every editorial meeting had as its main aim making *News at Ten* stylish and accessible.

No presenter could have been more assured about the quality of the show to which all ITN gave its most determined effort.

The rest was up to me. I buried all my fears about being given such an assignment by approaching it with the same pattern of intense hard work that had seen me through my years at ITN. I made a point of being involved in what we were due to broadcast later that day, sharing my views about the stories we might wish to cover at some point during mid-morning. And I tried to be at my desk by late morning. It was exhausting but I felt there could be no other way of doing the job.

The ITN approach was almost always the same. It may not have been very difficult to predict the day's news agenda, but what made *News at Ten* distinctive was *how* those stories were told. We challenged ourselves constantly by asking simple questions such as: how do we make the complications of the views of the opposing sides in the Middle East accessible? Why should our viewers care? How can we explain the Bos-nian crisis to a family watching *News at Ten* in Norwich or Aberdeen? Our discussions at free-flowing editorial meetings were aimed at deciding that above all. We paid high regard to our editor's views but there was a seductive, freewheeling democracy about ITN meetings. No one was afraid to speak, and everyone was heard.

I have always thought that that culture of openness was a significant factor in the success of the ITN brand.

ITN took great pride in the quality of its writers and I was particularly fortunate with the team on *News at Ten*. They shared a commitment to style of expression, and I looked for-ward to our discussions about phrasing and emphasis right up to the moment before I went down to the studio.

Despite the rigour of presenting *News at Ten* on weekdays, I tried to find time to keep up my contacts in the London dip-lomatic world and beyond – at the White House, the Pentagon and the United Nations. The status I had acquired anchoring the main evening news on ITV did me no harm.

Long before I became the *News at Ten* sole anchor, the bulletin had become one of the stars in the ITV schedule. Its ratings were equal only to those of the long-running soap opera *Coronation Street* and the reality show *Blind Date*, and I'm sure I was told that the advertising break in *News at Ten* was the most profitable in commercial television in Britain. I have often wondered whether, paradoxically, the success of ITN with its highly rated news shows created something of a problem for our bosses at ITV's network centre and by association for the ITV companies who had collectively awarded ITN the contract to do the news.

This perhaps needs an explanation.

It probably begins with the fact that reporting the news costs money and it's not always possible to predict how much. Costs rise, sometimes to an astonishing degree when journalists are assigned to cover wars in the Middle East which rage on forever, or outbreaks of civil unrest in Europe or a devastating famine in Ethiopia. Nearer to home, reporting the Troubles in Northern Ireland for years was a persistent drain on ITN resources. As a result the ITN budget occasionally slipped into the red. When that happened the ITV companies were asked to make up the shortfall. This did not engender abundant brotherly affection.

There was also the view, not always expressed in precise language, that ITN had acquired an inflated opinion of its own importance. ITN reported the news on ITV and in the hallowed chambers of Westminster ITN *was* also the news – a newcomer that had made a splash into the waves of news reporting, now rubbing shoulders with prime ministers and other senior politicians, and not abashed about using its influence to have a campaigning word in the right ear.

This was certainly the view of one ITV executive. Over lunch one day he suggested that ITN – a creature of ITV – had found methods of lobbying 10 Downing Street in ways which were not always sympathetic to ITV's broader aims. I listened politely on the basis that saying too much in response was probably above my pay grade. But what I heard amounted to a charge of disloyalty, plain and simple.

And then there was the seemingly perennial battle about whether *News at Ten* should retain its time slot. I never understood why this became such a long-running saga but for long periods it dominated our lives. Just when you thought the issue had been put to bed, up it rose again. At one time it was explained to me that *News at Ten* prevented ITN from scheduling big dramas at nine in the evening that would naturally go beyond ten o'clock, were it not for *News at Ten*. For a time, movies beginning at nine would be paused for the news before resuming.

I am sure that there were billboard ads suggesting that no one had proposed that I should be able to interrupt the nine o'clock movie on ITV with *News at Ten*. It was clearly not the most satisfactory solution then and would be much less so now in the multi-channel age.

One day someone from the ITV network centre, conveniently sited in the same Gray's Inn Road building, explained the problem to me in disarmingly simple terms. 'You see, Trevor, when you finish the news everyone switches off, and whatever we do after that fails to get as good a rating as it might have, had you not sent the nation to bed by saying goodnight.'

I thought it rather flattering that I could possibly have such influence on the nation's viewing habits, but decided not to say that. My question, though, was whether there was anything I could do.

It was suggested that I could trail the ITV programme that followed the news, in the hope of keeping the interest of our viewers after the news. It resulted in one of the oddest set pieces in my news-reading career. This is what I said for many weeks at the end of *News at Ten*: 'That's it from *News at Ten* tonight. Coming up next on ITV: *Bad Girls*', which was the name of the ITV post-*News at Ten* show. My friends found a way of making the association stick. They would say to me that even when they didn't manage to see *News at Ten* in its entirety they tried to make sure that they never missed the end to hear me sign off the programme by advertising *Bad Girls*.

After a long day at ITN I usually paused in the newsroom to collect my belongings and head off home. I never saw a single episode of *Bad Girls* and I never discovered whether my promotion helped the show to greater prominence.

Sadly, during my time at ITN the running debate about the *News at Ten* time slot did not end on a note of such hilarity. It was shifted to 10.30 and for a time predictably lost its lustre. It became the butt of not such good-natured humour. Being labelled *News at When* was horrible enough, but even more horrible was the truth behind the jesting.

Etched in my memory is the plastic noticeboard in our newsroom that told us when that day's late evening news would begin. The time varied slightly day by day. 10.30 45 it would read one day meaning forty-five seconds after 10.30. Much worse as the days went by were: 10.31 30; 10.31 50, and on and on.

News at Ten has regained its proper starting time and I was persuaded to relaunch its comeback. Alas, nothing stays the same. We had been warned that should ITV give up its precious time slot our eagle-eyed competitors would rush in to fill the space. The BBC did just that and *News at Ten* faces competition it never had before. For reasons impossible to describe, ITV never anticipated that the BBC would move with what might be considered such commercial speed. But the BBC did and ITN faced a situation it could so easily have avoided. That is all in the past now.

In personal terms, despite all the ups and downs I could never have anticipated such a career with *News at Ten*. Almost from the moment I first walked into its Wells Street office ITN gave me the chance to do everything I could have dreamed of. There were a few battles to be fought, but in retrospect they now appear mere skirmishes. Several opportunities came my way and I had the good sense to make the most of them.

The most important of them was that I was given the chance to be a world-travelling correspondent and for a long time, whenever there were important interviews to be done, I was asked to try to arrange and conduct them. That could not have always been the case, and it was without question the most fulfilling part of my journalistic life.

I remember I first went to America for ITN in the fading days of the Jimmy Carter administration. The crisis brought about by the American hostages in Iran had sucked all the energy out of the presidency. I remember the moment when the president, who had tried so hard to get the hostages back, realised that they would be released into the arms of his successor President Reagan. For the next twenty-five years I travelled across America reporting on presidential campaigns and high-level international summit meetings.

Presidential campaigns are the pinnacle of the American political system, but they are also fun. I loved listening to the way Reagan based his campaign speeches on his profound and deeply touching optimism about the inherent greatness of the United States of America. His election crowds always waited to applaud his description of his country as 'the shining city on the hill'. Conflating or sometimes confusing lines from old movies with reality, the former movie actor dropped them into his political speeches. Nobody seemed to mind. He delivered them so well.

I'll never forget that after the *Challenger* space disaster and the loss of brave Americans he uttered the lines written for him with such dramatic force. The president said of the lost crew, quoting the poet John Gillespie Magee Jr: 'They slipped the surly bonds of earth to touch the face of God.'

A senior administration official explained to me the way Reagan viewed the approach to the opening up of a dialogue with the Soviet Union. There were immensely complicated arms-control issues to be debated, but the president always felt he had the upper hand, the moral high ground in dealing with Gorbachev. He felt simply that America was better than the Soviet Union. He apparently felt that if he could take Gorbachev on a tour of America, the Soviet leader would immediately return to Moscow and would denounce Communism.

And, of course, Reagan believed in what came to be described as the 'Star Wars' nuclear shield. This was the theory, apparently never anything more, that the United States could be protected from any Soviet nuclear attack by an impenetrable shield way up in space that the Soviet missiles could never breach.

Following the Reverend Jesse Jackson's attempt to win the Democratic nomination to fight the presidential election was a roller-coaster ride lit by soaring oratory. We all flocked to the Ebenezer Baptist Church in Atlanta, where Martin Luther King once preached, to hear Jackson rail against the inequalities still tearing his country apart.

Jesse Jackson had not always been at one with Barack Obama when he ran for the presidency. But I was in my hotel room in Washington watching Obama's victory speech at Grant Park in Chicago. There was a tear in Jackson's eye as he watched proudly in the crowd. The battle that proved far too much for him had after all been won by a fellow African American.

* * *

My passion throughout my years at ITN was international politics.

I did want to be part of the biggest national news stories, too, and very early on I made no secret of wanting to be sent to Northern Ireland.

In the very nature of what was expected of general reporters I did my share of watching ministers arrive and leave 10 Downing Street, doorstepping other Members of Parliament at Westminster or in their constituencies, covering grisly murders, interviewing famous people and those seeking fame and following for what seemed to be at times never-ending seasons of industrial disputes culminating in strikes by workers in almost every sector of the British economy. I did not enjoy standing outside car plants in the Midlands in the dead of winter, vainly attempting to balance the competing claims of management spokesmen and trade union leaders.

But those were jobs we all did.

What the majority of us craved were international assignments. They carried prestige, perhaps even the faintest suggestion of glamour. The ITN I saw when I joined was divided unequally into the few who had earned the distinction of ducking bullets and reporting fearlessly on wars in the Middle East and Africa and the many who were permanently anchored to the home desk.

I was a slow learner. It took me a while to notice colleagues who always came to work armed with their passports even on what appeared to be the dullest and most routine of office days. The difference between the two groups could, of course, be explained by sound editorial judgement. The dispatches from well-known ITN reporters on the biggest foreign stories were acclaimed as among the finest in our industry. The majority of us were yet to show our mettle.

Money was a consideration, too. There were costs involved in sending reporters abroad, and foreign editors weren't keen on gambling on those of us yet to prove ourselves. Reporting on foreign wars never held much of an attraction for me. Almost every other kind of international assignment did. I was anxious to learn more about countries in Europe and the Middle East and Southern Africa and I was pretty desperate to be given the chance to immerse myself in the complexities of the international political world.

I put this down partly to the fact that I was born on a tiny island in the Caribbean and was always fascinated by the world beyond our shores. The confines of my island home imbued me with the desire to see more of the world. It was obvious to me that we were not immune from actions taken by governments thousands of miles away. Colonial ties had once bound us to Britain and British influences remained, as did those of the other European explorers who pointed their sailing ships westward centuries ago.

We were conscious of the fact that we lived in the shadow of the mighty North American continent. Our forebears had come from Africa and the Indian subcontinent, and when the Cuban missile crisis brought the world closer than ever before to a nuclear showdown between Washington and Moscow, we islanders felt the tremors of a possible East–West conflict.

My interest in the culture and politics of the outside world was consequently as natural as our geography was and as our history had been. For all that we could occasionally pretend that we were tiny specks neatly tucked away in the folds of the map of the world, we were still part of the world. I knew that and I knew we could not avoid the fact.

The smallest local newspapers in Trinidad recognised that, too. Right next to stories about murders, robberies and West Indies cricket matches were tantalising snippets of international news from Reuters and the Associated Press. The interest in foreign affairs I showed at ITN was nothing new.

Then luck played a winning hand. I was hired from Trinidad to work at Bush House in London as a current affairs producer, first for the Overseas Regional Service and later the World Service of the BBC. Here was the United Nations of broadcasting in a single building in the Strand with its antennae fixed on the world beyond. That effectively sealed my decision about how I wanted to spend my life in journalism. It lit up the path I would always follow.

So far as I can tell, I missed only one early chance to be sent abroad very shortly after I joined ITN. It was 1973 and one of the biggest stories around was the highly inflammatory political decision to expel Ugandan Asians to Britain. The man behind it was Uganda's president, Idi Amin. In no time he became, in the eyes of the editors of British newspapers who plastered his features over every front page, a swaggering, unprincipled bully. Television news, too, was having its fill of Amin's rambling press conferences and his brazen off-the-cuff pronouncements. And since his victims were being sent to Britain, the entire nation plunged into debating what the hateful Ugandan dictator would say or do next.

The ITN man in the Ugandan capital Kampala was, if I remember correctly, not an ITN employee but a freelance journalist who did a sterling job keeping our viewers intrigued about a Ugandan president of whom we previously knew little. At some point in this bizarre affair our reporter in Kampala was sounded out by my ITN bosses as to whether it might be a good idea if I were sent there to boost our reporting effort.

The thought probably had its origins in the fact that in my job interview with Nigel Ryan some weeks before we had talked about the proposed expulsion of Ugandan Asians. I did have some marginal involvement in the story at Bush House and I was quite outspoken. I told Nigel that although Amin showed all the signs of being a bombastic villain who was having a good time twisting the tail of the British lion, Ugandan Asians might have been in a much stronger position had they done a better job of integrating with the native Ugandans. It was a point made to me by someone who had spent many years in Kampala.

That in itself was no justification for what Amin was doing, and in the circumstances it was probably an unworthy thought. In the end it didn't matter in the least. ITN's suggestion about sending me to Kampala was turned down by our man on the spot instantly and with great force. It would be, he insisted, a most terrible idea. And that was that. As far as I can tell the suggestion was never raised again. It had been throttled before it was allowed to draw breath!

It came as somewhat of a surprise to me when I was later told of the outcome. Then it suddenly made sense. Protecting your patch from intruders is one of the cardinal rules in the journalist's survival kit. Here was a reporter sitting on the story of his life. Why on earth should he entertain the idea of sharing it with someone else?

I made up for that loss in more ways than I could have expected. I travelled frequently to Brussels and Luxembourg, Paris and Strasbourg. After being turned away at the altar once before by General de Gaulle of France, Britain's flirtation with Europe had blossomed again. The debate about whether Britain should join the Common Market was in full flood and there were opinions to be canvassed, party leaders to be interviewed – repeatedly – and an unremitting schedule of meetings to be followed in every continental capital.

I must confess that I remember few references at the time to 'loss of sovereignty', although there must have been some. One recurring theme was Britain's future relations with the Commonwealth if it acceded to the Treaty of Rome. Such a move, it was argued, would do irreparable damage to the economies of former British colonies. Anti-Common Market voices were untiring and unrelenting in championing the cause of New Zealand lamb and Caribbean sugar.

It is with a degree of embarrassment that I recall my delight at the widely reported view that joining the Common Market would at a stroke result in the availability of huge quantities of excellent, cheaply priced French wine. It was never scrawled on the side of buses, but it proved a great rallying point among my journalist friends, especially when a subject of such import-ance was discussed in the many bars around our Wells Street office. Adding to such pleasurable interludes was the fact that the London sophisticates had fallen in love every November with, of all things, French Beaujolais nouveau. Every year there was a frantic race – clearly staged to milk every ounce of publicity – among restaurant and bar owners to be the first to rush thousands of crates of the stuff to London. At the end of the supposedly mad dash everyone claimed victory and every year we rushed to noisy, overcrowded bars to boast that we were among the first tasters.

As a public relations coup it was brilliant. From what I remember, the wine was never worth the rush. I am told the French made no comparable fuss or great claims about their Beaujolais nouveau. It was drinkable but it was young and still maturing. Its youthful zest was known in some years to wreak havoc on the lining of the stomach and to resurrect less-than-welcome memories of the night before. Despite that, thousands of bottles were drunk to celebrate Britain's eventual entry to the Common Market.

It was the beginning of Britain's European adventure and the start of a new reporting adventure for me. There were summits and European Council meetings, and after a time speeches by our new members to the European Parliament in Brussels. They were unfailingly accessible to anyone with a television camera, eager to prove to their uncertain constituents in the Midlands, Essex or Northern Ireland that they were doing worthwhile jobs and that the Common Market or the European Economic Community – the EEC – and later EU was making an invaluable contribution to British life.

I have warm memories of the weeks and months after Britain signed up to join. Reporters who showed the slightest interest in EEC policies or institutions, and even those who did not, were invited to Brussels, cultivated, wined and dined. One Strasbourg mayor was in the habit of inviting us to join him on lazy trips along the river on bright summer evenings with the promise of fine champagne and excellent foie gras.

On one occasion, for no other purpose than having a little harmless fun at his expense, I advised the redoubtable Reverend Ian Paisley, who was known to take a dim view of journalists he suspected of having had a drink ('I can smell the devil's brew'), that if he wanted me to report his speech to the Brussels parliament, he must make the effort to seek me out in the Members' Bar, where I'd be waiting until the sitting commenced. Much to my surprise Dr Paisley did as I had asked, and about an hour later tiptoed into the bar with a knowing smile.

I would be less than honest if I didn't say that from my earliest assignments to Brussels or Strasbourg I thought I detected a less than wholehearted British commitment to what might be called in today's jargon the European project. We had joined the Common Market, but there was still Britain and then there was the rest of Europe. Somehow we always managed to stay apart. I felt at times the best we could say was that we promised to be good neighbours.

At meetings of heads of state and the European Council, there appeared to be a British point of view quite distinct from that of the other member countries. One memorable example of that was Prime Minister Thatcher's table-thumping demands at a lively summit in Dublin for a return of what she famously called 'our money'. That was a row about Britain's contribution to the common agricultural policy (CAP). Feelings ran equally high on other European policies and the demand for British 'opt-outs' continued right up to the referendum vote in June 2016.

British foreign secretaries with whom I had contact at the time were all serious political talents and people of stature. They earned the grudging respect even of those with whom they frequently disagreed. They worked diligently to square obvious differences with our European partners. But some differences in outlook never disappeared entirely.

Disputes with our EU partners made headlines. As a general rule, no such prominence was given to agreements on difficult technical issues hammered out in the councils of Brussels after hours of hard bargaining.

In a desperate attempt to discover the gist of long-running disputes, or merely to try to find out what really went on at EU meetings, I hatched a plan when I was assigned to cover Brussels meetings. Pressure of time permitting, I made an effort to attend the post-summit briefings of at least three member countries. Relying totally on Britain's interpretation could be less than adequate. In addition to the British briefing, I also tried to find out what the Germans and the Irish spokespersons had to say. Only when I managed to do that did I feel I might have arrived at something approaching a balanced view of what those high-level meetings accomplished.

It also allowed me to discover whether Britain's view on major issues had prevailed or not. On several occasions I discovered a distinct impatience on the part of other European countries with Britain's position on matters vital to Europe. In those earliest days we were semi-detached at best. Britain once had an empire. We were still in search of a role in the world of international politics. We were never quite sure whether we had found that role in Europe.

Any less effort on my part left me struggling to interpret the language of Brussels diplomacy. Important though it was, reporting EEC or EU affairs was not always the most exciting journalistic challenge. There was too much verbal jousting.

* * *

My assignment to cover a Communist Party Congress in Moscow about two years after the 1980 Soviet invasion of Afghanistan posed problems of a different kind.

There was minimal contact with party officials, and we were invited to nothing that could be considered an informative briefing. We were dependent on Russian television facilities. I was not allowed near the splendid hall in the Kremlin where the congress was taking place. I was forced to follow the proceedings as they were shown on television. I depended a lot on my producers and my more experienced British journalist colleagues.

The general secretary was Leonid Brezhnev. He was the latest in a long line of ageing Soviet leaders to whom the passing years had not been kind. His speech was the only public item on the agenda, and he slurred his words so badly that even my Russian-speaking friends weren't always sure they were interpreting them correctly.

I spent a few days in Moscow on that trip, but in the end I never got the chance to report on the general secretary's speech. I was asked by the authorities to leave Moscow. This was put to me politely but firmly. There was no opportunity to appeal. I blamed myself. I had committed the elementary error of ignoring the warning I had been repeatedly given that in Moscow walls have ears, and a few incautious remarks of mine were picked up by those whose job it is to listen to what foreign journalists say, especially if we are overheard making comments about the state of the Soviet Union.

I must explain.

I had been to the Russian capital a year or two earlier, but being driven from the airport to my hotel on that visit through what seemed to be the afternoon rush hour a random thought occurred to me. Moscow was a city with a great history and the Kremlin, the onion domes and St Basil's sitting in majesty along the Moskva River make up one of the most impressive capital sights in the world. It quietly oozes power, status and authority.

That day I noticed something else. The city centre was drab; the main streets were clogged with old cars and even older lorries. The lorries rumbled by impatiently, belching out clouds of dark, smelly diesel fumes. Taking in this unappetising scene from the back of my taxi I thought to myself that downtown Moscow looked like the crowded city of a Third World country, but one with enough intercontinental missiles capable of reducing the world to ashes. There was perhaps nothing inherently wrong in making such a comparison whether it was well judged or totally without merit. What was unforgiveable was that I did not keep the thought to myself. I made the disastrous mistake of advertising it.

A little too puffed up by what I considered a clever exegesis, it tumbled out quite loudly and repeatedly one evening at the Moscow flat of a friendly British journalist. I had after all made one of those journalistic observations and I wanted to boast about it. In truth it was not that clever. It was no more than a passing thought in the back of a taxi.

The following day Brezhnev made his speech to the Communist Party Congress. It would be the subject of my report. The general secretary said little or nothing about the invasion of Afghanistan – the raging international political issue of the time – and nothing at all about the Soviet economic malaise for which the invasion was blamed. Instead he devoted a significant portion of his address to an apparently new Soviet arms-control proposal to the West.

I have had problems decoding East–West arms-control proposals. They are usually loaded with technical jargon, they are made deliberately complicated, and when you get down to the business of deciding the number of missiles either side says it's planning to mothball, accuracy depends on who is doing the counting and what was being counted.

There were inevitable disputes about whether the Soviet Union or the Americans genuinely planned to discard as many missiles or warheads as they insisted they were. There were perennial problems, too, about inspection and verification. Every time the Russians made an arms-control proposal, Americans pleaded for time to let its experts study it closely.

I was not an expert and I frequently wondered whether the superpowers genuinely wanted to get rid of any significant categories of weapons systems. Talking about arms control became a routine item on every international agenda. Both the Soviets and the Americans had for decades believed in the theory of mutual assured destruction, or MAD. It was based on the chilling realisation that East and West would destroy each other in the event of a nuclear conflict, and that each side had more than the required number of missiles to do that.

And that – rather than new proposals to have another tally of American and Russian silos, missiles or warheads – is what really kept the two sides from firing off missiles at each other.

But back to my Moscow assignment and the Brezhnev speech. Having given prior thought to the matter of arms control, my report that night would ignore that passage in the speech. I was not in a position to judge if what the Communist Party leader said would make a real difference to the Soviet Union's nuclear arsenal. It was as simple as that.

Instead I concluded my report by saying that Leonid Brezhnev might be remembered more as the man who destroyed détente by sending the Soviet Red Army into Afghanistan and the leader who did nothing to arrest a decline in the Soviet Union's economy.

That didn't please the people at Russian television on whose technical facilities and all-round cooperation we depended. In expressing their displeasure at my take on the general secretary's speech one executive went beyond the mere content of my television report. He remarked acidly: 'Of course, you know all about the Soviet Union. We are a Third World country.' He was replaying word for word the view that I had expressed at the Moscow flat of a fellow journalist some evenings before. I could come no other conclusion but that my comment had been *overheard*.

My interlocutor had no need to explain or to raise his voice. His tone was matter-of-fact. The facilities earlier allocated to us were simply no longer available.

I have never forgotten how quickly and efficiently the Soviet system spread the news that I had incurred its displeasure and had in effect been told there was no longer any reason for me to remain in Moscow. On my return to the hotel the manager greeted me with the words: 'I hear you're leaving tomorrow.' I could only smile.

There was a bowling alley in the hotel basement to which in the company of my producer I retired most evenings after

work. In those days there was little else to do on spare evenings in Moscow. The nicest thing about the bowling alley was
that it was invariably empty. When I enquired about using it
that evening I was informed it was closed.

Had I been given the opportunity I might have got myself
into more hot water. There was an aspect of Brezhnev's appearance before the Communist Party Congress to which
I was itching to refer. Soviet television did a fine job in its
presentation of the event. Shortly after we watched Brezhnev arrive, the cameras cut to sustained images of delegates
standing and applauding warmly. That image was held for
several minutes. The picture we saw next was that of the
general secretary firmly ensconced at the rostrum. Missing
from Soviet television's coverage of the event, deliberately
not shown, was the scene of the old man being carried to the
platform.

I was on an assignment in Moscow when my father died
unexpectedly. Arrangements were made by Richard Tait, my
thoughtful editor back in London, to get me back to Trinidad
as quickly as possible. On my way to the airport, I stopped off
at an office in the Kremlin to explain to the relevant authorities why I was leaving so suddenly, having only hours before,
on my arrival, arranged a series of meetings and interviews
with senior officials and politicians.

The Russian press officer would hear nothing of my haste.
He nodded to the most comfortable chair in his office, poured
me a glass of vodka and insisted that I found time to talk
about my father's life. It was a gesture of surpassing kindness.
Dad, who had not the slightest knowledge of or interest in
what went on in the Kremlin, would have been thrilled and
bemused in equal measure to know that he was being talked
about in a government office in Moscow. I wish I could have
told him.

No repercussions followed my minor disagreement with
Soviet television. I returned to Moscow several times after

that, most notably when East–West relations had thawed visibly and Gorbachev and Reagan were exchanging state visits. Reagan had come to the presidency calling the Soviet Union the 'evil empire' and demanding that Gorbachev tear down the Berlin Wall. In Moscow, Gorbachev had introduced the policy of more openness – *glasnost* – and when he came to London, Prime Minister Margaret Thatcher, no less, concluded that he was a man with whom 'we can do business together'.

Reagan being Reagan believed that a fully functioning United States was the last, best hope for mankind. He is thought to have felt that if he were able to take his Soviet visitor on a tour to show him how the American capitalist system worked, Gorbachev would return to Moscow and denounce the Communist system forthwith. It didn't quite work out like that, but as I watched the two leaders stroll across Red Square like actors on a film set in the golden glow of the afternoon sunshine from my Moscow hotel balcony we gleaned a more hopeful sign for an East–West accommodation.

We reporters remained cautious but quickly felt the warmer temperature in our dealings with the Soviet Union. Party officials were more available. One expert on arms control, Georgi Arbatov, was always on hand to contribute to the debate and Gorbachev's principal spokesman, Gennady Gerasimov, became, by his frequent appearances on television in London and in Washington, almost as well known as his boss. And when Gorbachev came to see Margaret Thatcher, his interpreter was none other than a man who'd previously been my best contact at the Soviet Embassy in Kensington, Nicholai Ouspensky.

I was told by people in the State Department in Washington at the time that Reagan always felt he had a winning hand to play in his arms-control talks with the Soviet leader – beyond the fact that he learned a Russian proverb to impress his guest.

He then spoiled the effect by repeating it so often that Gorbachev begged for mercy.

American scientists had been talking for some time about developing a shield in space to defend against any possible nuclear attack by the Soviet Union. Its technical name was the Strategic Defense Initiative – SDI. If it was ever possible to protect the United States with such a shield it would, at a stroke, destroy the theory of mutual assured destruction. American nukes could still take out Moscow, but the Soviets would be unable to do equal harm to Washington or New York. The shield in space would knock out their intercontinental ballistic missiles.

It is important to point out here that the American scientific community was sharply divided on the issue of whether such a shield in space could be made to function as well as it was claimed. There was also the problem of cost. To no one's great surprise the project acquired the fictional name 'Star Wars.'

The one true believer in the SDI was apparently President Reagan and, the argument runs, it so scared the Soviets that it may have played a part in the eventual collapse of the Soviet Union. The extent to which 'Star Wars' can take credit for such a major foreign policy victory is debatable. It is almost certain, though, that somewhere along the line Reagan convinced the Soviets that they could never outspend America on arms and the Soviets finally acknowledged it.

For many years after the end of the Cold War it was discovered in one audit that the Pentagon continued to budget for the same weapon enhancement programmes as it had done at the height of the Cold War, as if there had been no change in the international political temperature. And to this day senators representing states whose economy is dependent on the sale or manufacture of weapon systems can never be counted on to give unwavering support to any arms-control proposal. 'Making our military stronger' is still a favourite chant in today's presidential vocabulary.

America responded to the invasion of Afghanistan by arming the mujahideen, the guerrillas who were doing their best to harass the invaders at every turn. Billions of dollars' worth of American weapons were shipped in through Pakistan and I had many conversations with Pakistan's President Zia and, after his death, Prime Minister Benazir Bhutto, about the battles just across their border.

The guerrillas became very efficient in the use of rocket launchers, and the Soviets faced increasing difficulty in subduing Afghanistan. Bogged down in inhospitable terrain fighting an enemy skilled in the art of unconventional attacks, the Soviet invasion bled Moscow for a decade.

Pakistan, meanwhile, was awash with weapons, no doubt parts of consignments intended for use by the mujahideen. I was shocked to be told on one visit to Karachi that it was possible to rent sub-machine guns by the hour.

There was increasing lawlessness in the sprawling cross-border areas and in towns on the Pakistan North-West Frontier. Dr Khan Abdul Wali Khan, a prominent political figure, described to me one afternoon, when he was sitting in the lobby of my Peshawar hotel, having to mediate between two warring villages about the ownership of a rocket launcher.

The fighting in Afghanistan allowed the cultivation of the opium poppy to flourish. Heroin came across the border into Pakistan in ever-increasing quantities. The drug, frequently in its raw state, was transported by the truckload down through the Khyber Pass, eventually ending up in Karachi and destined for shipment to the Near East and Europe. Afghanistan was on the way to becoming the world's first true narco-state. It supplied more than half the heroin smuggled into Europe and the United States.

In the North-West Frontier town of Landi Kotal, a place once favoured by the British for its delightful escape from the steaming temperatures further south in the hot summer months, I went to a market where large trays of heroin were openly displayed. The police perfected a routine to warn sellers of the drugs of the approach of unwanted visitors. I had sought permission to visit the market, and when it was eventually agreed I was accompanied by half a dozen uniformed police officers. As we were spotted walking up from the crest of a small hill, the heroin sellers could be clearly seen secreting trays of drugs under large sheets.

The heroin business was thriving and had become quite sophisticated. A Pakistani drug enforcement officer took me to a warehouse a few miles south of Peshawar where, under strict security, the authorities stored scores of canvas bags bursting with kilos of raw heroin. Some of them had been seized from smugglers, but he told me some had been handed over to Pakistani officials. There was, he explained, such a growing network of laboratories along the Afghan–Pakistan border that drug enforcement officers were occasionally invited to raid one of them so that they could be made to look as though they were having success in curbing the trade.

Pakistan no longer views the drugs trade with equanimity. Drug addiction is now a major problem. A few years ago the former Pakistan cricket captain Imran Khan, whose political party formed the government after the 2018 election, took me to a hospital in the city of Karachi funded by one of his charities. There were no addicts in Pakistan when the Soviets went into Afghanistan in 1979, he told me. Today it's a problem no president or prime minister can ignore. The United Nations states that the rate in the rise in addiction is one of the worst it has recorded anywhere in the world.

After more than a decade the Soviets were on the run from Afghanistan. Much later the Americans went in and the entire region changed forever. Pakistan has become increasingly unstable, and in Afghanistan itself the Taliban and Islamic State battle for supremacy while the American-supported government in Kabul finds itself a hostage in its own country. The results are bombs and bloodshed on an unimaginable scale.

Although my passion throughout my career has been international politics, sometimes it has been tempting to avert my eyes from the object of my obsession.

7

A New Birth of Freedom

'Reservation of Separate Amenities Act 1953:
Act to provide for the reservation of public premises and
vehicles or portions thereof for the exclusive use of persons
of a particular race or class, for the interpretation of laws
which provide for such reservation and for matters.'

My visits to South Africa were perhaps the most challenging
and instructive of my career as a television reporter. They were
dominated by a question that never left me. How could a state
in the twentieth century devise a system of government that so
ruthlessly excluded more than 80 per cent of its population?

The most persistent prediction, voiced quite openly when I
first went there, was that the poison in its politics and its race
divisions would propel the country to a mighty confrontation
between black and white, engulfing cities and townships in a
bloody war. Fortunately, that dark prophecy never came to
pass. Even more fortunately for me I met the man to whom
most of the credit is given for helping to avert such a ghastly
event in his nation's life. He was to become a South African
hero and one of the icons of twentieth-century politics.

Nothing like that seemed possible the first time I arrived in
Johannesburg.

It's not easy to absorb the shock of finding yourself in a country where the hospitals, trains, buses and public conveniences

you are not allowed to use, the park benches on which you are not allowed to sit, and the beaches you're not allowed to go to, are determined solely by the colour of your skin.

For many days on my first visit to the country, I felt I was drifting around, eyes wide open, but in the grip of a frightening and recurring nightmare. My colleagues thought they could extract some fun having me photographed on a beach close to a large sign saying: WHITES ONLY.

I played along for a while. I found nothing remotely funny about it.

To me here was incontrovertible evidence of life in a bizarre world where the deeply offensive could be passed off as disarmingly normal.

I had thought I knew a lot about South Africa before I went there for the first time in 1984. As a student I had written angry essays about the politics of the country. For years after that the actions of the authorities in Pretoria always found a way of grabbing international headlines.

That was certainly the case in 1968.

The South African government forced the cancellation of a visit by an MCC team that year because it included at the last minute Basil D'Oliveira, a coloured player who had come to live in England to escape the discrimination against non-whites in his own country. D'Oliveira, a talented all-rounder, was not allowed to represent South Africa because he was not white.

Here was the collision between politics and sport South Africa had always hoped to avoid, and it was being painted on an international canvas. Sport was a South African obsession. It was followed with religious passion. But passion could not be allowed to run roughshod over the rules about the separation of the races.

At a stroke, the cancellation of the cricket tour put the policy of apartheid in the unforgiving court of popular opinion. An entirely new constituency was forcing the country to confront its pariah status and the obloquy that surrounded it. This was big news. It played itself out over many weeks and purely by chance it coincided with the start of my career as a journalist in London.

Like most of my fellow West Indians I am a cricket obsessive (I was president of Surrey Cricket Club at The Oval in 2014) and I immersed myself in the story about the tour cancellation. The story polarised opinion in Britain. An anti-apartheid campaign was quickly formed and advocated cutting all sporting ties with South Africa. On the opposing side were South Africans and leaders in the English cricket establishment who insisted that politics should be 'separated from sport'. The problem with that argument was that it was proposing something impossible. Pretoria itself had made the connection and was holding fast by it.

Reporting on the cancellation of a cricket tour I was learning a great deal about the politics of South Africa. Even so, the public signs I couldn't fail to notice on my first trip to Johannesburg never lost the ability to surprise. I was stunned by their bluntness and in a strange way by their audacity. How could a state do that and not be forced to confront its majority population seething with anger and crying out for blood?

I cringed visibly at seeing so horrific a message spelled out in such uncompromising terms. They spat out exclusion. NET BLANKES: WHITES ONLY. SLEGS NIE BLANKES: NON-WHITES ONLY. No black visitor could view such a notice with equanimity.

To black South Africans they screamed inequality. I found them wounding and demeaning and yet at the same time they felt tawdry and mean-spirited. In one sense they were, because set against that vast canon of rules governing the separation of the races they were nothing more than examples of petty apartheid, nasty, niggling acts of officially sanctioned bias based entirely on race.

The killer regulations were contained in something sinister

called the Native (Urban Areas) Consolidation Act. That compelled black South Africans to submit every aspect of their working lives to the control of a white minority government. The Pass Laws subsumed within the Act banished black people to rural South Africa well away from white city areas and allowed for their forceful removal whenever that was deemed desirable. That meant whenever black townships edged too close to areas preserved for whites.

The problem of keeping the races apart was that in reality they could not be kept apart. The patterns of ordinary life made rules ordained by the state a glaring absurdity and it was clear to everyone.

White South Africa needed black labour. It was well-nigh impossible to imagine life without it. Without it South Africa would crumble. Black South Africans needed to work. They needed jobs to survive. So from its inception the Urban Areas Consolidation Act, despite its impressive name, had been a classic case of self-serving hypocrisy. To try to circumvent a rule that made nonsense of reality, black people were allowed limited access to white urban areas to work. That was not enough. Something had to be done to remind them that they were there on sufferance.

So black South Africans were required to carry a passbook, an identity card or internal passport, to prove they'd been given permission to work in white suburbs. It had to be available for inspection at all times and produced on demand. Failure to do so could result in automatic arrest and possible expulsion to the countryside.

One black South African told me his people called the passbook the book of death.

The Pass Laws framed my lasting impressions of how black South Africans lived, or more precisely how they managed to survive under the oppressive weight of rules and regulations handed down by the state.

To read about those rules and to hear them described to me

by black South Africans was one thing. To see them in action was quite another. I sat in a Johannesburg courtroom one morning watching a number of young black men convicted of flouting the Pass Laws. Defendants in courtrooms the world over appear diminished in stature when confronted by the trappings and the full majesty of the law. What I observed that day had little to do with majesty. Such a word would be surely misplaced. It seemed to me to be routine, rule-inspired humiliation.

No defendant spoke up or attempted to rebut the charges. I cannot recall a single defence. There were no defiant speeches. I suspected that the way the rules were applied left little room for legal argument or personal dissent. They were meant to restrict the free movement of black people in their own towns and cities and that is precisely what they did.

I felt the atmosphere thick with a sense of opprobrium.

Confused and ill at ease, the defendants gazed expressionless into the middle distance and spoke little if at all, dignity sorely affronted; pawns in a grotesque game, reduced to playing bit parts in the much larger tragedy of their haunted lives.

The presiding magistrate, white and in his forties, said even less, only occasionally looking up from his papers as he recorded the decisions of the court. Although he was responsible for implementing this important arm of government policy, his attitude was neither censorious nor sympathetic. What he did affected real lives but, to anyone looking on, his job appeared merely mundane.

Weeks later, nearing the end of a long day's filming, I watched one black colleague, for whose safety I felt partly responsible, tremble with the fear of not getting out of the city by nightfall. I was terrified at what my role would be if my colleague fell foul of the law. I have never forgotten how scared I felt for him. I almost sank to my knees with relief when he successfully made it out of town in time.

The arbitrary manner in which such rules were enforced

and the sense of injustice they evoked stirred opposition to apartheid from unexpected quarters. I witnessed that at first hand when, late one afternoon, I met a group of white women, some the wives of captains of industry. They had set up a charitable body known as the Black Sash. Through a network of offices and by attending Pass Laws court hearings it monitored how the laws operated and tried to help black people mired in their complexity.

To the South African government such white identification with the problems of black life was unwelcome. Apartheid had after all been designed to keep people separate and apart. Campaigns like those of the Black Sash posed a direct challenge to the system by doing just the opposite. As a consequence, the charity's members were not very popular in official South African circles. One of them, a middle-class white woman, showed me the evidence of a night attack on her family home by persons unknown. No one was ever arrested or charged in connection with the attack.

None of this was good news for a country always sensitive to international public opinion. More fundamentally there was always the nagging question: for how long could a majority of the country's population be kept under control?

By 1984, when I went there for the first time, opposition voices were becoming more strident. State security suppression could not silence the multitude forever. The architects of apartheid had been forced into rethinking the master plan. And that was how I came to be on an assignment in South Africa.

I had gone to report on plans to introduce a tri-cameral legislature. For the first time coloureds, those of mixed African and European ancestry, and Indians would be given a limited share of power. Black South Africans were excluded.

This was in reality no radical change to the system of apartheid. In fact, it entrenched discrimination by race and brought the two numerically smallest parts of the population into an alliance with whites against the interests of the overwhelming black majority.

If it worked, South Africa could chug along against the run of the tide of international criticism, towing the idea of the tri-cameral legislature. As ever the problem was that it excluded the majority black population of the country. It was felt that they had already been bought off or had foisted on them self-governing homelands where they could be responsible for their own affairs. 'Own affairs' was the key phrase. It formed part of the stock ministerial response to every question about the aspirations of black South Africans.

It was always surprising to me that no one in authority seemed embarrassed by the fact that these so-called homelands or Bantustans were then scattered, geographically disjointed territories marked out along ethnic and linguistic lines. By designating some of them independent the government had been able to wash its hands of anything to do with black empowerment.

The Bantustans in effect denied black South Africans any claim to citizenship of the country of their birth. By the time I went to South Africa for the first time, the Bantustans had come to be seen as part of an outrageous concept.

Despite that fatal flaw the government felt sufficiently confident in 1984 to describe its plans for a tri-cameral legislature as a 'new political dispensation'. To everyone I met I tried to say as carefully as I could that the word 'dispensation' sounded more than a little patronising. I got nowhere with that observation.

I had always been worried about going to a country where black people faced such open discrimination. But as ITN's diplomatic correspondent, South Africa fell squarely into my patch and I told myself I was never going to have to live there. It was, after all, an assignment. To those colleagues who questioned how I would fare working there I replied perhaps a little airily and without conviction that I should feel at home in a country where the majority of the people were black.

More seriously, as a journalist I had always been curious about the apartheid system and puzzled that it had survived in the face of outright condemnation from every significant political forum in the world. I was fascinated by the mechanics of state control, especially since administering a country along race-drawn lines in the glare and complexity of twentieth-century life was bound to throw up a mass of contradictions.

One of those had come to light in the 1960s when the government in Pretoria signed an agreement to sell large quantities of pig iron to Japan. It was quickly obvious that as part of the deal Japanese businessmen would make periodic visits to South Africa. But in a country so preoccupied by skin colour, into which racial grouping could the Japanese be slotted? They were not white nor were they coloured or Indian and as valuable trading partners they could not be subjected to the blunt regulations under which black South Africans were forced to live and work.

As ever, the theologians of apartheid found a solution. The Japanese would be designated 'honorary whites' and could travel, work and live as white South Africans. I can only surmise that Japanese businessmen were content with this formula.

On rare occasions and for a variety of reasons the South African government tried to apply such a designation to other non-whites. That was never easy. South Africa could not on a whim or caprice slip easily in and out of a system it had created with such meticulous attention to detail. In any event no self-respecting black visitor wanted to be called an 'honorary white'. I remember making it clear that I had no wish to be so described.

This meant, however, that I could only be put up in hotels or go to restaurants or bars operating under what was known as an international licence. Places without that official blessing were off-limits for me and if I ever got anywhere close, as I did on several occasions in error, and sometimes out of a sense of pure mischief, a hotel manager or restaurant owner would always materialise at the entrance in double-quick time to explain with pained courtesy why I was not allowed to eat or drink there.

After a while, my white English colleagues feigned mild amusement and shock. Native South Africans accepted the consequences of such acts of petty discrimination in their stride. To them it was unexceptional, just a part of everyday life.

One incident in relation to these rules made a great impression on me.

Two senior figures from the far-right Conservative Party invited me to lunch after a political rally on the outskirts of Johannesburg. I had gone to the rally to interview the party's leader, Dr Andries Treurnicht, and would have been delighted to escape as soon as it was done.

I encountered no hostility but the rhetoric from the podium, though entirely predictable, did nothing to warm me to the party or to its leader. I should perhaps confess that I also felt a little self-conscious as the only black face, prominently positioned, in a crowd of some fifteen hundred.

At the end of the rally I accepted an invitation to have a meal in the generous spirit in which it had been made. I suppose that deep down I imagined that my hosts would have made a quick calculation about where it might be possible to take me. They had not. I stood on the pavement and listened in consternation as the two party officers debated where they might be allowed to take me.

I am convinced that my hosts had no wish to embarrass me and would have been mortified and apologised profusely had I shown the slightest sign of discomfort. Their invitation had been made on the spur of the moment and with good intentions. Conservative Party members had probably not taken too many people like me to lunch before, far out of the city, and were simply dealing with a practical consequence of the rules governing their lives and which, by the way, I assumed, their right-wing Conservative Party strongly supported.

It turned out that neither man knew the area well and neither was sure which of the nearby restaurants had the international licence required to entertain me. One was eventually found. We ate and talked and didn't mention the business of international licences. I noted that the rhetoric at lunch was not the same as it had been on a public stage at a rally.

For a visiting black journalist such regulations were never burdensome and gave me the chance to observe the system at work.

Even before I left the airport in Johannesburg on that first visit I was drawn to an illuminating cameo. At the luggage carousel white travellers would stand awaiting their bags or suitcases. At the slightest hint that a traveller had recognised his or hers, there came the merest nod at which a black hand would appear as if by magic to whisk said bag or suitcase off to a waiting car. In the car park nearby, the boot would spring open and black hands would ensure that the item or items of luggage had been safely tucked away. There was little sign of acknowledgement by either party. The transaction ended as it had begun, in silence. There was nothing unusual about it. It was the accepted way bags travelled the short distance from airport carousel to waiting cars.

In a show perhaps amounting to nothing more than gesture politics, whenever I was assisted with my bags at Johannesburg airport I made a very public display of thanking the porter profusely and giving him a large tip. I was frequently moved to make such gestures on my visits to South Africa. Although they probably meant very little, I never managed to stop myself from doing it.

On the journey from the airport into town on my very first day I challenged my helpful guide and brilliant colleague, Cliff Bestall, who had a range of contacts with political operatives on every side, to a test on how accurately he could tell me whether people we saw in the street as we drove by were black or coloured. I had never been part of such an exercise before, nor was I quite sure that he had ever been. I was anxious to find out how accurately he could make the proper distinctions.

Cliff met my questions with impressive certainty. When he failed to make the designation at a glance, he apologised and assured me that the authorities had devised their own methods to have people placed in the correct colour classifications. One of those involved placing a pencil in the hair of the person whose colour could not be determined on sight. It is too tiresome and almost too ridiculous to explain the procedure in detail except to say that, if the pencil stayed in, the news for the individual and his family was not good.

No system could be absolutely perfect, however, and some decisions were occasionally so finely balanced that families were torn apart. A brother or a sister born to the same parents might have slightly different shades of facial colour. That simple consequence of unavoidable genetic fact could be disastrous. For one thing, it could result in siblings being forced to go to different schools.

South Africans of all colours were in the main amicably disposed to visitors and keen to talk superficially about life in their country and anxious to find out what the rest of the world thought about South Africa. However well-disguised, the sense of isolation, heightened by the drumbeat of international criticism and the more obvious pressure of economic sanctions, was keenly felt. And so white South Africans attempted to find anything resembling validation from the few outsiders they had the chance to meet. That was conspicuously so when I was recognised as an ITN television reporter.

It became tedious after a while to be asked repeatedly what I thought about the country (I invariably stuck to geography in non-serious approaches and praised South Africa's natural beauty) but it did throw up unusual encounters.

One morning a man I'd never met invited himself to my breakfast table in a Johannesburg hotel. After the obligatory question about my views of the country he proceeded to outline what he described as his 'big problem'. I was slightly confused about why I merited such a disclosure but I could do nothing to interrupt his story. He got to the point quickly. 'I married a white woman,' he confided.

I was less than stunned by that declaration because I would have put my last penny on the certainty that my interlocutor was a white South African. He was, he told me, looking around as though anxious not to be overheard, a very light-skinned coloured man, a fact which I assumed could and had been so proved by the relevant authority. He then went on for fifteen minutes or so to describe the official hoops he'd been made to go through to be permitted to marry. At one point, he told me even South Africa's foreign minister, Pik Botha, whom he'd managed to see through the helpful intervention of a mutual friend, was surprised about the nature of the 'big problem'. Like me the foreign minister also thought he had been talking to a fellow white South African. Colour classification rules were not meant to fail so spectacularly.

By placing such a stern emphasis on separating its population on the basis of minute gradations of colour, the apartheid system had unwittingly sown the seeds of its eventual demise. Relationships across the colour lines were one thing, but more significantly it was inane to assume that people of the same colour could be corralled into sharing the same political philosophy. And so it proved with the introduction of the tri-cameral legislature. It precipitated one of the most serious and sustained challenges to the concept of the separation of the races.

On my first evening in Johannesburg, I went to listen to a coloured man who had become one of the most trenchant critics of apartheid and of the government's new political dispensation. Allan Boesak, a Dutch Reformed Church cleric and a brilliant speaker, was urging a smallish but lively crowd of people of all races to boycott elections to the tri-cameral legislature. In ringing tones and with his audience applauding, chanting and frequently jumping around and dancing in approval, he denounced the government's latest initiative.

That was bad news for the authors of the tri-cameral plan. Opposition from such a quarter was a dagger to the heart of the South African government. Having invested all in the creation of a system to keep the races apart it had no way of dealing with people whose political outlook crossed lines which should have been dictated by the colour of their skin. Had the government's view held, Allan Boesak would have been seeking election to the new legislature. Instead the new political dispensation had energised another sworn opponent.

I talked to a number of candidates running for seats in the allocation for coloureds. Even those who broadly supported the government, and who hoped to enjoy the benefits of securing a position of political prominence, were embarrassed about the fact that their complicity in the new tri-cameral plan had consigned black South Africans to a state of political hopelessness. Indian candidates were particularly tetchy and hostile to the view that by agreeing to take part in elections to the new legislature they were selling out black South Africans for short-term political advantage. Reacting to that suggestion one candidate threatened to have me thrown out of his office in a manner he assured me I would not forget.

Incensed that I had been threatened, I stood my ground and in an uncharacteristic loss of temper issued a few threats of my own before leaving his office and slamming the door behind me. That was silly and unprofessional of me. The man had probably assumed that he was working for the good of South African Indians. I was convinced that he could not have failed to understand that his action was part of the plan to entrench the separation of the races by shutting out the majority black population for good.

In the barber shop at a maximum security prison in Indiana with Rick Pearish (on my right), who was serving a long sentence for burglary and kidnapping, and contract killer John Serwatke.

Mafia mobster Anthony Russo, who never discussed with his wife what he did for a living for a long way into their relationship.

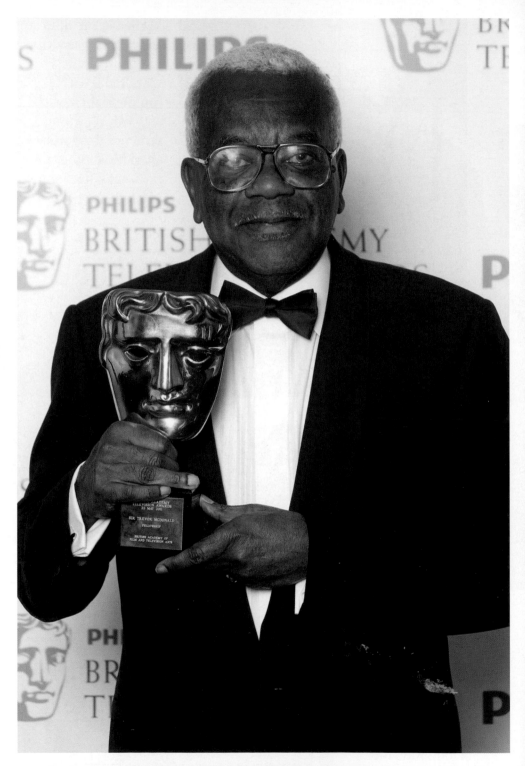

A proud moment – my BAFTA Fellowship in 2011.

I had the honour of meeting Her Majesty the Queen.

Cricket is a West Indian addiction, and I played the game into my sixties. I went on to write biographies of Clive Lloyd and Viv Richards.

Carrying the torch before the Beijing Olympics in 2008 on part of its journey across London.

With my friend Lenny Henry.

An evening with the actor Morgan Freeman, near his home in Clarksville, Mississippi.

On the *News at Ten* set in June 1993, a year after I had been promoted as its first sole presenter.

I was knighted by the Prince of Wales at Buckingham Palace in 1999 for services to broadcasting and journalism. Never in my wildest dreams growing up in Trinidad did I think I would ever become 'Sir Trevor'.

There was a history to Indian political calculations. As far back as the 1880s Indians began going to South Africa in great numbers to escape poverty in the subcontinent. When the then South Africa government sounded an alarm about the immigrant influx, the Indians initiated a campaign to make the case that, although they were not white, they should be regarded as superior to native blacks. Mohandas Gandhi, living in Durban at the time, became its chief spokesman. He argued with some success that his compatriots were a civilised people and bearers of an ancient culture who should not be looked upon as 'the raw kaffir whose occupation was hunting'.

Gandhi made no bones about the fact that, initially at least, he regarded South Africa's black majority as of a much lower social order than his fellow Indians. He probably saw apartheid as another declension of India's caste system.

Far from ushering in an era of political harmony the plan for a tri-cameral legislature sharpened general opposition to white minority rule. Black townships – overcrowded, impoverished and in the grip of despair – became the crucibles of open rebellion. I came to know the townships well, especially those around Johannesburg – Katlehong, Soweto, Thokoza, Alexandra, Tembisa and Sebokeng.

South Africa's security bosses had for years convinced themselves that black protests of any sort were Communist-inspired and responded to black township unrest as they had always done: with force.

The most notorious example had been at Sharpeville in the Transvaal in March 1960 when police fired on a crowd of some six thousand demonstrators. Sixty-nine people were killed. The demonstrators insisted they had been peaceful; that they had been protesting against unjust laws and had in no way threatened the lives of policemen. That was not the official view. One senior officer had reportedly explained the police response and the shooting by suggesting that the mentality of the natives was such that it did not allow for non-violent protests.

I was astonished to hear a similar version of that view when, almost twenty-five years later, I rode in the back of an armed police truck rumbling through the black township of Soweto. In uncompromising terms the police commander sitting next to me explained what he thought of black protesters. Shouting to make himself heard over the dull roar of the vehicle's engine he said: 'Troublemakers, violent troublemakers. They are all Communist agitators, Mr McDonald, all Communist agitators.' I remember saying to the commander with all the tact that I could manage in the circumstances that I had always failed to understand why it took belief in an imported political ideology to convince people whose lives were scarred by discrimination and mired in poverty that they were not being treated fairly.

It was impossible to know what the police commander made of what I'd said. He looked at me blankly and did not respond.

As a part of the concept of keeping the races apart, South Africa's black township strategy was brilliantly effective. It struck me from my first few days there that it kept the white minority in comfortable ignorance of where or how black people lived. This did not mean that white people were unaware of the existence of black townships, but they had no cause to get too close to them, nor could they even be glimpsed in passing as the country's fine network of roads took the unsuspecting at high speeds to their privileged, white destinations. The townships were close enough to supply workers to nearby cities but never close enough to impinge upon the conscience of white employers. Townships were off the beaten track and largely out of sight.

For some time I had thought that when white South Africans confessed to knowing nothing about black township life they were simply shutting their eyes to the obvious and were not being truthful. Very early in that first visit to the country I changed my mind. In many cases people were telling the truth. Black townships had been deliberately planted away from the view of whites. The system allowed, even encouraged, white South Africans to avert their gaze. It worked perfectly.

I was surprised at first to discover that even among South African journalists and their friends I could stop any animated dinner-party conversation dead in its tracks merely by saying quite casually that I had spent part of my day in a black township. I immediately became the focus of attention, the star guest. Everyone wanted to hear more. I was asked quite basic questions about what black township life was like, and there were more searching enquiries about the political mood of township dwellers. Some, desperate to find an appropriate retort to how I'd spent that part of my day, commented on my bravery; others wondered whether I had been foolhardy.

I vividly recall one visit to a township school.

Its plight had come to the attention of the South African government and an official from the Education Ministry had been dispatched to offer words of support and a gift of food. In the official visiting party was, by happy accident, someone I had known for months. He was a man in his late thirties who had been a prominent diplomat at the South African Embassy in London and extremely helpful to me in my dealings with his country's Foreign Office. His time in London had ended and he had begun the customary home posting before being sent abroad again.

Ours was a chance meeting at that township school. We greeted each other warmly and slipped easily back into a conversation about his time in London. He surprised me by confessing that he had never been to a black township before. He was astonished when I said that I had been to several and that they were all equally miserable. Looking around the run-down school in an environment seasoned in hardship and disfigured by neglect, his face was a study. 'Christ!' he said, after several minutes. 'This place is truly awful.' His expression was one of genuine shock.

My shock was that a young, bright South African diplomat, whose career was doubtless on the rise, and who had been given the authority to speak about his country and to explain its policies to journalists like me in London, had never been exposed to the reality of black township life. He had never before set foot in a black township less than an hour's drive from his office in Pretoria.

With Nelson Mandela still behind bars on Robben Island at the time of the introduction of the tri-cameral legislature, the most visible black political leader was Chief Mangosuthu Buthelezi. He had accepted the government's offer of the homeland of KwaZulu in Natal, set up a parliament and had become its powerful chief minister. In so doing Buthelezi had fallen in with the policy most cherished by South Africa's white minority rulers – the creation of a geographically disconnected patchwork of blacks-only Bantustans into which the government in Pretoria could pour money if it wished to bolster the pretence that black people had been afforded freedom to control their political destinies.

Buthelezi's acceptance of that made him a hated figure in the eyes of the majority of black South Africans. He was seen as a tool of the apartheid system. He travelled the world speaking out against the swelling chorus for international sanctions against South Africa and at home his Inkatha party waged a bloody war against supporters of the African National Congress, which never ceased to recognise the incarcerated Nelson Mandela as its head.

I saw one result of the violent turf war between Inkatha and the ANC.

One afternoon I was taken to a village a few miles outside Durban where the night before Buthelezi's supporters had set fire to a number of homes. Some twenty families had taken refuge in a nearby school with no idea of when or where they might be rehoused.

I still have in my mind's eye a picture of the bespectacled old woman – she reminded me of my mother – who described to me how her house had been burned to the ground. She said she'd been given due warning and allowed time to escape to safety. What made her indignant, she explained, was that her attackers lacked what she felt would have been the common decency of hiding their faces. They were happy to be identified as Inkatha henchmen.

The ANC had always insisted that those in Buthelezi's party who perpetrated such shameless violence had been allowed a free hand by the South African security forces. It was even suggested that the security forces used Inkatha's supporters – armed with machetes, spears and ceremonial Zulu clubs – to fight an unrelenting war against the ANC. Thousands were killed.

Buthelezi was always happy to see me and treated me with courtesy. One afternoon he interrupted what seemed an important meeting with colleagues to welcome me to his homeland capital, Ulundi. At one of the annual celebrations of the Zulu people, he once picked me out in a small crowd of journalists, stopped mid-procession and came forward to greet me warmly and to introduce me to his wife. He later invited me to have tea with the Zulu king.

There was a strange sequel to that display of warmth by the chief. When the celebrations ended I stood within earshot of a small crowd solemnly intoning what's called in the television trade 'a piece to camera'. By that time of day gallons of drink had been consumed and people had become excitable. Something I said speaking to the camera included a reference to the chief and it was overheard. A small group in the crowd considered it blasphemy to hear an unknown foreigner speaking of their chief in a language and in a context they did not understand. They charged, tribal weapons in hand, threatening loudly to beat me to death.

The slightly comic element to the scene, which was not really comic at all, was that, unable to understand their dialect or to discern the cause of their wrath, I had stupidly stood my ground in total ignorance of any impending danger. Fortunately, our South African cameraman Ian Robbie realised that, crazed and in their cups, they were intent on making light work of getting rid of me.

I was hustled away through what had by then become a mob baying for blood and into the relative safety of the back of a van. Trying vainly to explain to my would-be attackers that I meant no insult to the Zulu people, I apparently kept shouting as I was rushed away that I was a friend of the chief's. In the confusion my South African colleagues tried to make the same point, to no avail. They made sure that I was safely behind the locked doors of the van, convinced that the threats to my person were serious. I said nothing about the incident when I later had tea with the king.

Buthelezi's blueprint for the future of South Africa did not include the important condition of one man, one vote. His reason was obvious. Like everyone else he suspected that the majority of the black vote would go to his party's sworn opponents, the ANC, and his political capital with the government in Pretoria would be lost forever. Whenever he and I spoke, his comments about Mandela were therefore models of diplomatic phrasing.

He was more outspoken on the question of economic sanctions. He was against them. He said they would hurt his people. Again he was falling into line with Pretoria. That brought him modest success. His position on the issue informed Margaret Thatcher's view when she was Britain's prime minister, and she waged an unremitting battle against her Commonwealth colleagues who favoured taking a tougher line against the South African government. But Buthelezi's days as the country's most respected black voice would begin to fade as South African politics edged towards recognising the inevitable.

We had one tense meeting a few months before Mandela's release.

The chief had made some anodyne comment about the future of South Africa and I had replied by saying the ANC leader might not necessarily agree. Peeved that I had injected a Mandela thought into our conversation, he insinuated that I had become what he called a 'Mandela spokesman'. I was having none of it. I said so and stopped the interview. The chief was somewhat taken aback but, gracious as he always was in our meetings, he apologised. One of his ministers who had overheard our exchange solemnly informed me afterward that chiefs of the proud Zulu people are not in the habit of saying sorry.

When our conversation ended, Buthelezi briefly disappeared into his office and returned carrying a Zulu shield and spear. With due ceremony he presented them to me, proclaiming me 'a son of Africa'.

I managed to get the items safely to London. Today I would not dare risk getting a Zulu shield and spear through airport security at Heathrow.

The introduction of the tri-cameral legislature, bringing into the system of government coloureds and Indians but excluding blacks, was the last throw of the political dice for the rulers of white South Africa. Township violence was becoming uncontrollable. In ever more security crackdowns, the numbers of people arrested and jailed went up but the volume of the unrest only increased. The economy was not in good shape and South Africans were beginning to grow weary of the constant sting of international disapproval.

Most frustrating of all for the South African government were the ceaseless international demands for the release of Nelson Mandela. Cooped up in a prison on an isolated island off

Cape Town, Mandela seemed to pose an even bigger headache to the authorities than if he was free to attend ANC strategy meetings and make public political speeches in Johannesburg or Cape Town. This constant pressure finally caused the South African government to crack.

Barely a year after the tri-cameral legislature was hailed as a 'new political dispensation' there was a dramatic development.

President P. W. Botha, a man not usually impressed by campaigns waged outside his country or within, was forced into agreeing to what was for him a major concession. He announced that he would agree to release Mandela if he unconditionally renounced the use of violence as a political weapon.

Mandela's response, in a letter read out by his daughter to a heaving political rally in Soweto, was cutting. 'I cherish my own freedom dearly, but I care even more for your freedom. Only free men can negotiate . . . I cannot and will not give any undertaking at a time when I, and you, the people, are not free. Your freedom and mine cannot be separated.'

It was probably the moment the South African government knew it had lost the ability to control its political future without the cooperation of its turbulent though partially silenced adversary. 'Only free men can negotiate,' Mandela had written. It was a stinging rebuke to Botha and to everything the ruling National Party stood for. Mandela's words confronted the government with an unpalatable choice. There were no escape routes.

At no point during my many visits to South Africa after 1984 was I given the slightest hint that Botha's ruling National Party had begun to explore the possibility of talking constructively to Mandela. Public pronouncements suggested that the government had reverted to its customary uncompromising stance. His offer to release Mandela having being rejected, Botha fell back on the rhetoric that had always worked for him.

He attacked all those, including the banned ANC, who had denounced the idea of a tri-cameral legislature. He called them 'barbaric Communist agitators and even murderers who perpetrate the most cruel deeds against their fellow South Africans because they are on the payroll of their masters far from this lovely land of ours'. Straining to control his anger at Mandela's rejection he gave a little too much away in explaining the real thinking behind the government's latest initiatives. He declared that he was not prepared 'to lead white South Africans and other minority groups on the road to abdication and suicide.'

Even by Botha's own standards it was an extraordinary outburst.

The South African capital markets digested the president's thoughts and their implication for the country's future and went into freefall.

I continued my visits to black townships, always in shock at their unpromising landscape and listening to the despair of their residents. Such places were thick with the air of poverty and hopelessness; they held thousands of stories of lives in ruinous neglect. Township life could be brutal and frequently caked in blood. But I saw little raw anger. Perhaps it had been dissipated by time, punctured by resignation and a lack of belief in anything better.

Apartheid's firm hand had wielded its power to oppress and was squeezing the ability of black South Africans to protest, too. For some the cost of speaking out was simply too high.

On my journeys around the country I saw evidence of that. One afternoon we had driven for several hours to follow up on a story about cases of severe malnutrition in a part of KwaZulu-Natal where, given the government's black homeland policy, such a problem should never have occurred. We had been told we could find a hospital where the story could be verified and I had been encouraged to make the journey by the fact that some doctors there were British.

We eventually found the hospital and the British doctors. They recognised me as an ITN reporter and were instinctively inclined to be helpful. They were, however, concerned about saying anything that might jeopardise their position. They did not want to be interviewed on camera.

Sensing my disappointment at having come a long way to end up without a story, one of the doctors asked me whether I knew anything about the government's 'removal policy'. I said that I did. He was referring to the fact that when black townships expanded too much and began to encroach on designated white areas, black residents were removed sometimes forcibly, and dispatched to the countryside. The doctor suggested that if we were prepared to drive for a further two hours or so we would find clear evidence of the site being prepared to receive the next black township.

The very word 'township' was a misnomer because the entire area to which we had been directed was barren, bleak and deep in the heart of the countryside. I asked the doctor how we would know when we had got to the place to which he was directing us.

'You'll know,' he said, 'watch out for the corrugated metal latrines.' With a fine sense of the need for hygiene the authorities apparently always put in the latrines before people moved in. Discouraged at not being able to verify the story we'd originally set out to find, we'd driven on as directed, half-heartedly, on what might easily have been another useless chase.

About two hours later we arrived at the place one of the British doctors had described.

From a distance of half a mile away we saw, gleaming in the South African sunshine, some twenty or thirty galvanised iron latrines perched on a desolate hillside. I could not believe my eyes. It was an indication of the perverse sense of the planning required to drive black South Africans out of the cities.

I took great care to deliver my report about the latrines factually, in measured tones and without a flicker of emotion.

Some stories, profound in their own meaning, need no exaggerated show of disgust. They have a voice of their own and speak volumes.

Even so, my report about the latrines did not endear me to the South African High Commission in London. For a time I was denied a visa to return to Johannesburg. It was a mere slap on the wrist. The word 'banned' was never used although over lunch one day the second-in-command at the High Commission said, as we sipped our wine, he hoped I would understand that my report about the latrines didn't go down too well. I said I understood.

A little more strangely, I was also mildly rebuked by the high commissioner himself for sending back to London reports about his country that were too depressing to his children, who were looking forward to living there sometime in the future.

It was impossible for any government to keep treating its people as the National Party had done for years. Putting international criticism to one side, it was stretching any concept of basic humanity to its limits. It was also bad economics.

I remember an encounter with the mayor of Grahamstown who explained to me how his municipality had been affected by a boycott of white-owned shops by residents of black townships in the vicinity. I mischievously suggested that Grahamstown should be able to cope with such a boycott because apartheid had been designed to keep people separate and apart. With my tongue firmly in my cheek I suggested that his town should be able to ensure its economic survival without a dependence on black custom. 'But that's not possible,' he said.

He had made my point. I told the mayor that if South Africans of all colours and creeds depended for their continued existence on a degree of cooperation by their fellow citizens it was obvious that a fairer system of government had to be devised. Repression and exclusion could never successfully be the sum total of public policy.

The South African government was running out of time.

The introduction of the tri-cameral legislature had not done what it was supposed to do. It had failed to stop the growing unrest at home and international opinion about the proposed legislative change was sceptical. It had become much too late in the day to tinker with the system of apartheid and to dismantle a few of its structures.

It is never easy to manage change. The process invariably acquires a momentum of its own. A government that fails to keep pace faces revolutionary chaos.

And so, reluctantly and with grave reservations and in secret, the National Party government had begun talking to prisoner number 46664.

There were few clues about the discussions between Mandela and a small group of National Party officials. The first, tentative contact had begun in 1986, but by the beginning of 1990 it was clear that the thinking in the ruling National Party had undergone a significant change.

By February of that year F. W. de Klerk, who had replaced Botha as president, was ready to make a dramatic announcement. The ban on the ANC was to be lifted and Mandela was to be released. No firm date had been announced, but with barely concealed excitement the world's media gathered up its notebooks and its cameras and headed to Johannesburg.

My ITN colleagues and I got there two days before Mandela walked from prison a free man.

8

Looking Beyond the Past

'. . . there is a dark
Inscrutable workmanship that reconciles
Discordant elements, makes them cling together
In one society.'

William Wordsworth, *The Prelude*

The decision to talk to Nelson Mandela would not have come easily to South Africa's ruling National Party. Having invested so much time and legislative energy erecting elaborate structures to support the policy of racial segregation it could not appear to be reckless in tearing them apart. To do that would mean going back on everything the country stood for. It would also mean repudiating the very basic principles of white rule on which the government had relied for nearly half a century.

It meant above all entering into a dialogue with the representative of an organisation branded terrorist, committed apparently to nothing less than the violent destruction of the South African way of life.

That's how the African National Congress and its leaders had been described to National Party supporters for years. It was even the view in some areas of British politics. Talking to Mandela would be a monumental gamble. It had to be done with clear purpose, and to cover the possibility of it all going badly wrong it had to be done in secret.

Secrecy was important, too, because apartheid had given succour to and helped sustain a combustible mix of religious zealotry and political extremism. Discussing the mere possibility of bringing black South Africans into the political process was an apostasy and there were people prepared to fight to the death to defend the status quo. Some said it openly.

The good news for the government was that the diehards were always a minority of the minority, stridently vocal at times, frequently threatening and capable of the most vicious criminal acts, but never more than a fanatical fringe.

Despite that, the atmosphere surrounding any political discourse about South Africa's future was frequently doom-laden and brimful of images of blood-soaked streets. When black townships rioted and the security forces repelled protesters with tear gas and bullets, I understood the genesis of such grim prophecies. I was not convinced they'd come to pass.

Untutored though I was in the many complexities of South African political life, I saw enough to make me doubtful of the view that it would all end in mayhem, with bodies piled high in the streets.

Apartheid had succeeded in oppression. It had blighted black lives. That was plain to see. But it had never managed, as its core philosophy intended, to keep its peoples entirely separate. That was in very obvious ways impossible.

Black and white South Africans needed each other. They were interdependent. They had been thrown together, and some way down the line they were destined to live together however their fates decided.

Something else led me to believe that there was always the possibility of an eventual political accommodation. In my travels around the country, through the most depressing black townships and in the face of the most terrible hardship, I was surprised by the absence of hate – the bitter hate of the kind I saw in the eyes of opposing sides across the barricades in Belfast and Londonderry.

Black South Africans hated their government and its policies. They railed against the policies of a government that treated them with contempt. They felt no burning hatred of their white compatriots. There was, as far as I could see no desire to kill them or to run them out of town.

The system had another flaw. It was being undermined from within. A number of white South Africans openly opposed the system. Senior white political figures like Helen Suzman and a host of others spoke out constantly against black repression. So, too, did courageous academics, and when the drama of the life and opposition of the great newspaper editor Donald Woods was celebrated in an award-winning Hollywood film in 1987, *Cry Freedom*, audiences around the world saw the lengths to which the South African government was prepared to go to stifle white dissent.

White opposition posed a unique challenge to the policies of the ruling National Party. White people were after all supposed to be grateful beneficiaries of the system. They were not meant to swell the growing ranks of the protesters.

Prominent white protesters got under the skin of the government and, as Donald Woods discovered, those deemed to have done that were to be shown no mercy. They were to be hounded and punished for their heresy.

Woods had befriended the Black Consciousness leader Steve Biko, who died in a South African prison in 1977. The suspicion that Biko had not suddenly died in the night of natural causes was taken as fact. Government propaganda, purposeful though it was, could do nothing to change that belief. The dirty work of silencing anti-apartheid activists in or out of prison had to be done in more clandestine ways, and it was.

The story of how a special counter-insurgency unit planned the kidnapping, torture and deaths of people who opposed the system is one of the gorier chapters in the history of modern South Africa. It would not be fully disclosed until the Truth and Reconciliation Commission took evidence from key witnesses in 1994, well after Mandela's release. Before that, only scraps of information were available to journalists.

No government can hide its darkest secrets, nor can it silence its critics forever. In South Africa too many people knew the truth.

I once spent an evening at the home of a young white lawyer who'd agreed to assist me with a story I'd been chasing about torture in South African prisons. There had been, as I've suggested, persistent talk about the practice but little hard evidence. That evening I was given the proof I was looking for.

I have a clear recollection of the interview. I remember thinking the man looked much too young to have been a seasoned lawyer. We sat in a cluttered living room where his daughter, no older than five or six, played about distractedly and noisily, seeking to catch her father's eye. The evidence he provided about the torture of black prisoners was as convincing as I could ever hope for. It was supported by a bundle of legal documents, including affidavits signed and witnessed by a young white prison doctor.

The doctor herself must have been a particular annoyance to her superiors. She had concluded her medical training with the help of a South African government grant. And she it was who had tipped off the lawyer about the torture of black prisoners.

As an expression of my gratitude to the lawyer I offered the services of ITN and said I'd be delighted to buy him lunch or dinner if he ever came to London. Thanking me, he explained that he'd run foul of the government before and had been forced to surrender his passport to the authorities in Pretoria. He was not free to travel outside the country; he had paid the price for challenging the system.

By 1985, when P. W. Botha made his offer to release Mandela if he agreed to renounce violence, South Africa was in trouble. White opposition could no longer be swept under the carpet, black activism was making governance extremely difficult – despite the heavy hand of the security services – and from almost every international forum the criticisms about the obscenity of the apartheid system had been unrelenting.

Governments of every complexion seek international approval at some time. They may do their best to disguise it, to pretend it does not amount to much, but disapproval stings. South Africans knew they were living on the edge of codes of decency and were forced into thinking about change. A new strategy was required.

Turning the great ship of state around required delicate skills and for a time politics appeared becalmed. We know now from various accounts of the period that the National Party was in turmoil. There were deep internal divisions. Ministerial meetings degenerated into shouting matches. P. W. Botha had become a liability, but he clung stubbornly to office, while black unrest was making the country ungovernable. A State of Emergency allowed South Africa's security forces to do their worst, but they couldn't stem the chaotic tide.

F. W. de Klerk, who was destined to play a major role in reordering his country's priorities, captured the atmosphere in his autobiography. He writes:

> The uprisings were frequently led and driven by a new generation of teenagers. They sometimes turned on their own parents and teachers whom they despised for having acquiesced in apartheid for so long . . . The result was that in hundreds of black communities there was a breakdown of normal services. There were many areas in which the police could not maintain a sufficient presence except for quick forays in armoured vehicles. Education in thousands of schools was seriously disrupted . . . Principals and teachers who did not agree with the disruption

of education were simply expelled from their schools by
their radical pupils who were motivated by their slogan
'Liberation before Education'.

In other words, South Africa teetered on the edge of anarchy.
The National Party could no longer pretend to hold the country together. It had become weary of the hammering it took
in the councils of world opinion. Exasperated that its calls
for political change had gone unheeded, the United Nations
declared that what South Africa had done to its majority black
population was 'a crime against humanity'.

Great political movements can sometimes turn on unexpected events.

President P. W. Botha suffered a stroke in 1989 and left office
reluctantly. His presidency ended in embarrassing episodes
of rambling incoherence. His declarations were beginning to
affect confidence in the economy.

His successor was F. W. de Klerk. I had met de Klerk on my
first visit to South Africa in 1984. He was then a government
minister. He had gone out of his way to find time to see me
and had been charming and courteous while making it absolutely clear that the participation of black South Africans in
the governance of the country would be limited to control of
what he termed their 'own affairs', the euphemism for the
Bantustan homeland policy. By 1989 that game had run its
course.

Times change and so do political perceptions. In his autobiography de Klerk explains his change of heart by citing a
concatenation of circumstances, not least of which he says was
the fall of the Berlin Wall. That deadly blow to Communism
and to the influence of the Soviet Union in Southern Africa
meant that liberation movements like the ANC could no
longer count on Moscow's money and political support. Thus
weakened, the ANC could be safely enticed into the councils
of responsible government.

We must take the former president at his word. What is undeniable is that, within a few months of becoming president, de Klerk radically altered the course of his country's history. In what must have been a legislative whirlwind his party repealed the hated Separate Amenities Act, announced a moratorium on the death penalty, allowed once-prohibited protest marches to go ahead, released a number of political prisoners, including the ANC leader Walter Sisulu, who had been imprisoned with Mandela, and unbanned the ANC. As if to emphasise the dizzying pace of change, de Klerk notes tersely in his book, 'Mr Mandela had been fully apprised of our proposed action.'

The drama in that statement could hardly be more breathtaking. Mandela was after all still a prisoner but had been brought into the political loop. This was incredible. In the wake of those announcements it seemed barely necessary for de Klerk to add that Mandela, too, would soon be freed. The two men had met for the first time in secret only a few weeks before. They had taken the measure of each other and had concluded that they, too, could do business together. That meeting had set the tone for de Klerk's dramatic moves.

The National Party was throwing in the towel.

The secret of what the president was about to say had been kept within a tight circle of his closest advisers. The president himself took great pleasure in the fact that his critics in the more liberal newspapers were caught completely off guard. The far-right Conservative Party was aghast. True to its beliefs to the last, it implied that the president had taken leave of his senses and was guilty of treason. The rest of South Africa digested what it had heard, stopped in shock and then breathed a collective sigh of relief.

In black townships across the country the joyous noise of spontaneous celebrations could be heard for hours.

Mandela's release on 11 February 1990 gave the world the first glimpse of a man who'd been talked about but not seen for nearly thirty years. It quickly became one of the more memorable images of the twentieth century. In today's parlance, it went viral.

In a smart suit, hand in hand with his wife Winnie, Mandela smiled a little diffidently and raised a fist to the waiting crowds and photographers. There were no banner-waving demonstrations by those who had campaigned so long for his release and no triumphal declarations from the man of the hour about the onward march to justice and freedom. Given its national significance it was a decidedly low-key affair and turned out to be rather chaotic.

Neither the National Party nor the ANC had any experience of managing an event of such magnitude, added to which there were heart-stopping worries about security. As a result, Mandela's walk to freedom was two hours behind schedule. Everything else ran late, too. A meeting with the world's press had to be put off until the following day, a political choreographer's nightmare, and by the time Mandela arrived to make his first appearance in a Cape Town square the crowd had shrunk to a disgruntled fraction of its expected size.

Mandela's speech nearing the end of that heady day was not his best. He had never been a great public orator. His rhetoric and style lacked the power to move crowds to peaks of excitement and his body language, restrained and undemonstrative, gave the impression that he was deliberately trying to avoid doing that. It was immediately obvious that he preferred the lawyer's logic to the high-sounding phrase. He had dreams of what his country could become but he lacked the ability to give them full voice.

Nelson Mandela was no Martin Luther King.

What he said that evening achieved what it was intended to do. It reassured both the National Party and the African National Congress. Mandela made it clear that the policy of the separation of the races would come to an end. But he also said that he would strive to put all races on an equal footing and that his release from prison should not be taken as a signal that South Africa's black majority would act to subdue the white minority.

He would act in the interests of all South Africans.

That night I anchored the main ITN news from the top of a flatbed truck in the heart of Soweto. It had been an amazing day for my colleagues in the ITN team in Johannesburg and one of the most exhilarating moments in my life as a journalist.

Reporters who travel to the far-flung corners of the world become accustomed to hearing lofty expressions or slogans about freedom, democracy and justice. In so many instances those ideals remain distant, unrealisable hopes. In Soweto that evening we dared to believe that we might be about to witness the first practical steps to translating such lofty ideals into a political reality.

That was the cause of great excitement.

We had taken a room in lodgings directly across the street from the house to which Mandela would return on his first full day of freedom. It was the first-ever live broadcast from a South African township, and the first time we had been allowed to bypass the eagle-eyed attention of the authorities at SABC, the South African Broadcasting Corporation.

Over the years SABC had become part of the state apparatus and it took a close interest in what foreign broadcasters said about the country. Throughout the apartheid years South Africans maintained a keen interest in what was being said about their country. Run in close collaboration with the Ministry of Information, SABC had a front-line role in that listening process. With our own satellite dish parked in the middle of an angry black township, we had no need of the corporation's transmission services, and SABC could no longer monitor what we said or attempt to interfere with our technical ability to do as we pleased. For those of us who'd had contact with the South African broadcasting authorities before, this was a significant point of departure.

A few years before, I had involuntarily caused a security alert by managing to walk unescorted into one of SABC's broadcast control areas. Now, suddenly there was no need to go anywhere near those premises.

The speed at which everything had changed was astonishing. It had occurred with the suddenness of a thunderclap. Even before Mandela had shaken off the dust of his island prison, another crack had appeared in one of the pillars of apartheid.

Our adventurous evening had only just begun.

My colleague David Mannion had gone to the house of Archbishop Desmond Tutu to escort him to the flatbed from the top of which we would be broadcasting live to *News at Ten* in London. The archbishop's house was only a few hundred yards from our truck.

Having Tutu on the ITN news on the evening of Mandela's release was a great coup for us. What we failed to anticipate was the reaction of the people of Soweto on seeing one of the heroes of the anti-apartheid movement who had spearheaded the campaign for Nelson Mandela's release.

At the first glimpse of their famous neighbour, the crowd, already ecstatic, went wild and according to Mannion neither he nor the archbishop touched the ground as they made their way to us. They were lifted into the air from the moment they left the archbishop's house and carried shoulder-high all the way to our outside broadcast truck.

Anchoring the news that night in front of a cheering mass I struggled to hear myself speak above ululating waves of noise. Amid the historic scene, it was hardly the ideal place from which to make oneself heard in a live broadcast. The editor of ITN, Stuart Purvis, who understood the medium so well and the importance of matching words and pictures as much as anyone else I knew, was sitting in the control room in London and sensed my difficulty. He sent a terse message down the line and into my earpiece: 'Tell Trevor he can't fight it. Go with the flow.'

I heard that message from London with immense relief. I was never going to win a battle against Soweto's wall of joyous noise.

Getting Tutu at last through the throng and on to the flat-bed to stand next to me, it seemed obvious after hearing his reaction to Mandela's release to ask whether Mandela or any single individual could ever fulfil the hopes of the millions who'd groaned under the yoke of apartheid for so long, people whose joyful voices, suffused with relief, we had heard so insistently all evening. Was that not too much of a burden to be placed on the shoulders of any man, however brilliant?

The archbishop was having none of it. He gently scolded me, asserting that it was no time for journalistic scepticism. He said the man who would lead South Africa to democracy was free and it was a time to rejoice. The words were spoken in that familiar high-pitched tone and with the happy laughter so characteristic of Tutu's manner. At that the archbishop broke into an impromptu celebratory jig and suggested I should join him. His exuberance, totally in character, captured the mood of the moment perfectly. The crowds all around us seemed to shout and sing even louder. *News at Ten* had never ended with a dance like that before.

If that was a fitting coda to a memorable day, I remember it too as the moment in our live transmission to ITN in London when the gods decided they'd seen enough. The heavens opened, lightning struck and lit up the sky, and a Johannesburg thunderstorm poured down on us in all its fury. The rain didn't stop the dancing and the singing, and we stumbled out of the Soweto darkness and made our way back into the city centre only by the flashing streaks of light from a fearsome sky.

Before leaving London we had been warned by a press officer at the South African High Commission in London about the ferocity of evening storms in the area around Johannesburg at that time of year. I had confidently urged my colleagues to ignore what the press officer had said, believing that his ominous forecasts were clearly meant to scare us away from an outside broadcast, using our own satellite dish in Soweto and bypassing the censoring eyes of the South African Broadcasting Corporation. I may even have gone further and suggested that the press officer was guilty of a transparent untruth. I've always felt chastened when I recall how wrong I was. The press officer's warning was based on hard fact. Evening thunderstorms in Johannesburg are forces of nature and at their worst, as they were on that unforgettable night, magnificently tempestuous.

Mandela returned to Soweto the following day – his convoy of sleek limousines kicking up a swirling cloud of dust as it snaked its way into the township. A few hundred feet above, a security helicopter wheeled and ducked perilously close to the ground. Only weeks before such a sight would have sent township residents scurrying into hiding. Now they rushed into the street to celebrate their hero's return and to embrace the dawn of a new age. The crowds converged on Mandela's unremarkable Soweto house in pulsating waves of joy.

A scattering of ANC officials, as if totally caught out by the galloping speed of an event they'd prayed for all their lives, found themselves struggling to deal not only with their own high-spirited supporters but also with a small battalion of television journalists jostling to have the first sit-down interview with the great man.

American television stations had sent their formidably famous senior anchormen to make the pitch. There's nothing in the world quite like a large body of journalists desperately chasing a single prize. In this case the decision seemed to hinge on whether the prize should go to a British or an American journalist.

No superior arguments prevailed. The matter was eventually settled by the toss of a coin. We called correctly and I was to have the first interview with the man from whom the world was waiting to hear.

Everything about Mandela was immediately impressive. Even on that first day, in those first few hours back in Soweto, he exuded an air of quiet authority. It floored us all.

With the evidence of nothing less than a political revolution breaking all around him, he was the calmest man of all. Such composure was not expected of someone who had been locked away on an island off the coast and in other prisons for twenty-seven years. I dissolved into a bag of nerves merely to shake him by the hand. If he had the slightest tinge of nervous anxiety about all the fuss around him, he hid it well. He seemed thoroughly at ease.

For a man of such indomitable will, Mandela's voice was gentle. He was warm and approachable. Not yet exposed to the art of political evasion he addressed questions as they were put with careful, precise responses.

To me the most striking thing about him was his humility. It was obvious to the world that he would be the leading voice in shaping the policies of the African National Congress but he referred to himself in unwavering terms as a servant of the movement. Time and time again in our conversation he said his future role would be determined not by him but by what his party wanted. He would in future do what he was asked to do by his comrades.

My first question was the obvious one. How on earth could the ANC and the National Party ever arrive at anything approaching an agreement, given the years of bitterness and, more to the point, their diametrically opposing views on almost everything?

That drew from Mandela the first extraordinary statement. Without in any way dismissing my reference to the long years of bitterness, he said that once the two parties had agreed to enter into serious negotiations, compromises were always possible. Surely not *all* compromises, I shot back. Flexibility could be shown, for example, on a host of peripheral issues but surely not on basic, fundamental principles.

Mandela heard me out and said it again. The second time, more deliberately and with quiet emphasis. You must, he told me, be prepared to compromise even on fundamental issues once you begin to talk seriously. There was, of course, a tactical dimension to that answer. The National Party, having released Mandela, was never going to suggest the unthinkable. It would not even begin to think that the ANC would abandon the core principle of one man, one vote. Mandela knew that and was setting out in unambiguous terms the spirit in which he would talk to the South African government.

He wished to make it clear from day one that he was prepared to meet his political opponents on equal terms. He wanted to signal a readiness to compromise and to make it abundantly clear that in him the National Party would find a serious interlocutor.

Mandela repeatedly stressed that in the South Africa of the future no one race should dominate another, as had been the pattern during all the years of the ANC's struggle. He went out of his way to say that his vision was of a multiracial society inclusive of all South Africans. He wished there to be no thought of retribution against those who by the colour of their skin were deemed to have been the oppressors. Those days had gone and gone forever, he said.

Because of South Africa's history of discrimination and violence against the majority of its people, these were amazing words from the leader of a black liberation movement. In short Mandela was conveying the message that he saw no insurmountable obstacles to setting South Africa on the road to democratic pluralism.

Whenever during my questions I expressed doubt about what might be possible in the politics of the future, he listened carefully and exuded that brand of philosophical optimism for which he was to become so well known. If you are prepared to talk in good faith, he told me, everything is possible.

I was stunned and impressed in equal measure.

Having failed to uncover any ideological roadblocks on the path to democracy, I went in search of more populist responses. I was acutely aware that I had been granted the very first interview with a man who, despite his great fame, had never been heard before.

I asked Mandela to tell me about the atmosphere at that first secret meeting with P. W. Botha. Botha had for some time been a dinosaur of the age of apartheid and for nearly all of his political life would have considered it anathema to talk to a prisoner he regarded as a political terrorist. He might well have been perplexed by the indestructibility of the Mandela myth and might have wanted to see what the myth looked like in the flesh, but never in a million years would he have relished a conversation with the man.

With that in mind, I tried to get Mandela to be more descriptive about their meeting. How did it go? What did he say to you? Did he offer you tea? Mandela replied: 'He was very courteous.' And that was about all he would say. I was almost at the point in the interview when I would be driven by the convention of such things to be slightly more aggressive and ask different versions of the same questions over and over again.

In the end, good sense stopped me from doing so. I noticed that on coming to the end of a sentence or a thought Mandela simply stopped speaking. It is frequently the intersection at which people being interviewed, anxious about the pause in conversation, carry on speaking if for nothing else to fill the uncomfortable void and it is sometimes the point at which they may say something they had not intended to. Mandela did not. He finished a sentence or a thought and stopped speaking. The void in the conversation troubled him not one bit.

I ploughed on. What, then, about the meeting with F. W. de Klerk? There was a suggestion of a gentle smile. I was on to something. 'Ah!' Mandela said, 'when I met him we got down to business.' Not a bad news story, I thought, but no blockbuster headline. After all, had the meeting with de Klerk not gone well we would not have been having a conversation in the garden of his Soweto house so soon after his release.

I decided to shift the conversation to an area which I was sure would yield results. I tried the emotional route. It must have been absolutely terrible, I suggested, to spend such an unconscionably long time in prison away from family and friends and cut adrift from the day-to-day lives of your associates and your countrymen. How bad did it get in the worst of those dark, depressing days? Surely there must be a story here, I told myself. Doing time on Robben Island was never meant to be a picnic.

'Oh, that's all in the past,' Mandela responded. I paused, in the hope that he might rush to fill the silence by saying something more. I tried several variations of the same question. His answer was always the same. 'That's all in the past,' he said. 'We must now look beyond the past, to the future of the country.'

I shifted uneasily in my chair with more than a little disbelief. I was finding it impossible to think that I had failed to draw a single word out of him on the hardship question. That might have nagged away at me for years, had there not been a sequel to my persistent questions about the pain of prison life.

Five years later on the occasion of the 1995 rugby World Cup made famous not only by South Africa's demolition of the All Blacks of New Zealand in the final but by the president's appearance on the pitch in the No. 6 shirt of the Springbok captain, I saw Mandela very early one morning at his official residence.

I had been sent to South Africa not because of my knowledge of rugby but because ITV had, for the first time, won the exclusive rights to show the games. In advance of the first match, and to stir interest in its coverage, ITV had planned a special programme about South Africa as a suitable opening to the tournament. An interview with President Mandela would be a part of that broadcast, and it was thought that, having met him before, I would be person to secure such an interview.

Fortunately, I did.

Before I could begin the interview the president asked several times whether we could dim the arc lights. We did our best to comply with his request, but he continued to insist that they were much too bright. I was on the point of explaining to him why, in the unsurprising gloom of the room to which we'd been assigned, our cameras required some degree of light when he apologised. 'I know, I know,' he said. 'I understand totally. It's not you,' he said, 'it's me. I've had trouble with my eyes for many years because of the dust and the splinters from breaking rocks on Robben Island.'

In fact, the dust and the splinters and the punishing glare of the sun, shining off the limestone rocks on which he worked day after day for years, had done permanent damage to his eyes.

In several meetings over the years,, it was the first and only reference he'd ever made to one of the physical hardships of his time in prison. He could so easily have talked about what breaking rocks had done to his eyes at our first meeting two days after his freedom. He had conspicuously, and to me quite remarkably, not done so.

His gaze, literally, was fixed on high during

And that in essence was a fleeting glimpse of what Nelson Mandela was about. He would refuse to dwell on the past. He would think of what the future of his country could be. And he would continue to believe, as he told me when we first met, that everything was possible in a new South Africa if there were compromises on all sides.

Back to that eventful day in Soweto and at the end of serial interviews, an impatient crowd, who had sung themselves hoarse and danced through most of the night before, now clamoured for a speech from their celebrated neighbour.

Mandela showed no sign of wanting to rush to the microphone. He never lost his smile, but nearing mid-afternoon his pace had slowed noticeably. Freedom had been intoxicating and tiring. He was exhausted. His comrade-in-arms, Walter Sisulu, made a sound judgement of the situation. It would be impossible for his friend to bring down the curtain on the day of his return to Soweto without speaking to his supporters.

It was clear to anyone within a mile of the township just what the crowd wanted to hear. Mandela – free at last – was expected to give a rousing speech, replete with the required lofty phrases about the enormous political significance of his release. He would be expected to make a stirring declaration about the dawn of the age of freedom and justice, now only just around the corner. It was to be the 'Uhuru' moment. Some hope!

Mandela took a few short, reluctant steps, walking from the tiny front garden of his house and on to the pavement to address an expectant crowd. There was no rostrum, no lectern, and Mandela spoke without notes. He thanked the crowd for their welcome. Pausing before he said anything else and looking around at the eager faces, he would have noticed the high percentage of young people of school age. His first words were aimed directly at them. 'I have one thing to say to you today. Go back to school.'

A hush swept the place. For many months young black South Africans, as a protest against chronic underfunding on education, sub-standard school facilities and what in general amounted to a deliberate policy of state neglect, had been boycotting classes. Black schools had been, like everything else in black South Africa, second rate. The student protest had been acknowledged as legitimate and proper in the context of the privations of township life.

Now, hundreds of young people listened stunned as Mandela went on. 'Walter and I are old men now and we shall not be here for very long. The future belongs to you. But to embrace that future, to achieve anything, you must go back to school.'

There was, of course, sound logic to his admonition about going back to school. But was it really possible that after all those years in prison and only in the first hours of freedom that Mandela, the man of all their political futures, was giving sound advice to the young but also expressing intimations of mortality?

I felt at the time, and I still do now, that they were in a way the most extraordinary words I've ever heard from the lips of any political figure in any country. The harsh, unforgiving sobriety of his message to young black South Africans was a hint of what we would, in time, come to regard as vintage Mandela.

My interview warranted no sensational headlines. Perhaps that was precisely as Mandela intended. When he was eventually called to play his role in South Africa's future, he would be calm, judicious and not given to political hyperbole or grandstanding. Mandela would be realistic and would never miss opportunities for accommodation. He would be a pragmatist who would always recognise the need to engage.

When he put on the South Africa rugby World Cup jersey and cap in 1995 at Ellis Park Stadium, that cathedral to white Afrikaner sport in Johannesburg, it was not as a stunt but as a symbol of the all-embracing ethos of his presidency. He had studied Afrikaans in prison, not only to get into the minds of lunatic white supremacists in his country but also as a courtesy to those with whom he might have to talk.

His greatest talents were his humility, his willingness to compromise and his lack of any sign of bitterness.

Journalists who traverse the unpredictable world of international politics are warned to proceed with caution. We are taught, quite properly, to question, to challenge and to doubt. We are told to be sceptical of anything that sounds too glib and everything that looks too good. Nelson Mandela – the man – the president – changed all that. He was as good as his word. He raised the bar of political deportment. He left his mark on everyone who met him because he was exceptional. The widest possible cross-section of people felt good just to be in his presence. He radiated benevolence.

I was always terribly proud that many years after our first meeting, Mandela's greeting, on seeing me across a room bursting with admirers anxious to shake his hand, was to call me by my first name. I once pushed my way through a throng at a party in London to introduce him to my wife. Looking squarely at her and exuding all the charm he dispensed so effortlessly, he said: 'And tell me, my dear. How on earth did you have the good fortune to be married to such a fine man?' Not very long ago I discovered that the line had become something of a Mandela special. It was his response on being introduced to any spouse and used repeatedly. But to this day I remember it with a silly, boyish pride. Casting all thoughts of merit aside a genuinely fine man had said that about me!

One night at a dinner in Central London at Apsley House, the Duke of Wellington's home, I had a long conversation with President Mandela about how the new South Africa was making the adjustment from the apartheid system to a democratic one. He thought the change had gone reasonably well, although he was worried about the violence still claiming too many black lives. I asked him about the country's economy. He confessed that economics was not his strong suit, and that he left such matters to his more competent ministers.

He was on splendid form that night. Our host was the South African conglomerate De Beers, famous for its diamond mining.

One of my many memories of that evening was of an unexpected encounter. I had left the first-floor dining room and gone downstairs to find the toilet. Inching my way gingerly in the semi-dark I suddenly became aware of the presence of someone else. Coming face to face with a man, I assumed that he, too, was on a mission similar to mine. 'Are you looking for the loo?' I enquired, eager to appear as helpful as I could. Back came the reply: 'No. I'm the Duke of Wellington. I live here.'

Mandela enjoyed the company of great men, of captains of industry, and they were honoured to be in his presence. He was proud to be able to command the attention of princes and pop stars, supermodels and sporting celebrities. In and out of office he raised millions for his Children's Foundation and was not shy about making his influence count.

He had great belief in his ability to bend people to his will and was puzzled when he failed to do so. Shortly after he became president, he asked at the end of one of our meetings whether I had any knowledge about how he might go about getting the quadrennial football World Cup to South Africa. I was sorry to disappoint him but I confessed that I didn't have a clue. The president said: 'I had a conversation with the head of FIFA the other day, but he was unable to give me an assurance that we could have the competition here.'

Mandela was surprised that FIFA had not then and there been able to make a firm promise to him to take the World Cup to South Africa. The president must have been relieved when the competition was eventually staged in his country and would have been terribly distressed about all the stories of the alleged corruption involved in the South African bidding process.

Just after he ceased to be archbishop, Desmond Tutu described to me an incident that illustrated the way Mandela was prepared to use his influence.

On my way into tea at Tutu's home in Soweto one afternoon I noticed a very expensive looking new car in his drive. I teased him about it, commenting that former archbishops appeared to live in some style. It was not seriously meant, and Tutu, a man of unfailing good humour, knew that. But nevertheless he felt compelled to explain. He, too, had seen at first hand a revealing side to Mandela's personality and wanted to share it with me.

He'd had lunch with Mandela at a hotel in downtown Johannesburg and, as they prepared to leave, Mandela, with a wave of the hand, had asked the lobby staff if they would summon the archbishop's chauffeur. Tutu explained that he did not have a car and would be heading back to Soweto by taxi. Shaking with laughter the former archbishop told me what happened next. The following evening Mandela phoned him to explain that he had not intended to embarrass his friend by calling for a car he didn't have. 'Anyway,' said Mandela, 'I've had a word with the Anglo American company, and they're sending one round to your house in the morning!'

I never quite gave up on trying to get Mandela to say more about his time in prison, and I sensed a splendid opportunity when I was asked to accompany him one evening to Birmingham, where he was to be given the Freedom of the City. It was a time when cities everywhere were queuing up to invite the great man to any number of such events.

I had been asked because it was discovered late in the planning that there'd be a hiatus between his arrival and the start of the evening's ceremony. I was invited to help fill the time. Foreign Minister Alfred Nzo was with us, but it was clear that he was not in the habit of saying much.

The president asked me about my early life in the West Indies, about school and the books I'd read, and we talked about his growing up in South Africa. I gently steered the conversation to his time on Robben Island, and wondered whether he was ever fearful of the guards and whether he was concerned that even now some hitman from an extremist right-wing Afrikaner political or military movement might try to kill him. Mandela told me quietly but firmly that, despite his long years behind bars and the general violence around him, he never feared for his life. Then reminding me that we'd talked about Shakespeare, he recited some lines from *Julius Caesar*:

> Cowards die many times before their deaths . . .
> Of all the wonders that I yet have heard,
> It seems to me most strange that men should fear,
> Seeing that death, a necessary end,
> Will come when it will come.

He paused and, changing tack, proceeded to tell me to my great surprise that he'd seen some of my television reports from South Africa while he was still a prisoner. He had been moved from Robben Island and held in a prison close to Cape Town in preparation for his eventual release. One of his luxuries was a video player. I knew about the video player because Winnie Mandela had talked about it in one of our conversations. But how did tapes of my reports come into the hands of the prison authorities?

One of my colleagues at ITN's office in Johannesburg provided a straightforward explanation.

One afternoon the office had been raided. To spare the police the trouble of ransacking the place, it was suggested to them that it might be helpful if they said what they were looking for. My colleagues offered to cooperate.

'We're looking for all of Trevor McDonald's reports,' was the retort. They were found and handed over and the South African police left the office.

I never found the courage to enquire what Mr Mandela made of my reports.

What is not generally known is that one of Nelson Mandela's sternest challenges was to convince ANC activists, who had been fighting a guerrilla war against the apartheid government, to put down their weapons and agree to his conversion to a peaceful, negotiated settlement. Many of his colleagues told him in forthright terms that he was making a terrible mistake and that they could no longer trust him.

At his treason trial he had said he was prepared to give his life, if needed, to continue the battle for freedom and equality for his people. Now here he was, talking about peace and reconciliation even before he was certain that there would be a deal about the core ANC demand: one man, one vote.

Moreover, even after his freedom South African security forces were still hunting down and killing ANC activists. The country's security apparatus never gave up the ambition to eliminate the ANC as a fighting force for all time. And South Africa continued to stand aside while other political parties waged war against members of the African National Congress.

Mandela worked assiduously to bring the militants on his own side to his point of view. Perhaps his clinching argument was that if no political accommodation was found, South Africa would be forever engaged in a perhaps unwinnable, bloody war. Mandela's calm reasoning eventually won the day.

ANC hardliners were appeased when, responding to a speech in which F. W. de Klerk talked about all the things he had done for black South Africans, Mandela spoke for an hour, rounding on the apartheid years and told his people that he would settle for nothing less than a government led by the ANC.

That was a point of departure.

Mandela's place in the pantheon of world statesmen is assured. Perhaps like no other South African he possessed the temperament, the humanity and above all the vision to lead the process of change in his country. Countless others rendered invaluable service. Among those I am fortunate to have known well is Archbishop Desmond Tutu.

The archbishop confounded many in his country by rising to the heights he did, and he pursued the struggle against apartheid armed with the power of his preaching and the sword of profound Christian belief. How is it possible, he asked over and over again in a voice unmistakeable in its conspicuous sincerity, for white South Africans to oppress their black brothers and sisters with such a canon of unjust laws? No answer could be found to that basic question and certainly not one that conformed to Christian teaching.

While Nelson Mandela languished in his island prison, Tutu kept the flame of hope alive. Mandela's release vindicated his faith. He knew that in the end humanity would triumph over violence.

Of course, justice was far from done. The unbanning of the African National Congress and the release of Nelson Mandela did not put an end to the evil at the heart of apartheid. A secret counter-insurgency unit established sometime after the death of Steve Biko in 1977 was ordered to do all it could to tarnish the image of the ANC and other liberation movements.

One of its priorities was to increase the level of black-on-black violence. That became one of the biggest headaches for Mandela after his release. In a now famous public speech he stated angrily that while the South African government was negotiating with him and his ANC colleagues, a 'third force' was killing black people by the hundreds. In many cases the counter-insurgency unit used Russian weapons to implicate the military wing of the African National Congress.

The scale of these planned killings became public during hearings of the Truth and Reconciliation Commission established in 1996 as a public forum for restorative justice. By testifying before the Commission a perpetrator could be granted relief from civil and criminal prosecution. The Commission's chairman was Desmond Tutu. The tales it heard were horrifying.

Eugene de Kock, who commanded the counter-insurgency unit, told the commission how black activists were tortured and killed and their bodies set alight on pyres of wood and car tyres while his men sat around eating and drinking. One journalist described de Kock as the Commission's polygraph machine. He was found guilty on eighty-nine charges and sentenced to 212 years in prison. Granted parole and released from jail in 2015, it was perhaps one of the most unlikely consequences of the work of the Truth and Reconciliation Commission.

In the years following his appearance at the Commission, de Kock apparently gained the trust of many of the relatives of his victims. He had done what so many of his unit's colleagues had refused to do. He had testified about the calculated evils of apartheid. His release caused hardly a stir in the body politic of modern South Africa. Were he alive in 2015 might Nelson Mandela have considered de Kock's release a natural extension of the Mandela creed of forgiveness?

A few weeks after de Kock was given parole, the questions of reconciliation and forgiveness came up again. This time it did so in a spirited and racially charged debate about symbols of South Africa's past. A 112-year-old statue of Queen Victoria outside the city library in Port Elizabeth was vandalised, and another of Cecil Rhodes on the campus of Cape Town University was covered in excrement and finally removed from its plinth after a boisterous campaign. When the huge stone structure crashed to the ground, people danced and sang in celebration.

South Africa had been catapulted into the post-Mandela age. The memory of the country's first black president is more ambivalent. There is high regard for all that he did to bring South Africa back into the brotherhood of democratic nations and for his humanity. But there is a persistent view that those who followed Mandela have not done enough to further the cause of black empowerment or of national unity.

The African National Congress that Mandela led is no longer the body it once was. High offices reek of scandal. Charges of corruption are rife. Some have reached the courts.

In common with many other parts of the world, South

Africa's economy has been through turbulent times. Crime stalks the land. More gated communities are springing up again with the specific purpose of putting secure distances between those who are well off and those who live in the bustling towns.

It is perhaps understandable, but still a shock to me, that the infamous ghastly slums and shanty towns – huge, unmissable blots on the landscape – have not disappeared. South African prisons are overflowing.

Deprived of the Mandela magic, questions are being asked about whether real change has come to the lives of most South Africans. The answers to those will inform the ongoing debate about the future of a country one man did so much to steer. Today that debate is more fervent and more relevant than ever.

The patience of those who placed so much hope in a new South Africa is growing thin. It is darkly unedifying to read in 2017 that the office Mandela once graced with such dignity was for many years held by a man who now faces 783 charges of corruption. How could a man who calls himself president be so venally corrupt? It is a scar on the body politic of a nation still struggling to rid its collective memory of a horrible past.

I returned to South Africa shortly after Mandela left office, and on several occasions during the presidency of his successors. His passing in 2017 was mourned throughout the land, and Johannesburg and other towns and cities marked his status as 'father of the nation' by erecting statues and a variety of memorials in a conspicuous show of love and devotion and gratitude – if not always in the finest artistic tradition.

Although he was no longer around, his countrymen did not forget that in July 2018 Mandela would have reached the age of one hundred. That, too, was duly celebrated.

But something else is happening in South Africa today.

Talking to a number of people in the making of two

television programmes I found the country in moods of deep introspection, and I was surprised to find that a number of his supporters were beginning to take a more questioning attitude about the accomplishments of the Mandela presidency.

Much of this, it is argued, can be traced to the fearsome difficulties he faced convincing his own diehard ANC activists of the benefits of compromise and, more crucially, what he himself came to regard as the duplicity of the white National Party and its President, F. W. de Klerk. Simply stated, Mandela discovered that his release from prison was only the first step in a long and tortuous road to South Africa's eventual freedom.

In the first place the armed wing of the ANC, Umkhonto we Sizwe, was deeply distrustful of the ruling National Party and its president, and for good reason. Long after Mandela had been released, and while he and de Klerk were ostensibly discussing the formalising of a peace accord, South Africa's security forces and its notorious hit squads were hunting down and killing ANC activists.

The talk was about peace in the heat of open warfare.

Jessie Duarte, a senior member of the ANC who worked closely with Mandela, told me early in 2019 that ANC colleagues bluntly demanded to know the deal he had signed up to, which seemed to allow South African security forces to continue to wreak havoc by murder.

It all came to a head at a conference called to discuss possible progress towards a democratic South Africa when Mandela, furious at a speech de Klerk had made, rounded on him in angry, uncompromising terms.

In the first place de Klerk had been suspected of fixing the agenda so that he would have the last word. Mandela was having none of it.

'The members of the Government persuaded us to allow them to speak last . . . and it is now clear why.' Mandela went on to attack de Klerk directly. 'He has abused his position . . .

he must not think that he can impose conditions on the African National Congress.'

At the heart of Mandela's response to de Klerk, who in his speech had talked about all he had done for black South Africans, were these words: 'You have a strong, well-equipped, efficient police and defence force. Why are you not using that capacity to stop the violence? The perception exists amongst our people that in the forefront of this violence are elements of the security forces ... Their main task is to eliminate freedom fighters in this country. So many activists have been killed without trace. The killers have never been traced ... and in those massacres not a single member of the National Party was even grazed with a spear.'

Days after his dramatic release from prison, Mandela made a point of emphasising the importance of the willingness to compromise. At that conference more than a year later he was warning de Klerk that trying to take advantage of that belief in compromise was 'extremely dangerous'.

Long after he became the first black president of his country, Mandela's battles with the National Party, and more specifically with the security forces, continued. They took a heavy toll on his administration and what was expected of it.

Among his most devoted supporters, the discussion goes on today about the Mandela presidency. The major question of land redistribution is still to be resolved. One township resident told me: 'We have the vote but we have no freedom, no jobs and no land.'

The question about land redistribution has become one of the most contentious parts of the political dialogue. The facts need no explanation. Under apartheid, white South Africans who make up about 10 per cent of the population possessed 70 per cent of the land.

South Africa began legislating to deprive its black majority of land in 1913. In that year it passed a Native Land Act, well before the introduction of apartheid in 1948. In the succeeding years the issue has become immensely complicated and, if it's not handled with care, the country's economy, which has already gone through so many rough passages, could be ruined.

The bottom line, however, is that the travesty of current land ownership cannot be allowed to continue forever.

Some progress has been made in improving black education, but so much more needs to be done. In August 2018 there was a shocking incident at an elementary school in Middelplaas when students staged a protest and confronted the government minister for education when a six-year-old first-grader fell into a dilapidated pit latrine. Millions earmarked for building and maintaining new schools and improving the level of education have disappeared. The system has been undermined by rampant corruption.

It is painful to recall that on his first day back in Soweto after his release from prison, Mandela talked about the crucial importance of education.

Archbishop Desmond Tutu told me that he had once paid a visit to his old school and found it impossible to hide his distress at how little had changed since his time there. He told me he found that the desks at which he once sat still looked the same, and he thought he could detect no great changes to the classrooms or to their furnishings.

Tutu left his old school disconsolately and in tears.

Mandela served only one term as president, as he had always said he would, partly because by the time it ended he had been exhausted by the unending struggle. He had after all been negotiating with government officials since July 1986, as he was keen to remind questioners. He was still in prison then and would not be freed for another four years.

He oversaw and was the inspiration behind the transition to democracy. His great hope was that having done his part he would hand over the reins to a younger man imbued with the same passion to improve the lives of all South Africans.

And yet the old proverb springs to mind: 'The many fail, the one succeeds.'

9

Facing Saddam

'Thus bad begins.'

William Shakespeare, *Hamlet*

In all my years as an ITN journalist I can think of no single event that has stirred more international controversy than the decision by America and Britain in 2003 to invade Iraq.

My opinion probably has something to do with the fact that for a long time I had been involved in reporting various aspects of the story. Closeness to an issue can lead to a far-from-impartial point of view. And yet I am convinced that the invasion precipitated one of the biggest disasters in the bloody history of the Middle East. The region lives with the horror of the aftermath of the war to this day, and certainly will for generations. None of us can escape the consequences. It has spawned networks of terror around the world. We are all beset by more issues of international terror and are all – wherever we live in the world – less safe than we were before 2003.

The decision to invade Iraq was one of the worst American foreign policy decisions ever and the worst by a British government since Suez.

Every week I cringed at the news that hundreds more had been killed in suicide bombings in and around Baghdad. So frequent were they that they became mere footnotes to the world news, but for the hapless people who lived there endless days and nights were enveloped in crisis and drenched in blood. Years after the Americans thought their mission had been accomplished and withdrew their soldiers, they have been forced to send more troops to act as 'advisers'. In reality the Americans still in the region are there to help the Iraqis and others in the battle against a far more dangerous enemy than we ever imagined – the pernicious Islamic State, Isis. The hopelessness of the situation can be seen by the fact that even where Isis has been driven out, what's left is nothing more than a complex patchwork of ungovernable ethnic, tribal and religious militias that lay claim to parts of the country.

There is no functioning central authority. Sectarian strife and the violence of murderous militias have dismembered Iraq. It has virtually ceased to exist as a country. The fragmentation is probably irreversible. Hardly anyone feels a sense of belonging to what might be called an Iraqi nation.

It is ironic now to think that the fall of Saddam Hussein was greeted by President Bush with the words: 'Iraq is free.'

Today the international community, once so fixated on the virtue of getting rid of a dictator, looks on in helpless exasperation, wringing its hands, making scarcely believable excuses, powerless to arrest the consequences of what it started.

The reasons for attacking Baghdad were part of a twist of political logic that began with the deadliest attack on the United States since Pearl Harbor. On 11 September 2001, al-Qaeda, a terrorist group preaching a poisonous concoction of hatred and religious zealotry, flew planes into the World Trade Center in New York, attacked the Pentagon – the heart of America's military establishment – and aimed to complete the humiliation of the proudest democracy in the Western world by hitting its seat of government in Washington. The last of those plans failed by a whisker.

We all have memories of that day.

Summoned back to the office from lunch, I watched from

my desk at the ITN building in London as one of the planes crashed into the World Trade Center, and started planning how soon I could to get to New York.

Al-Qaeda and its leaders were heartless about the loss of thousands of American lives. They knew what they did would goad the US into retaliation, and they were right. Wounded to its core, America's entire chain of command went into blind panic. America could not appear impotent. A blow had been struck at the cherished belief that among all nations on earth America was exceptional, and someone would have to pay a price for its injured pride.

The problem, as ever, was how.

The terrorists had roamed and done their planning in caves and crevasses in remote, mountainous areas of Afghanistan. Going after them would not be easy and it would not be a popular war. Not one that could be followed blow by blow on CNN, anyway. And, as in Vietnam and in the first Gulf War, Americans wanted to be able to sit in their living rooms and watch pictures of enemy military assets being pounded to destruction in a hail of bombs, with belching smoke and roaring fireballs.

The battle to avenge al-Qaeda's attacks on New York and Washington had to be no different.

Easier said than done.

In one of the first meetings of the War Cabinet after the attacks on New York and Washington, Deputy Secretary of Defense Paul Wolfowitz, one of the most vocal hardliners in the administration of President George W. Bush, explained that Afghanistan 'was so primitive that there were few targets'. Indeed, to fight a television war one did need visible targets. Wolfowitz concluded that it 'would not be a particularly satisfying place to wage a war'.

Less than two weeks after 9/11, the president found a way to circumvent the concerns of his cabinet colleague. America would have to find a more satisfying place to wage a war, one that would offer a range of excellent targets to be destroyed in full view of television news cameras.

American retaliation had to be sold by a clever presentational device. One was quickly found. The president broadened the scope for American military action by describing al-Qaeda as 'heirs of all the murderous ideologues of the twentieth century'. That opened the way for a Western military alliance to go after any of those murderous ideologues.

George Bush was immediately given the support of British prime minister Tony Blair, who agreed to stand 'shoulder to shoulder' with the president and said the world had a duty to curb the activities of ideologues.

The one who came most easily to mind for Bush and Blair was President Saddam Hussein of Iraq, that well-known troublemaker in the Middle East. His credentials as a murderous dictator were impeccable.

There was one small problem. Saddam Hussein had nothing to do with the attacks on New York and Washington. No matter. Such a consideration should not be allowed to stand in the way of the march to war to avenge the attacks.

It was hardly surprising that the decision to attack Iraq divided world opinion. There were huge anti-war protests in cities in America, in the Far East, in the Middle East, in Australia and in almost every European capital. They were marked by boisterous anger.

Here in Britain the government was divided. The leader of the House of Commons, Robin Cook, resigned.

The decision to attack Iraq again delighted some members of the Bush administration – Vice-President Dick Cheney had for years been obsessed with Saddam Hussein.

The 9/11 attacks on Washington and New York had taken place while President Bush was out of town and the vice-president coordinated the initial responses from the White House. Deeply shaken, Cheney had visions of Armageddon and in his one-to-one meetings with the president never lost the chance to press for action against Saddam Hussein.

In her book *The Dark Side*, Jane Mayer, investigative report-er for the *New Yorker*, provides an illuminating account of a meeting between top-level British and American intelligence experts very soon after 9/11. According to Mayer, the team from London had arrived on the first flight allowed to break the ban imposed on flights into the United States after the attacks on New York and on the Pentagon. The British team included Sir Richard Dearlove, head of MI6, Eliza Manningham-Buller, deputy head of MI5, David Manning, Prime Minister Tony Blair's foreign-policy adviser, and a number of other experts on fighting domestic terrorism. Mayer writes: 'CIA officials listened intently as their British counterparts issued the first of several well-meant bits of advice. After an eloquent toast and a vow to work together against this new terrorist scourge, Manning told the group, "I hope we can all agree that we should concentrate on Afghanistan, and not launch any attacks against Iraq."'

Jane Mayer's account of that meeting in Washington, as the smoke was still rising from the World Trade Center, is not contested.

On my visits to New York and Washington, journalists were told nothing about David Manning's advice against hitting out at Iraq. Manning's boss Tony Blair shared President Bush's toothpaste at Camp David and happily went along with America's plan for attacking Iraq, and even agreed to try to sell the idea to Britain's partners in the European Union. He had no luck with that.

Two years of planning followed, during which we were fed a diet of news about the work of United Nations inspectors, speeches in the Security Council, CIA reports of questionable value and dodgy dossiers and falsehoods about weapons of mass destruction.

The last of those – the issue of Iraq's weapons capability – remains one of my most painful memories about the path to war. United Nations inspectors found no conclusive evidence that Saddam Hussein had a store of chemical and biological weapons. That was also the position of our own intelligence services.

Four years after the invasion, Lord Butler, the former cabinet secretary, took broad aim at Tony Blair's role in giving his support to President Bush and in particular at the prime minister's statements about what he had been told by British intelligence. In a speech to the House of Lords he said: 'The United Kingdom intelligence community told him on 23 August 2002 that "we know little about Iraq's chemical and biological weapons work since late 1988. The Prime Minister did not tell us that. Indeed, he told Parliament just over a month later that the picture painted by our intelligence service was extensive, detailed and authoritative."'

Lord Butler's conclusion was that the prime minister's treatment of the facts was 'disingenuous'. He talked at one point of Iraqi weapons that could be activated 'within forty-five minutes'. That had no foundation in fact.

In London and in Washington reporters listened to the riddles in which other misinformation was disguised. In the US Secretary of Defense Donald Rumsfeld, a seasoned bureaucrat who had worked in the administration of four American presidents, framed the debate about going to war against Iraq with no hard evidence of the existence of a threatening arsenal by sermonising about 'known knowns', 'known unknowns' and even 'unknown unknowns'.

Having found no smoking gun in the rush to convict Saddam Hussein, Rumsfeld had resorted to the use of language as a smokescreen.

The defense secretary's next observation was more disturbing and the precursor to an American tragedy. Intoxicated by his mastery of the political discourse, he boldly declared that the absence of evidence is not evidence of absence. At a stroke, all logic about the conduct of international affairs was turned on its head. America, he implied, could go to war on any pretext of its choosing. Nothing impelled it to prove the existence of weapons of mass destruction in Iraq before taking military action to stop their possible deployment.

The paradoxical strength of such a position was that it eliminated the need for any consideration of legality. There was certainly no need, as experts in international law had argued, for a specific United Nations resolution.

Surely that was a minor detail when the overriding issue was your president's global war on terror.

There remained, of course, the serious problem of how to justify an attack on Iraq. The murderous Saddam Hussein had nothing to do with 9/11 and more to the point had nothing to do with al-Qaeda. It is doubtful whether such a competitor for world attention would have been given house room in Saddam Hussein's Iraq. Baghdad ran a one-man show and its leader tolerated no interlopers. The CIA came to the rescue. American intelligence found ways of suggesting links between Saddam and al-Qaeda, and in any case, after 9/11 it would be irresponsible to leave a stockpile of dangerous weapons anywhere within reach of Saddam Hussein.

Rumsfeld was not alone in his sermonising. Other members of the administration weighed in. Vice-President Cheney, that most hawkish of hawks, believed invading Iraq was as much of a no-brainer as his later advocacy of the routine torture of enemy prisoners, hidden away from public scrutiny at 'black sites' in unnamed countries.

National Security Advisor Condoleezza Rice raised the stakes by slipping into a comment about Iraq's alleged hoard of weapons the words 'mushroom clouds'. The implication was clear: Iraq must be attacked before its president and his bombs attacked Iraq's neighbours and jeopardised the peace of the world.

I listened one afternoon to a presentation to the UN Security Council by Secretary of State Colin Powell that he came

to regret. Powell dramatically held up a vial of anthrax to il-
lustrate the danger Saddam Hussein posed, and stated as a fact
that the Iraqi leader had been placing orders for uranium in
Niger in West Africa. The French, who have traditionally kept a
close eye on the activities of their former colonies, warned the
Americans that although Niger has one of the world's largest
reserves of uranium, it had done no business with Iraq. That
cut no ice. Powell had been misled into making the charge by
the American Central Intelligence Agency. The CIA and its
torture experts had also provided Powell with evidence of a
confession by one of the prisoners in their custody.

Colin Powell's stature as a former chairman of the Joint
Chiefs of Staff gave credibility to the misinformation that
shaped administration policy. With little need for actual facts,
President Bush, armed with the support of Prime Minister
Tony Blair, set off resolutely on the road to war. To borrow the
words of Shakespeare's Hamlet, 'Thus bad begins'.

President Bush had made up his mind about attacking Iraq a
long time before Colin Powell's appearance before the Security Council. In April 2002, almost a year before the war, I did
a television interview with the president in the White House.
After evading several questions about his thinking on Iraq, he
told me bluntly: 'I've made up my mind that Saddam needs to
go.' The war began on 20 March 2003.

Baghdad was pounded into submission by American bombs
in an operation designed to cause 'shock and awe'. The battle,
insofar as it might be called that, was decided quickly. The
occupation was longer and more ruinous. Thousands of American and British soldiers lost their lives. More than a hundred
thousand Iraqis were killed, and planning for the peace was
ill-conceived, haphazard and inefficient. One illustration of
that was the attack on the UN mission in Baghdad.

Before she became America's esteemed Permanent Representative to the United Nations, Samantha Power wrote a
biography of the Brazilian diplomat Sérgio Vieira de Mello,

who headed that UN mission in Iraq after the invasion and was killed when it was hit in 2003. That the bombers were able to penetrate the security thrown around offices so crucial to America's post-invasion plan for Iraq was in itself a grave indictment. Power's anger was expressed in harsher terms. In an account of the attempt to rescue the diplomat from the rubble and to save his life, she wrote: 'The most powerful military in the history of mankind was forced to rely for rescue on brute force, a curtain rope, and a woman's handbag.'

It was an appropriate metaphor for America's unpreparedness for what happened after its pious declarations of intent and the spectacular television images of 'shock and awe'. If the attack on the UN mission in Baghdad and the death of a fine public servant shocked America and the United Nations family, much worse was to unfold across Iraq right under the noses of its American occupiers. In chaotic convulsions the country was torn apart in an orgy of bloodletting. Sectarian strife made it a breeding ground for a mutating terrorist threat that never existed in Saddam Hussein's day.

Today the legacy of a calamitous war stalks the Middle East like a medieval plague. Bloody massacres have wiped out entire communities, millions have been displaced and a refugee crisis of unprecedented proportions threatens the stability of nearly every state in the region. It also inflames the political debate in every country in Europe.

A war that sought belatedly to justify itself as an excuse to rid Iraq and the world of a ruthless dictator has spawned images of human misery as desperate as the world has ever seen.

Back in 2003 the warlords of the Pentagon were still living in a world of their own. Rumsfeld turned his attention to detainees in American custody. In April that year he approved a 'torture memo' written by a senior Pentagon lawyer. The memorandum found legal language to get around the fact that some interrogation techniques were not authorised by military regulations. Rumsfeld wrote in its margin: 'I stand for 8 to 10 hours a day. Why is standing (for detainees during interrogations) limited to 4 hours?'

In other words, he cared as little about the fate of detainees as he did about planning for post-invasion Iraq.

We now know from a report by the American Senate Intelligence Committee that forcing prisoners to stand for hours on end was a minor crime in a catalogue of incidents in which prisoners were routinely subjected to every manner of human degradation. It included something particularly nasty called 'rectal hydration'. The Pentagon had outsourced its obligation to enemy prisoners to freelance specialists in the psychology of torture. Parts of Iraq the invasion forces found too difficult to control were left to the mercy of trigger-happy killers, accountable to no one.

In one of the darkest incidents of the Iraq war a private American contractor, described by the United Nations as a mercenary force, killed seventeen unarmed civilians at a crowded traffic junction in Baghdad.

* * *

I had become involved in the Iraq story thirteen years before 2003. Saddam Hussein had made a serious political miscalculation. Just before dawn on the morning of 2 August 1990 he sent 100,000 men, tanks and planes across the border into Kuwait.

He had invaded his neighbour for a combination of reasons, some to do with the state of Iraq's economy. The eight-year-long war with Iran – ended only two years before – had been draining: 680,000 people dead or missing, more than 1.5 million wounded and maimed, and billions of dollars, nearly half of it because of the loss of oil revenues. Iraq claimed a victory of sorts, but the country had been worn down by the struggle and was broke. Saddam Hussein owed the Kuwaitis hundreds of millions of dollars – a debt he felt they should forgive in gratitude for his stand against the spread of Iranian influence. His creditors felt he was duty-bound to honour his debt. Saddam was in no mood to oblige, especially as he was convinced that in addition to wanting their money back the Kuwaitis were deliberately flooding the market for oil by over-production, thus depressing the price and depriving Baghdad of desperately needed foreign currency. Iraq interpreted that as a declaration of economic war. As if that wasn't bad enough, Saddam Hussein renewed the charge that for years Kuwait had been stealing oil from Iraq's Rumayiah field close to the border by 'slant drilling'. That brought up an old bone of contention. The president and his ruling Baath Party had always regarded the border separating the two countries as an imperialist fudge that gifted to Kuwait land and resources that were rightfully Iraq's. Baghdad was determined to settle the matter once and for all. A few days after his troops crossed the border, President Saddam Hussein proclaimed Kuwait the nineteenth province of Iraq.

On a more personal level, Saddam had acquired a bristling dislike of the Kuwaiti ruling elite. He considered them pampered playboys who lived like princes at home and shamelessly squandered their country's wealth in the fleshpots of Europe.

I became convinced that there was another significant factor in Saddam's miscalculation. Among his own people the Iraqi dictator inspired fear. It was obvious to anyone who'd spent even a few days in Baghdad. Once the president had set his mind on a course of action, no one would have been brave enough or crazy enough to try to persuade him to change his mind. The president's inner circle was small, tight and ruthless with dissenters, regardless of their status. Family members who crossed the president were summarily executed. The regime was notorious for its brutality.

One of the things I noticed on my first visit to Baghdad was how the mere mention of the president's name in any conversation could send the most genial Iraqi into robotic silence. On the Iraqi side of the border crossing with Jordan – one I made several times – you could get tea and biscuits in a pleasant waiting room while your papers were checked. I once tried a little small talk with one of the attendants. He was middle-aged and was pleasant and chatty as he went about his duties. At my one passing reference to something vague about the Iraqi president, the man froze and scurried into a back room at breakneck speed. I found him sitting with his head in his hands when I pursued him to offer him a tip for his hospitality.

Saddam Hussein had scared his people into cowing acquiescence.

Dictators have no need of high regard or popularity. They re-quire no mandates to justify their actions; they're accountable to no one. Saddam Hussein lived behind the secure walls of his palaces from where, with the help of a handpicked clique, he issued his orders. They went unchallenged because his people were terrified of their president. He occasionally appeared on national television at events staged for the government media, and Baghdad was rife with stories of the president dropping in unannounced on Iraqi families. He might well have done that but in no sense did he have any real contact with the Iraqi people. He had no need to. His most faithful servants were hesitant about responding to the simplest questions. One story circulating in Baghdad during my time there was that if the president asked his foreign minister what time it was, the minister's stock reply would be: 'Mr President, what time would you like it to be?' The story is probably made up. But like fables of old, it carries a nugget of truth.

Iraq laboured under a greater curse – its president's isola-tion from the world beyond the walls of his palaces. Save the occasional visit from American congressional delegations, the president's contact with international politicians of note did not extend beyond the Middle East. He rarely travelled outside the region and few of its fellow leaders were regular callers to Baghdad. President Hosni Mubarak of Egypt had gone to see him to urge him to lean more towards diplomacy in his quarrel with Kuwait. King Hussein of Jordan had conveyed much the same message. The Iraqi president listened and made them both promises on which he promptly reneged. His interlocutors eventually left him to his own devices believing, regretfully in some cases, that he was unworthy of their trust. In a world where effective diplomacy is measured partly by the warmth of personal relations cultivated over time by presidents, prime ministers and their representatives, Saddam Hussein saw few leaders and none of the diplomats accredited to his capital. Given that Baghdad was such a socially active capital and that the Iraqi people went out of their way to be friendly, I was surprised to learn that there were no set-piece ceremonies where the president could rub shoulders with ranking foreign dignitaries. There was no custom of set-piece presidential receptions or dinners. Saddam Hussein had few opportunities to take the international temperature.

I first went there in 1990 to interview the Iraqi president. It would be the only interview he ever gave to a British television journalist. I had been given the job of persuading the president to see me by my editor, Stuart Purvis, who surmised, quite correctly as it turned out, that at some point after the invasion of Kuwait Saddam Hussein would seek to justify what he had done to an audience outside the Middle East. My contact in London was Nael Hassan, who ran the Iraqi Cultural Office at an address in Tottenham Court Road, a convenient five-minute walk from ITN in Wells Street.

For weeks I saw Hassan every morning on my way to work. He was immediately taken with the proposal of an extended television interview with his president and from our first meeting offered to do all he could to make it happen. He was as good as his word. A recurring difficulty in our conversations was that Hassan clearly enjoyed the entertainment that came the way of a young diplomat posted to London and he was never able to find, in the mountain of papers on his desk, the replies to his urgent messages sent to Baghdad on my behalf – replies, he assured me, which had been received only a few hours before my arrival.

Our meetings were also held against the distracting din of two television sets fixed to a wall facing his desk and took place in a swirling fog of cigarette smoke. In a metal tray in the middle of his desk, jostling for space with Coke cans, half-empty coffee cups, newspapers and stacks of what looked like official documents, there was always a volcanic mound of cigarette ash.

My conversations with Hassan became more of a ritual and less obviously useful as time went on.

I turned up at his office more or less at the same time every morning; he offered me coffee, charm and courtesy and referred to messages he'd received from his masters in Baghdad but could never find. I came to treat his assurances with equanimity, though I never lost hope of a meeting with his president. I felt he had decided that arranging such a meeting would enhance his status with his superiors in the Information Ministry at home. I kept reminding myself of that whenever I lost my patience at Hassan's inability to locate at least one message from Iraq about my request. He never lost patience with me. Only once did he come close to showing anything resembling a flash of anger.

The Iraqi Cultural Office had been attacked by demonstrators one weekend and had been barricaded and placed under guard. In the wake of the attack it could be entered only through a large reinforced metal door. Hassan felt besieged and under threat. And when one morning I said something about oilfields in Kuwait being set ablaze, he let fly. 'Why are the Americans so concerned about Kuwaiti oil? Don't they realise that if they start a war, all that oil will go up in smoke? We have mined all those oilfields and we'll blow them up as soon as an invasion begins.' To make absolutely sure I understood what he'd said Hassan looked up from his stack of papers and said again: 'We will blow them all up, Trevor.' In subsequent meetings I evaded all references to Kuwaiti oil. Still I could point to no hard evidence that I was any closer to an interview with President Saddam Hussein. I was suitably vague whenever I was asked about the time I was spending at the Iraqi Cultural office.

Then, out of the blue one Saturday morning, Hassan rang me at my home to say: 'Baghdad will see you now.' He, too, I thought with mischievous glee, had avoided using the words 'the president'.

By the time I arrived in Baghdad in the autumn of 1990, international opinion had moved decisively against Saddam Hussein, and nothing less than a military showdown with Iraq over Kuwait was looming. Within days of the invasion a resolution in the United Nations Security Council had called on Iraq to withdraw its forces from Kuwait. There followed in quick succession a trade embargo, a naval blockade and on 29 November an ultimatum from President George H. W. Bush. Iraq was ordered to leave Kuwait by 15 January or face a ground war with American, British and French troops. During all the diplomatic activity at the United Nations, American troops under General Norman Schwarzkopf had begun flooding into the Gulf.

From the Iraqi president came the predictable bluster of soaking the desert sands with American blood. Away from the president's palaces and his spokesmen, Baghdad was consumed by anxiety and disbelief. The anxiety was understandable. Iraqis had been battered by the tribulations of a recent war with Iran. What I found more difficult to fathom was the sense of disbelief among senior government officials that their country faced another potentially more disastrous conflict. I felt it was based on an outmoded view of the nature of international relations and expressed itself in a simple question:

how could America support Iraq in its long war against Iran and only a few months later threaten to wage war against a one-time ally?

I was given a hint of that when after a convivial dinner one evening the head of the Information Ministry in Baghdad, Naji Al-Hadithi, persuaded me to sit with him in his car, even though we'd arrived back at my hotel, to listen to the midnight news from the Voice of America. The lead item was predictable. It was about Schwarzkopf's preparations to liberate Kuwait by force. Al-Hadithi could hardly contain himself. Trembling with conviction, he told me that any attack on Iraq by Western military forces would presage a disaster of international proportions. I was told it would almost certainly suck Israel into a wider Middle East conflict. I remember being terribly relieved when Al-Hadithi allowed me to leave. I rushed off into the lobby of my hotel as he sped off into the night muttering ominous warnings, dismay and incomprehension of what the Americans were about to do.

Although I was unaware of all its implications at the time, a significant event in the run-up to that first Gulf War was a meeting between the Iraqi president and America's ambassador to Baghdad, April Glaspie. Summoned to see Saddam Hussein, apparently at short notice and late one evening, Ms Glaspie expressed the view that Washington had always hoped Iraq's quarrel with Kuwait would be settled peacefully and with the help of the good offices of diplomatic councils in the Middle East. Ms Glaspie may have given too much emphasis to the State Department's belief that problems in Iraqi–Kuwaiti relations should be resolved in the region. However, it has always been alleged by senior Iraqi ministers that President Saddam Hussein interpreted the ambassador's comments as meaning that America had no wish to be involved, nor was it seeking in any way to intervene militarily in the dispute between neighbours. In short, Iraq felt it had been given the green light by the United States to do as it pleased in Kuwait.

Such a view seems hardly credible now, but it might go some way to explaining Saddam Hussein's bullish mood about his fighting chances. It was another terrible miscalculation. It emphasised how far removed he was from the reality about to crush him.

On my arrival in Baghdad I had gone straight into a round of meetings at the Information Ministry. Its officers could not have been more courteous. To my surprise and that of my colleague, ITN producer Angela Frier, I discovered that the matter of the interview had not been as firmly settled as I had been led to believe on leaving London. We learned quickly that all talk of its possibility had to be approached obliquely. This was disconcerting but understandable in the context of the way the country was run. A decision about an interview had been taken in principle but no ministry official had the authority to commit the Iraqi president to a meeting with a British journalist, and certainly not at a fixed time and place. That could come only from those closest to the seat of power and did not include, so far as we could make out, people at the Ministry of Information. And since our only line of contact to Saddam Hussein was that very ministry, we were never able to determine how or when we'd be told about the president's availability. We were stumbling about in the dark. That was how Baghdad worked.

My colleagues and I faced another problem. Our competitors at the BBC had received word of my arrival in Baghdad and were understandably furious that ITN would be given an exclusive interview with the Iraqi president. BBC correspondent John Simpson had been doing brilliant work reporting from Iraq for several weeks, and here we were turning up on what was virtually his patch after doing a deal in London to see the man whose actions formed the basis of his dispatches. Simpson protested strongly. He insisted that the interview should go to the BBC or at least be shared in a joint facility with ITN. When that approach failed, the BBC suggested that the Iraqis had made a terrible miscalculation in giving the facility to ITN since the BBC would command a larger audience than we possibly could. Baghdad checked with its office in London and when the BBC's assumption about ITN's audience reach was challenged, Simpson came up with another idea. He promised that if he was given a chance to interview the Iraqi president it would, in deference to our agreement with Baghdad, only be broadcast by the BBC forty-eight hours after mine. This was desperate stuff. How could the BBC, a television station frequently equated with the greatness of Britain itself, not be allowed an interview with the Iraqi president? And how could it go to the internationally lesser known ITN and to Trevor McDonald?

The head of the Information Ministry was coming under enormous pressure. He did his best to strike a deal to satisfy the interests of us both, but Angela Frier and I held his feet to the fire and insisted that there could be no going back on the promise to ITN at daily meetings in London weeks before. There aren't, as we pointed out, too many variations to the idea of an exclusive interview.

Still the talking went on, consuming hours in repeated visits to the ministry where, fortified by frequent draughts of coffee, the same points were raked over time and time again, day after day. Then, late one morning, the talking ended and we were told to return to our hotel and stay in our rooms to await further instructions. We should be prepared to leave at a moment's notice.

Culture and the language difference probably gave what was intended to be gentle advice the sound of a harsh command, and I remember thinking how much I've always hated the slightest hint that I was being bossed around by government officials in any country. However comfortingly self-regarding that thought may have been, it was entirely inappropriate. We had no choice but to do as we were told. What followed was one of the oddest experiences in my career as a journalist.

The telephone in my room summoned us down to the hotel lobby and to two waiting cars. The ITN crew piled into one and Angela and I got into the other. In the passenger front-seat of ours was an Iraqi army major. Our driver, also in uniform, was a younger man. His obvious nervousness betrayed his lower rank. The major added nothing to a perfunctory greeting as we swept briskly out of the Al Rashid Hotel forecourt, and on a sunlit afternoon headed off on to the open road taking us out of the city centre.

The journey was marked by its strained silence. Fishing for scraps, I may have ventured the mildest of enquiries about our destination. The major felt no need to reply in any informative way and my questions hung in the silent air. I did my best to compose myself, but I could not rid myself of the sense that it was all extremely odd. I was desperate to overcome a fear of the unknown and, more significantly, my cowardice.

In a feeble attempt at humour I asked Angela in a whisper whether she'd ever willingly got into the back of a car with strangers in a foreign country and with no knowledge of where the vehicle was taking her. She was not amused.

We'd hardly travelled any distance when it became clear that our driver was as much in the dark as we were. He had no idea where his major had been instructed to take us. While I pondered the implication of that, a game of cat and mouse ensued. As he approached every intersection or roundabout our driver slowed to a crawl, clearly waiting to be told which exit he should take. His instruction came eventually from the major, and not a moment too soon, to the sound of a short tap on the dashboard. 'First left,' the major would snap, or 'Second exit on the right.' Accustomed to barking out orders to underlings, the major was not inclined to be generous. Not once did he allow the driver the luxury of a comfortably early instruction.

That cameo went on through not much traffic for what seemed an eternity. In fact, it could only have been a journey of about forty minutes. Our driver was visibly relieved when his ordeal ended, and with the major's final tap on the dashboard he turned off the main road into the secluded driveway of what looked like a smart, upmarket residence. We had arrived at a presidential guest house on the outskirts of Baghdad and it was about four o'clock in the afternoon.

With no hint from our friends in the ministry or from our tight-lipped major we surmised, or at least I did, that we'd be kept at the president's pleasure for a few hours before seeing him sometime that evening. It was rumoured that Saddam Hussein kept unusual hours and was known to summon visitors to see him at midnight or in the small hours of the morning. The maître d' at the guest house – round-faced, bespectacled and impeccably attired in a dark suit and bow tie – immediately disabused us of the idea that there would be any presidential summons that evening. With exquisite courtesy and a toothy smile he enquired if we had given any thought to what we'd like for breakfast. I committed the unpardonable faux pas of attempting to correct him by suggesting he'd meant to ask what we'd like for dinner that night. Still smiling and without missing a beat he said with quiet emphasis: 'I meant breakfast.'

So that was that. At last we had one scrap of information. We'd be staying the night. There'd be no interview with the president that day. Two hours later we were joined by an Information Ministry minder, sent to keep us company during an interminable evening. Of course, he knew absolutely nothing about the possible timing of an interview. A charming man, educated in Britain, he talked about his love of London, shared his reminiscences of watching English football and of the delights of Trafalgar Square and St Martin's Lane. He, too, though, was struck dumb at the mere mention of the words Saddam Hussein or interview. So we sat and talked discursively, laughed too eagerly at the strain of half-made jokes and dined well. Another surprise awaited us.

As politely as I could, I asked whether it might be possible to have a bottle of whisky sent over from our hotel in the middle of the city, seemingly not too far away. A television crew from the Republic of Ireland had been billeted on the same floor as ours at the Al Rashid and I knew they'd be sympathetic to a request for drink. The presidential guest house was well stocked with drink but alas there was nothing resembling booze. I felt a glass or two of something strong would calm my fraying nerves. The smiling maître d' was unflustered by my request. To my considerable surprise he said the cars in which we'd arrived were still outside, so the question of the transportation of the whisky from the Al Rashid Hotel would be no problem but that he'd have to reconnect the telephone line to the guest house. He explained that it had been disconnected on our arrival. I decided after a moment's consideration that it would be futile to ask why. Paradoxically, I felt it wise to be kept in the dark. There is indeed a weird kind of bliss in ignorance.

At several points during the evening in that surreal setting, with servants appearing in changed uniforms from time to time and hearing what I assumed to be the faint ring of telephones, although I'd been told the lines had been cut, I did wonder if in some strange and mysterious way we had been catapulted into a parallel universe built around figments of our own imagining. In reality we were somewhere on the outskirts of the Iraqi capital and totally out of contact with our office in London. We had been unable to inform anyone where we were. The good news was that the whisky arrived.

We retired to our rooms just before midnight; mine was spacious and comfortable with a large television set and what looked like an elaborate, dial-studded radio and music sound system. I failed to get a squeak out of either and I drifted off to sleep in troubled silence.

The following day after the much advertised breakfast we were bustled into leaving the presidential guest house at annoyingly short notice but with the consoling thought that the wait to see the Iraqi president was coming to an end. That was naive. Nothing in Baghdad involving President Saddam Hussein would have ever been that simple. We were instructed to move quickly and to leave our cameras behind. My patience snapped. How on earth, I exploded, were we to set out to do a television interview without cameras? In our many meetings at the Information Ministry, which suddenly seemed an age ago, we had been made to provide detailed information about every piece of equipment we'd be taking into the presidential meeting. We had been also told that we would be on our own and would get no assistance from Iraqi television. To my continued shouting there were quizzical looks but no response. No one appeared too concerned about my cries of anguish. There was no alternative but once again to do as we were told.

My good fortune in an episode that became more bizarre with every passing moment lay in the composition of the ITN team. Angela counselled me against losing my temper. Phil Bye, senior cameraman, was professional and imperturbable; Jim Dutton, assistant cameraman, was the ideal team player in a crisis and saw the lighter side of the darkest moments, and Peter Heaps, our brilliant engineer, believed that no problems were beyond technical solutions.

We made a short journey to a large, splendidly appointed house, were given a routine security check, shown to an equally well-appointed room and instructed to be ready to receive the president of Iraq. And, lo and behold, there were television cameras and Iraqi technicians to assist us as we wished.

Getting the hang of the contrarian ways of operating in Baghdad, we shut our minds to the fact that we'd been told by the Ministry of Information only a few days before that we could expect nothing of the kind. The presence of the president's interpreter convinced us that his boss would not be far behind, and while we waited we entered into a good-natured conversational duel. My purpose in the exchange was to disguise the fact that one of the conditions on which the interview had been agreed was that we would not submit my questions to the president in advance. It was a point of editorial principle on which ITN had quite properly insisted, although the president of Iraq would have been in little doubt about the questions he'd be asked. Acknowledging the point of principle, the president's interpreter said he hoped that my questions would not be phrased in words with which he was unfamiliar and could not faithfully translate. I saw that, perhaps quite wrongly, as an attempt to get around the basis of our agreement about submitting questions and I assured the interpreter that he had no need to worry. The interpreter thanked me and turned to leave. As he did so, I felt that I had been forced too quickly on to the defensive and called him back. I explained that one unfamiliar word I would almost certainly employ was 'disembowelling'. The interpreter smiled faintly and asked why I'd be using such a word. I said there'd been reports that pregnant women in Kuwait had been disembowelled by invading Iraqi troops and that I would put the allegation to his president. I added, half jokingly, that I might also draw my fingers across my stomach to indicate precisely what I meant, if I felt my question had not be fairly translated. He assured me that there'd be no need for that and walked away.

We must have waited around for about ninety minutes or so when all the energy in the room ebbed away. Quietly and without fuss people began to shuffle about and then to leave. Not long after that, an aide quietly informed us that the president had been detained on urgent business and that we should return to the guest house. Nothing else was said. Somebody mentioned dinner. There were no takers. We hid our disappointment in the elaborate pretence of fully understanding the many calls on a busy president's time and, wordlessly and emotionally drained, dragged ourselves back to our temporary presidential abode.

The next time we were told to be prepared to leave, later that same day, the atmosphere had changed. For one thing the major who we had initially encountered when we left our hotel had reappeared, this time with a small security detail. Everyone around him was jumpy. The atmosphere of deep anxiety seemed infectious. We were again ordered to leave our cameras and recording equipment behind, and as before our protests were to no avail. We would again be putting our trust in Iraqi television. Overburdened by worry about so much I didn't understand, I imagined having to explain to my superiors back in London that we had turned up at the president's palace for a television interview arranged over many laborious weeks without our television cameras. What joy that explanation would be!

The next ninety minutes offered another glimpse of life in our parallel universe.

It was early evening and half dark as our small convoy set off at speed. Within seconds we were joined by a number of other cars in close pursuit. It soon became clear that none of the drivers knew where they were supposed to be going. Along the route they would have to be told by the major. We had covered a distance of no more than a couple of miles when, with a smack of his hands, he brought our lead car to an abrupt halt, got out and spoke to all the drivers in our wake. They, after following us blindly, had now stopped, too, albeit with engines running. To each in turn the major passed on what must have been information about the route but probably not our final destination because the process had to be repeated three or four times.

And so it was that in a flurry of stops and starts we travelled for the better part of an hour before we all turned into the inner courtyard of one of President Saddam Hussein's palaces. It was immediately obvious that the place to which we had been taken earlier that day would never in a month of Sundays have been a suitable location for a meeting with the Iraqi president. We had arrived there with no sign of the paranoia about presidential security that we had just witnessed along the route.

This place, on the other hand, looked the part. The entrance to it was wide enough for a small runway. It was dimly lit, and, even from what little I could make out, heaving with armed guards and not a smiling face among them. With little ceremony and hardly a word we were escorted through a line of what looked like metal detectors and hauled into an anteroom to be strip-searched. To the president's men, with bulging armpits and a stern demeanour, security mattered more than civility. My pockets were gone through and anything criminally incriminating such as my watch, pen and notebook was confiscated. Protests went unheeded. The soles of our shoes came in for particularly close inspection. It made no sense to us that evening in 1990 – a long time before airports around the world invested in machines to try to make sure that passengers' shoes were free of explosives capable of blowing planes out of the sky.

The palace's main reception room, into which we were eventually ushered, was spacious and sparkled conspicuously with gold fittings. It was perfectly lit for our purpose and it sprouted a small forest of television cameras. My colleagues descended on them with relief.

The room was crowded: about twenty or thirty people were milling around twitching nervously. I understood the need for security guards, technicians, palace keepers and interpreters, but about half a dozen others had lined up chairs barely feet away from where the president and I would eventually be positioned. They would in effect be sitting in on the interview and I could make no sense of their presence. Already rubbed raw by the concatenation of events of the last two days, my nerves were about to give way, and the equanimity I'd done so much to preserve since I'd arrived in Baghdad was beginning to desert me. None too politely I asked one of the close sitters encroaching on my interview space why he and so many of his colleagues had come to watch the interview. I may even have gone as far as asking whether they could find no better use for their time.

The man to whom I addressed those questions took me aside to one corner of the room and spoke in the kind of whisper that suggested he was sharing with me nuggets of priceless information. What he said told me a great deal about the Iraqi regime. My interlocutor explained that he was a member of the president's inner circle and said: 'We never get the chance to see him asked questions to which he feels the need to respond. You must understand,' he went on, 'this is a rare occasion for us.' He said again: 'We never see him questioned.'

It was, of course, a rare occasion for us, too, but I was silenced by what he'd said. Even to my overworked mind it made sense. It told me that, in general, meetings with Saddam Hussein were not meant to be forums for robust debates or for tough questions about how the president had come to a particular view. The president's word held. There were no dissenting voices or contradictory views. Meetings of the carefully chosen members of the inner cabinet were never, ever noisy, overheated affairs. Iraq had no presidential version of Prime Minister's Questions. Those members of his inner circle at the palace that evening were anxious to listen to their president being questioned about what he had done in Kuwait, and how he would deal with the response of the United States and its allies.

It was, I suppose, staggering to think that I would be asking questions they would never dare ask. Was it any wonder, I thought, that the mere mention of the president's name sent the most amiable Iraqi into stuttering incoherence?

We had been waiting for about forty minutes when the murmur of random conversation subsided and a hush swept through the palace in waves. There was a short, pregnant silence and signs of movement at one end of the room. People shuffled to stand to one side, as if responding to some barely spoken command – heads bowed, eyes cast down as if wary of even glancing up.

Almost as if it had been rehearsed, a human corridor formed, through which the president of Iraq strode, smartly suited, confident and smiling.

Saddam Hussein was a large, broad-shouldered man and his presence filled the room. Everyone stood. No one spoke. The president exuded total command. He had a penetrating gaze, though his eyes betrayed what I took to be signs of fatigue. His handshake was firm as his interpreter made the formal introduction and we posed for the obligatory pictures. The president never lost his smile and I fixed my eyes on his and tried to look at ease. I was not. I had, after all, come face to face with a murderous ideologue. I had prepared for the moment for weeks, going over in my mind what it would be like. Now that it had arrived, I was as nervous as I can ever remember.

The interview itself was not my only concern. There'd been murmurs in the UK about whether the Iraqi dictator should be given time on British television. They began as these things usually do, with one questioning comment picked up by one newspaper, eventually swelling into a tide of criticism. I felt they were hardly worth the bother and in exasperation had replied to one questioner by saying I would have been just as keen to interview Adolf Hitler or Joseph Stalin had I been a journalist in 1939. I also recognised a few of the criticisms as self-serving. No newspaper and none of its commentators would have turned down the chance to question the Iraqi president.

A much more serious worry to me was the nagging thought that one or two companies in the ITV constellation, frankly jealous that they had been beaten to the interview by ITN, were threatening not to broadcast it if it was not deemed sufficiently robust. I had nightmares about doing an exclusive interview that would never see the light of day. I was annoyed at having to cope with the unnecessary pressure. Try as I might, I could not banish those worries and they played a significant part in how I approached the task of facing the Iraqi leader.

I began by asking him whether it was an Arab thing to invade a neighbouring country and to rape its people. On reflection, it was not only insulting to the president but to all Arabs. To say he appeared unimpressed is an understatement. His eyes locked on to mine, he half smiled, stuttered and eventually turned the question round to ask whether it was a British thing to do.

Many months later I learned that the president and some of his ministers sitting in on the exchange had not been too pleased about my opening lines. If that was the case, Saddam Hussein disguised his displeasure well. He explained at length his reasons for attacking Kuwait and predicted that America and its allies would be defeated. He thought it incredible that the Americans were now defending people who had stolen Iraq's oil over many years, and he denied that his troops had been treating Kuwaitis with outrageous brutality. One story circulating at the time was that Iraqi troops had been un-plugging the incubators of premature babies in hospitals in Kuwait. I later learned that the report was part of a Kuwaiti propaganda campaign to make sure the invasion was utterly condemned.

It had been thus reported in newspapers in Britain and I had decided to use it in a feeble attempt to lure the Iraqi president into a rhetorical trap. It was not particularly subtle. It ran like this. I would repeat the story about how badly Iraqi troops were conducting themselves in Kuwait, he would deny it, and I would follow up by saying that the only way we could be absolutely sure of the facts would be to be given the chance to see for ourselves what was going on across the border in Kuwait.

President Saddam Hussein spotted the trap immediately. He said he understood the point I was making, but added that the security situation made a visit by an ITN team impossible.

I have thought of that exchange with the Iraqi president many times over the years, and I have come to the settled view that my suggestion about being allowed into Kuwait was as absurd as any I made in my career. It was crass and fraught with peril of the worst possible kind.

Sometime after my interview with Saddam Hussein a Pentagon official in Washington described to me with the help of stark black and white images the ruthless efficiency and the mechanical superiority with which the Americans defeated Iraqi soldiers in Kuwait. It was not an official briefing. We were passing the time while I waited to interview General Colin Powell, who had only just been appointed chairman of the Joint Chiefs of Staff. As the man from Pentagon told it, when Iraqi tanks were hit they imploded and shrunk into pathetic blobs of molten metal. I remember shrinking visibly as this was described to me. It would have been insane for a journalist or anyone else to be in the vicinity of one of those tank battles.

At our meeting in one of his Baghdad palaces, President Saddam Hussein staunchly defended Iraq's position in the dispute with its neighbour. He said America and its allies had been taken in by Kuwaiti lies and was scornful of those Arab countries that had openly supported military action by the West. Saddam Hussein sounded repentant about the Western hostages he was holding in Iraq, and attempted to make light of it by saying that they were enjoying Iraqi hospitality. When I replied that the hostages would prefer their freedom to Iraqi hospitality, the president went into an account of how the Japanese living in the United States had been incarcerated during the Second World War for no other reason than the fact that they were Japanese. Unpopular actions had to be taken in times of national emergency. I remember thinking it was a good response.

The president refused to be drawn on how far Iraq was prepared to go to defend itself when I enquired about the possibility of the use of nuclear weapons, and he was coy about bringing Israel into the conflict. 'We shall see' was all he would say. In his every response the president showed little real understanding of America's determination to drive his forces out of Kuwait. He sounded out of touch. He felt the battle would be long and attritional and that the West would tire of being bogged down in the sands of Arabia.

I suspect that even his closest advisers would not have told him anything to the contrary. No one would have hinted to their president that Iraq and its policies were doomed. The look on the faces of those encroaching on my space at the interview told their own stories. Like fans at a tennis match their eyes darted to and fro, from question to answer. Their interest never sagged. As I'd been told earlier, they had not been witness to too many such encounters with the leader of their country.

The length of the president's answers and the need for translators meant that our conversation went on for what seemed like the better part of two hours. I was relieved when it ended and thought of how quickly I could make a decent escape. The president stopped me in my tracks. As we rose from our chairs and shook hands again he said: 'I would like to have a word with you', at which point he gripped me firmly by the arm. I had no choice but to follow him as we began to walk to the furthest corner of the room. I was sure that I was about to be reprimanded for the bluntness of my first question. To my relief the president launched instead into a rambling lecture about the personal greed of the leaders of Kuwait. It was clearly an issue about which ministers in Iraq felt passionately. Saddam Hussein even went into a description of the style in which members of the Kuwaiti royal family lived in grand palaces with separate entrances for their many servants.

We walked the length of the room back and forth for some thirty minutes. The president never stopped talking. It occurred to me that there were moments when he seemed acutely aware of his own isolation from the ever-changing swirl of international decision-making. Several times he affected disbelief that his invasion of Kuwait had caused such outrage in the West. At one point he seemed to suggest that a diplomatic solution might still be possible. Why wouldn't someone come to talk to us? They'd be welcome here. Why don't they come to talk?

I never interrupted the president's monologue, but I've always speculated what the outcome might have been if Secretary of State James Baker had gone to Baghdad to talk to Saddam Hussein. Baker was first and foremost a political fixer. He favoured diplomatic solutions over conflict. After the invasion of Kuwait, diplomatic overtures to Iraq were put in cold storage and Saddam, isolated again, was left to rue the consequences of his own policy. No one came to talk any more. On the eve of the allied offensive, Foreign Minister Tariq Aziz did meet James Baker in Geneva in a last-ditch effort to avoid a shooting war. In reality no one had the authority to cut a deal about an invasion that the Iraqi president himself had authorised. Baker gave Aziz a list of demands to take to Baghdad. Aziz knew his president too well to return home with a document spelling what would be in effect an American ultimatum.

To this day I remember how distraught I was at the news that talks in Geneva had broken down and that the 1991 American invasion was inevitable. I was at an airbase in Saudi Arabia when the news came. My spirits sank. I was depressed that talking had failed. Most of all I hated the obvious implications of the start of another conflict with its predictable images of large-scale destruction, savagery, loss of life and all the other declensions of human misery. It was much worse than I could ever have thought. An entire country was about to be destroyed as a functioning unit. Iraq was about to split into warring factions who would never seek peace. At the risk of sounding too prescient about it, I never thought any good would come of the second invasion of Iraq.

Returning to my hotel that evening after seeing the president, and totally drained by the experience, I was surprised to be met by several members of staff from the Ministry of Information. I assumed rather selfishly that they had come to hear how my conversation with their president had gone, and I began to make a long speech describing in some detail the structure and content of the interview, the questions I asked and the general tone of the president's replies. It took me some time to realise that I had gone off on the wrong track with the men from the ministry. They were not too concerned about the content of the interview or how I felt it had gone. They wanted to know what impressions I had formed about their president. They had been waiting to ask me: what was *he* like? How did he strike you? Was he confident? Did he ever smile? Did he shake you by the hand? What did you think of him? Did he say anything about the work of our ministry? That is why they had come to my hotel room. Then it dawned on me. I had just spent two hours or more in the company of a man for whom they worked, in some cases for years, but someone they had never met and would never meet. I had been given an opportunity they would never have. None of them had ever seen him close up. Saddam Hussein had never popped into the Ministry of Information for a chat with the people who worked for him.

The saga of my encounter with the president ends in London and Baghdad. I didn't see Nael Hassan of the Iraqi Cultural Office again until a few weeks after my return to Britain and then only after a diplomatic incident. His career in London had taken a turn for the worse. He had been declared *persona non grata* by the Foreign Office and given twenty-four hours to leave. He'd made a statement about the consequences of the invasion of Iraq spreading to cities in Britain and it was deemed to have broken one of the rules of diplomatic protocol. In the pre-invasion atmosphere it was not a difficult decision for the Foreign Office.

I felt sorry about the way Hassan's London posting had come to an end, and wanted to thank him for his help in getting our interview with his president. I wanted to say goodbye. Late one evening I left a party in the middle of town and went to his flat in St John's Wood. The place was in the disorder that is quite predictable when someone is asked to pack up and leave in a hurry. Hassan put a brave face on his going but he couldn't hide his sadness. He had enjoyed living in London. I had grown quite fond of him and said I hoped we would meet again in Iraq. As he walked me out of the flat and down a flight of stairs, he turned to me and said: 'Trevor, you know there's something I always wanted to say to you. You know you were fucking rude to our president.' I was surprised at how blunt he was but I tried to make light of it, laughed unconvincingly and took my leave.

What he said didn't bother me, but I've reflected many times since on how I approached that interview with the Iraqi president and particularly about the opening question. For what it's worth, my view today is that it was too combative an opening. There was a reason for that, but the purpose of an interview should never be to shock but to prompt a disclosure of facts or views. I could have been just as forceful in my opening question if I had asked the president whether the invasion of a neighbouring country was not an outrageous and unforgivable breach of international law. There was no need for the 'rape its people' bit. It lacked style, conveyed needless aggression and was cheaply provocative. Interviews are not fist fights. Strong challenges are frequently inevitable, especially when in answers to pointed questions politicians make well-rehearsed speeches. Even then, in my view, journalists should always be conscious of and scrupulous about tone and language. I have no wish to begin a dialogue with colleagues who feel differently. It is simply my view, and it goes with the memory of my encounter with Saddam Hussein.

The Baghdad end of the story concerns Naji Al-Hadithi, who ran the Information Ministry and with whom we had endless conversations about 'the interview'. I had kept in touch with Al-Hadithi over the years and when sanctions against Iraq were at their most effective I had sent him books as presents through ITN friends travelling to Baghdad. In the era of sanctions he'd told me he missed books most of all. He had always kept up with the latest publications from New York and London. He'd been a professor of literature as a young man. Since I had last seen him, he had served as his country's ambassador in Austria and had become foreign minister.

For several days before the start of the second Gulf War I found myself close to the Iraqi Foreign Ministry and tried many times to see Al-Hadithi. I never did, nor was I ever told anything that resembled a convincing explanation. 'The foreign minister is very busy' would have been adequate in the circumstances but the minder outside his office would not even say that.

I later discovered that I had been attempting to see my old friend at the worst possible moment. In those very days when I was near the Foreign Ministry he must have been in the throes of finalising secret plans to get out of Iraq. He had decided to make a run for it, to leave the service of his country and his president and to seek a new life abroad. A meeting with an old contact would have been unnecessarily invasive and the last thing he would want.

He was embarking on an adventure fraught with danger. Had he excited the faintest suspicion of what he was about to do, he would in all probability have been hauled out of his office and shot. President Saddam Hussein did not take kindly to defectors. Just after that second Gulf War had begun, Al-Hadithi turned up in Damascus. He had managed to get there through a difficult route and was bound for Cairo. The news to me was that for some time he had been a top CIA source in Iraq and had been assisted by the Americans in reaching safety.

To this day I retain sharp images of the confident bluster of the Saddam Hussein I met that night in Baghdad in 1990 and I have frequently thought of how they contrast with pictures of his Republican Guard retreating in dishonour from Kuwait under a hail of fire from American helicopter gunships. So easy a target were members of Saddam's elite fighting forces that the Americans called a halt to what had become in their words 'a turkey shoot'. So much for the valiant Iraqi army soaking the desert sands with American blood.

I think, too, of how my memory of the smartly attired man I saw in his gilded palace all those years ago differs so much from the scene of his being unearthed and brought to the surface from a common spider hole in which he took refuge after the second Gulf War. Those later images were suffused with ignominy and loss. The president wore the haunted look of a hapless fugitive. Shorn of dignity, dishevelled and disorientated, he appeared distinctly unpresidential.

And then there was his so-called trial, its verdict all too obvious before a single accusatory word had been spoken. Then Saddam Hussein's unavailing protests, balefully proclaiming himself still president of a country that had changed utterly while he'd been in hiding. And finally there was the searing image of his hanging that was beyond the grotesque.

The new Iraq had shown its hand. It would be as bloody as the worst of Saddam's dictatorship, although we'd be told that the allied invasion was supposed to have done with all that.

The folly of post-invasion American administrators left Iraq in chaos. All too frequently it appeared to be drowning in blood, perpetually attempting to evade the bombers and mountains of rubble. It is easy to understand why the occupying forces wanted to purge the country of the worst influences of the previous regime, but the reckless disbanding of the army and smashing of all that remained of the Baath

Party destroyed all structures of effective administration. The war and the occupation had sucked dry every influence that made a country function.

The new government in Baghdad was viciously sectarian and there was nothing America could do. Rather than striving to be more inclusive, the governing party waged war on its opponents. It was riddled with cronyism and corruption. It was powerless to stop the bombings and the killing. Nearly five million Iraqis were displaced. Worst of all, the Baath Party members kicked out by the American occupiers left in anger with stacks of weapons and embarked on a campaign of creating mayhem. Some may even have been responsible for the rise to prominence in the region today of Isis, or the so-called Islamic State.

So much of what ails the Middle East today can be traced to the decision to invade Iraq in 2003 with no properly worked-out plan of what should follow after the bombs had produced shock and awe, and after the images of a hated dictator were wrenched from their plinths.

On my visits to the region after 2003 it has been painful and chastening to hear people talk almost wistfully about the possibility that Saddam Hussein would never have tolerated the level of disorder that scars the lives of millions of Iraqis today. Such is the depth of despair.

It is perhaps futile to speculate. It is possible, of course, that a brutal dictator was probably the one who could have kept the country from falling apart. Answers to world problems frequently involve much more than getting rid of ruthless dictators and making brave but foolish claims about freedom and democracy.

Even when I believe I have rid myself of every trace of the Iraq story, my visits to the country and my meeting with the Iraqi president somehow find a way of continuing to track parts of my life.

A few months ago, I was making my way uncertainly down

the steps of a Knightsbridge hotel in the West End towards the Underground station when I bumped into a rather hearty man, who put his face very close to mine to ask whether I remembered him. After a rather convivial evening with friends I had not seen since that rainy evening when Hong Kong was finally handed over to China, I confessed, perhaps a little too quickly and certainly without looking at him too carefully, that I sadly did not. I also indicated that perhaps my memory was never at its best when I had drunk some excellent red wine. I may have also said that, in my case, at least memory does not improve with age. It was a feeble attempt at self-deprecating humour. It didn't work.

Now with his face even closer to mine he declared almost triumphantly: 'I was your interpreter when you met Saddam Hussein.' The sobering effect of his words was immediate.

Haitham Rashid Wihaib rose in his service to the Iraqi president to become his chief of protocol. He saw Presidential Palace life close up and witnessed the merciless brutality of the regime. He survived an assassination attempt and his mother and his sisters were imprisoned by the regime. He managed to escape, partly because of his status as a diplomat, and now lives in Europe.

Wihaib and I exchanged notes about the evening I met his former president and I recalled how surprised I was that so many members of the president's inner circle were keen to sit in on the interview. He confirmed what was explained to me that evening in Baghdad. For people who worked closely with the president, it was unusual to see him challenged with questions of any sort. Wihaib told me they would never miss it for the world.

He capped it all off by confirming the details of a story about which I had been aware, though only sketchily.

At one of the regular meetings of his cabinet, Saddam Hussein had taken out and shot and killed a minister and returned to continue the meeting as though nothing of note had occurred. 'It was the minister of health,' Wihaib said. The minister had made a suggestion about the president disappearing for a while, as a way of confounding his enemies, who would for a time be left wondering what had become of him. The president gave every indication that for a few seconds at least he was giving the proposition serious thought. He evidently concluded that it was nothing but a plot to permanently get him out of the way. Presidential circles were never free of paranoia.

Very calmly the minister was eventually asked to step outside the room. Apparently without saying very much, Saddam Hussein unholstered his revolver and killed his minister with a single bullet to the head. The president then walked back in to continue the meeting with hardly a flicker of emotion.

There were never any other suggestions like that. At meetings of his inner circle the president spoke; others listened and gave their assent.

Wihaib told me that presidential palaces were fortresses stuffed with cash. They were like banks, he told me. The president's sons made good use of the money. Automobile magazines were read avidly and, of course, availing themselves of the latest models was never a problem. Of all the assignments I undertook in the course of my work, the world which Saddam Hussein and his henchmen had constructed remains to this day the most extraordinary.

10

Encounters on Death Row

'. . . the strange and sinister embroidered on the very type of the normal and easy.'

Henry James, Preface to *The Altar of the Dead*

One of the joys of journalism is its unending ability to surprise.

We can never accurately predict what we're getting into and we treasure the notion that plunging into the dark and the unexpected can be rewarding.

At the same time we are models of contradiction. We convince ourselves that all stories conform to a general pattern, although at the back of our minds are tiny, persistent voices suggesting that one day, and perhaps when we least expect it, we'll hit the journalistic jackpot and the one assignment for which we are least prepared would throw up the revelation to shatter all perceptions, be the envy of our colleagues and send our editors into ecstasy.

Natural caution mixed with a touch of superstition prevents us from putting anything like that into words, but hope is a powerful personal driver. Journalists are adventurers at heart, forever seeking the thrill no one has experienced before. We all believe in scaling new heights and setting new marks.

When not drowning in hope we settle for quiet resignation and an enduring belief in our native sound judgement. That view can run very deeply, and it is so often mistaken.

I surprised myself by an interest in crime and crime stories because I never read them in the newspaper, nor do I think about them very much. But when I was asked to report on some of these hideous stories, I became fascinated by the personalities involved, by the curious edges of human nature to which they exposed me.

When I became involved with a documentary on the Fred and Rose West story I couldn't get a sense of some of the detail of what went on in their lives. To drive around and pick up people off the street, take them to their home and then eventually mistreat them in such a hideous way and be responsible for taking their lives is a most unfathomable thing to do.

I found the same thing with the Beverley Allitt story in another documentary I did. Here was a young nurse who was responsible for looking after young children. Now what could be more natural? And then to discover that this young nurse, who became a godmother to some of the children because she looked after them so well, was responsible for the death of these same young children. I couldn't get my mind around that.

I also found absolutely fascinating that people in the hospital had great difficulty understanding that very fact, that this nurse was responsible for the death of some of these young kids, and it was a police detective who never left the case and never forswore his belief that maybe *she* was the one who was responsible. And he came to that view because he thought that whenever there was one of these incidents *she* had always been on the spot – and although his colleagues in the Met and in the force suggested to him that he should drop the case, he persisted. I thought it was a very good example of what splendid work people in the police force do with their painstaking follow-up of leads, and in the end bringing somebody to justice. I thought the Beverley Allitt case was an absolute prime example of that.

In 2012 I was involved in making a documentary at a maximum security prison in Indiana in the United States. On the two and a half hour drive from Chicago to the appropriately named casino hotel, the Blue Chip, with its car park capable of swallowing up several football fields and about two miles from the prison, I had formed in my own mind a few general views about entering such a place.

Security, I told myself, would of necessity be thorough, time-consuming and tiresome. I was not wrong. A machine blew hot air through my hair to make sure I was not concealing drugs. Shoes had to be temporarily disposed of, and another electronic contraption made sure we were concealing nothing in our pockets or on our bodies. I endured those procedures with an exaggerated show of patience, occasionally muttering under my breath that by any reckoning we would be the last people on earth to try smuggling anything unlawful into a maximum security prison.

Once, sometime after we had become well known to the security guards and their system of checks, I was emboldened to enquire of a prison officer how, after all their prevention efforts, it was still possible for drugs to be smuggled into the prison. Without missing a beat he replied: 'Staff.'

Drugs found their way into the prison quite easily, smuggled in by people who worked there.

As for the rest, I was not unfamiliar with images of the ugly sprawl of prison buildings, the abundance of brickwork, watchtowers, prison guards with guns and miles and miles of ugly, rolled-up wire.

I was cautious about meeting prisoners on death row. I'd never been to a death row prison and I was sure that doing so would go beyond the range of anything I had ever experienced. In fact, I have always had a horror of prisons. The idea of incarceration has probably been the worst of all my nightmares. So the notion of visiting death row, where people are waiting to be killed by the state, appalled me. And yet something propelled me into accepting the commission to do it.

No one has ever convinced me that the state should be involved in killing people. I have always been repelled by the mechanics of the process, the orchestrated waiting about in the claustrophobia of the room right next to the execution chamber, the condemned man's contemplation of his last hours on earth, and what seemed to me to be the obscenity of having the choice of a last meal. It is as though a prisoner's favourite food could be dressed up as a last-minute show of concern, or that culinary choice is so important when facing death.

Everything about it is horrifying, right down to the meticulous arrangement of seats for those who have come to witness someone's final moments. I know I am on shaky ground here because there are expert medical views about this, but I have never quite fallen for what must be the public relations spin that executions are done with painless, clinical care.

What a fearful thing it must be to be holed up in the excruciating seclusion of a prison cell, awaiting an undignified end at the hands of a state-appointed executioner.

When criminals kill, it is an abomination and a stain on the soul of man. The heavens themselves cry foul. When the state responds by putting the killers to death, it looks less like just punishment and more like the degradation of some ancient code of vengeance made possible with the aid of the worst of modern poisons. Over the years and around the world I have heard all the arguments to the contrary. Not one has altered my view.

In every other way, though, I felt that prison life would conform to what I'd read in newspapers and seen in films.

So much for my vague thoughts.

I was, in fact, totally ill prepared for walking into Indiana State Prison.

Surprise number one.

I was certain that every prisoner I met would try to convince me of his innocence. I would, I told myself, walk through rows of cells with men in uniformly drab prison attire, wearing looks of studied boredom, rendered anonymous by their number, explaining to me that they were not guilty, that it had all been a case of mistaken identity and that they had been wrongly convicted. After all, in the film *The Shawshank Redemption* the great Morgan Freeman himself, playing Red, had declared that to be so.

Whether or not that line had been rendered with a touch of irony, Red was wrong. None of the prisoners I talked to in Indiana protested that they had been wrongly convicted and incarcerated. Many were keen to suggest the extenuating circumstances that brought them to such a place, but none claimed innocence.

That was, for me, only the beginning of an unforgettable experience.

Walking through the prison yard on my first morning I encountered a young man whose life story has never left me. We had come upon Ronald Sanford as he was being locked into a fenced-in portion of the exercise yard, a bit of ground about twenty yards square. That is to say, he had been taken from his cell in handcuffs and shown into a secure area where, for an hour or so, he could enjoy the freedom from his stricter confinement and a little fresh air, if anything could be so described in a closely guarded maximum security prison.

Handcuffs were not removed until Sanford was safely locked into his tiny exercise area whereupon he would meekly surrender his hands through a hole in the fence to be uncuffed. In that single act I had a glimpse of the almost casual, ritual humiliation that underscores so much of all prison life.

I had barely begun to ask how he came to be in prison when the story of his appalling crime and his incarceration tumbled out it in an unstoppable torrent.

Sanford was thirteen years old when he killed a neighbour

because she turned down an offer to have him cut her grass. He had not been acting alone but his accomplice turned state's evidence and somehow managed to escape punishment. He was sentenced to 170 years and sent to Indiana's maximum security prison at the age of fifteen. One hundred and seventy years!

With a pained smile of helpless resignation Sanford recited the number of things on which he has missed out in life: 'I've never driven a car, I've never been out of the state, I've never had a passport, I've never been on an aeroplane, I've never been to a prom, I've never been to a bar.' He added, with what sounded like a tone of regret, that he had never filed a tax return. He was thirty-five years old.

On the morning I unexpectedly met Sanford at Indiana State, I had been in prison for less than an hour.

There's a death row at Indiana's maximum security prison and the warden agreed to take us on a tour to give me the chance to talk to some of men condemned to die. Death row is sealed off and its occupants are isolated from the rest of the prison. To the ever-rattling and disquieting sounds of keys being turned and iron doors being slammed shut behind us, off we went in a little party: film crew, director and producers. If the inmates were taken aback at seeing us they hid it well.

The prisoner at the furthest end of the row was Frederick Baer, who had cut the throats of a mother and her daughter whose home he had entered on the pretence of wanting to use the telephone. He was convicted for murder, attempted rape, and theft. I have never forgotten that later on in my visit I sat beside him on his prison bed one evening when he confessed to his ghastly crime, in a manner that confounded even the prison authorities hardened to listening to the most horrific crimes.

On our morning trip, the warden introduced us and began his conversation with the prisoner by asking about his health and a few other issues that he had raised with the authorities.

Baer suggested they had all been settled. It was not quite an over-the-garden-fence chat between neighbours, but not too dissimilar.

I was taken aback at what I could only describe as a civilised exchange between the warden, who would eventually be involved in that prisoner's execution and the prisoner, Baer, who would be strapped to a gurney after midnight and injected with a cocktail of lethal drugs. I would never have expected anything like that. Although on reflection, I understood why there would be little point in having an abrasive relationship.

Baer told me that he was fully aware of the part that the warden would someday play in his execution, but he said that he saw it as no reason for open hostility. He understood that fate had thrown them together in some extraordinary way. 'I know', he said, 'that one day the warden will be responsible for taking my life. I hold no grudge against him because of that and until that time comes we are forced to get along together.'

The warden, who had described himself as a practising Christian, agreed. Fate had brought them together and had decreed that they come to an accommodation.*

Five years later when I went back to Indiana State Prison I was caught totally off guard by the latest arrival on death row.

William Clyde Gibson is a serial killer who had been convicted of the murder of three people. In a sparsely furnished visiting room bathed in the harsh light of naked bulbs so that nothing and no one is unobserved, we sat feet away from each other as he talked about the crimes he had committed. His description of the murders of which he was guilty was almost casual.

His terse, declarative sentences were punctuated by an unnerving half-chuckle. He appeared to make every attempt to be boastful. With prison officers standing close by and listening

---

* In January 2018, Baer's death penalty was reversed as he was deemed mentally unfit at his original hearing.

to his every word, he said that despite his eventual capture he had made fools of the police. They had underestimated the number of people he had killed by at least ten times.

'That means,' I enquired, 'that you killed thirty people?'

'Something like that,' he replied calmly, again with that chilling half-chuckle. Then he drifted into what seemed a brief moment of self-examination. 'I don't know what it is about me, but I could kill someone and go off to dinner and think nothing of it.'

That confession was meant to shock, and it did. I could only stare at Gibson. He was almost smiling.

Journalists are no strangers to clichés and vastly overused words and phrases. Quite a number are attributed to us. This was different. There was no need here for exaggeration. I was distressed that the word 'evil' came so easily to mind and that, even worse, it probably showed in my expression which I had worked so hard to control. The men I had been permitted to see had, after all, been judged and convicted. They needed no further sanction from me.

I thought I saw evil and all the contorted villainy of mankind in the face of William Clyde Gibson.

Before meeting him, I felt I had been exposed to the darkest corners of a man's mind and of prison life when I interviewed Paul McManus in 2012. He had killed his wife and two daughters and was awaiting execution. I would later learn that beyond those simply stated facts there lay a tragedy far greater than anything the Greeks could have imagined.

We didn't talk about his crimes at that first meeting. He was keen to tell me about his life on death row. He was very proud, too much so I remember thinking, of the fact that his cell was spotlessly clean. 'I don't watch television and I don't read, you see. So I clean. That's how I spend my time, cleaning.'

He invited me in to inspect the cleanliness of his cell. I declined. He wore a slightly haunted look and no smile escaped his dull, serious expression. He lightened up almost imperceptibly when he explained that as a diabetic he was escorted out every day to be given an insulin injection. He enjoyed that brief escape from the isolation and separateness of death row, he said, because of the chance it gave him just to see prisoners moving about in the general population.

When I saw McManus five years later his circumstances had changed and, according to him, not for the better.

An Appeal Court had ruled against his sentence of death on the grounds of his mental state and he had been taken off the row. The new judgement was life without parole and when we sat on a bench in a quiet spot in the prison yard McManus's frustration, too tortured to comprehend, was close to breaking point.

It was a chilly afternoon and autumnal tints embroidered the trees beyond the prison walls. Much closer to where we sat were the long fences topped by rolls of barbed wire, occasionally glinting in the pale sunlight whenever the clouds rolled by.

McManus was attempting to come to terms with spending the rest of life in a prison that was in many ways a strange place to him. He had spent his prison years in death row isolation.

Words didn't come easily. He talked somewhat obliquely about the finality of a death sentence and the fact that, however dreadful it appeared, there was always a date in the future on which everything would be brought to a close. The dull, recurring pain of incarceration would end.

All death row inmates knew that despite appeals to higher courts, they would in all probability die at the executioner's hand and that someone would someday set the time. There was a brutal certainty about that. And everyone prepared to face it.

Now McManus asked looking around: 'Am I expected to live out the rest of my days in this prison?' Locked away for years in the seclusion of death row he had formed no friendships in the wider prison. Such associations can be a vital part of a prisoner's survival kit. Having not had that, he had no wish to share his life with the men he didn't know in the general prison population. In a way he looked down on them. He felt sure he had nothing in common with them. Many he regarded as common criminals.

There was a bizarre privacy to life on death row. With the Appeal Court's ruling, that had disappeared. He was now one of the herd and he was hating it.

It was one of the strangest conversations I'd ever had. I thought I understood what Paul McManus saw as his predicament. But I found it odd, nevertheless, to find a man so palpably distressed at the fact that he had escaped dying at the prison executioner's hand.

With little encouragement from me, he launched into a rambling account about killing his wife and daughters. His voice dropped and the words fell from his lips – unsure, jagged and in an unfiltered dirge.

He alleged that he had left one daughter in the care of a friend. The friend molested the child. McManus blamed himself and was overcome with guilt. To rid himself of his guilt and his daughter's shame, he killed her.

The dead girl's sister had been deeply affected by the course of events. McManus felt even more guilt at his initial lack of parental judgement. He had, he reasoned, caused so much pain that he thought it best to put an end to her trauma by killing his second daughter.

To his wife all this was impossibly unbearable. To end her emotional turmoil McManus killed her, too. However, he omitted to mention that his wife had served him divorce papers that morning.

He then attempted to take his own life by jumping off a bridge. He fell softly and survived.

I remember our conversation that afternoon drifting to an uncertain end, because it was getting quite cold and because neither he nor I could find anything further to say.

I was relieved. I guessed that he must have been, too. He had attempted to dredge from his past episodes of the most unbelievable pain. Yet he was facing a new dark night of the soul. And to that, there'd be no court-dictated end.

I left the maximum security prison at Indiana later that day wondering whether I could ever find the courage to visit it again. Many months have passed and at the slightest mention of the place I still see the faces of the men I met there. Men like Rick Pearish, a veteran of the Vietnam War who now runs the prison barber shop. He's now well past the age of seventy, and has spent some thirty-five years behind bars. He was cheerful when we last met but in failing health. He tried to be philosophical about prison life, telling me how civilised it was to work in the barber shop. He talked wistfully about the few personal items he would be sure to take with him when he is released, but without plausibility.

There were thoughtful pauses and intimations of mortality.

His was a case of cruel misfortune, he said. He had committed armed robbery, his getaway car failed to start, and the one he stole had a mother, her daughter and niece in the back seat. He drove the car across state lines, making that a Federal offence of kidnapping.

Ronald Sanford, who drowns his despair in his appetite for reading, and Rick Pearish, who survives largely on memories, may find freedom a struggle every bit as difficult as the relentless monotony of life behind bars.

The breathtaking pace of modern life and the uncompromising demands of our new technological age make it reasonable to wonder whether men locked up for decades will ever be able to find fulfilment on the outside.

At Indiana's maximum security prison I thought that for the first time I understood the true meaning of the world 'institutionalised'.

I remember one young prisoner said to me, 'Do you know, I've been thinking about the pattern of my life and probably I would always have ended up in a place like this, because I'm not a very good person. And if I were to be let out and I had no money and I had a weapon, I might do something awful and end up in a place like this. And this is what I have thought about my life.'

I thought that was an extraordinary thing to say to me. Having been involved in it for some time, I felt that I was terribly fortunate to gain the confidence of these people and that they would tell me so much about their lives.

* * *

No such problems faced the Mafia whose grisly murders and racketeering scarred so much of American life. Again, I was surprised, not only by the willingness of former members to talk openly about what they had done, but the pride they showed in their commitment to an obnoxious criminal fraternity. That spoke volumes about the degree of my incomprehension.

Members of the various Mafia families I met never saw themselves as criminals in the accepted sense of the word, but as apostles of a higher calling, part of a brotherhood, a family – an exclusive club to which they had been inducted in a blood ceremony, and to which they had sworn undying loyalty.

One of the more extreme examples of what this meant was explained to me in the story of a twenty-year-old girl who would not speak to her father for two years because he had in her eyes betrayed the Mafia and broken his oath of loyalty.

The constant references to loyalty amounted to nothing more than a continuing distraction. Betrayal was as commonplace and as frequent as those secret ceremonies and pledges sealed in blood. What broke many of the most powerful Mafia families was the number of their members who were prepared, when the chips were down, to break ranks, to look after themselves, to do deals with the law enforcement authorities and to try to sneak away into hiding. Doing deals this way usually meant a reduction of harsh prison sentences in return for information otherwise too difficult, and too time-consuming, to obtain by usual investigative methods.

Almost all the men who spoke to me had achieved their freedom by telling tales about life in the Mob and incriminating their former friends.

John Alite was one of those. He once worked for the notorious Gambino crime family. I met Alite in a part of Brooklyn he claimed as his former territory.

'Nothing went on in this area that I wasn't a part of. There were shootings, killings, all kinds of things. I was part of it all.'

'Were you involved in any murders?' I enquired.

'Sure,' he replied. 'One time the order went down that this guy had to be taken out. I took him to a bar, got him drunk, put him in the front seat of a car beside the driver and put a bullet in the back of his head.'

He told me all this as we walked along the sidewalk.

'What became of the body?' I asked.

'We pushed it out of the car.'

No attempt was made to hide the body, I was told. It would be common knowledge that this had been an execution and it would serve as a warning to anyone who stepped out of the line imposed by the Mob.

Alite had an expansive career in the Mafia. From the proceeds of only one job he was able to afford a secluded house in the country for his wife and children, with a garden pond and a swimming pool and all the toys. He had warm memories of the luxury, especially the lavish weekend parties.

He no longer owned the place, but the latest residents allowed us to look around, camera crew in tow. I was shown the cupboards where he kept his guns. I was a little surprised at the size of the arsenal. I was assured that they were essential tools of the trade.

He clearly enjoyed recounting to me a story about the

bedroom. It reminded him of what his life was like at the pinnacle of his Mafia power.

On one occasion when he was away, a workman he'd employed used it to entertain a girlfriend. Alite was not amused. In a fit of rage, he stripped the man of all his clothes, threw him into the garden pond and fired a number of shots over his head. He made a point of explaining to me that he never intended to kill the workman, because had he so wished the man would certainly have had no chance of survival. Coming at that point in our conversation I got the point immediately.

That was not the end of the workman's punishment. He was dragged out of the pond, and, still naked, tied to a tree in the garden. He was left there while Alite went off to dinner. The errant workman managed to wriggle free and made his way down the long path from the house and on to the highway. Before too long he attracted the attention of a passing police vehicle.

It was just as well. Almost midnight, on a February evening, the winter temperature in that part of New Jersey was below freezing.

For many years Alite kept one step ahead of the law, travelling the world on false passports. It came to an end in Brazil when he was arrested and thrown in jail.

Alite told me that conditions in the Brazilian prison were terrible. An open sewer dripped filth into his cell and the place was crawling with rats.

John Alite decided to call the Feds back home and, despite his pledge of loyalty to the Mob, to strike a deal.

Just when I thought I was beginning to understand what life was like for mobsters like Alite, he surprised me by telling of another instance when he had been ordered to take a man's life. The way the story unfolded felt quite matter-of-fact. Perhaps I was getting too used to Mafia-speak.

Alite had been out driving with his son, who was five or six at the time, and his brother when he was ordered to take somebody out. The manner in which these stories are told suggests that there is never room for discussion once such an order is given. So Alite made his way to the fearful rendezvous, barely apologising to his passengers.

He reached the place, left his son and his brother in the car and did the job. The man was shot. His dispatch from this life was apparently a quick one. To be honest I didn't ask, so stunned was I by the course of events.

On returning to the car he was asked by his young son who'd heard the gunshot what the noise was. Alite told his son it was a firecracker and the three continued on their way. Strangely, had the story ended there and in the light of all I'd heard before about how the Mob dealt with people who crossed them, it would have elicited no additional interest from me. I was beginning to think that I had heard it all.

What Alite said next was a shock. He told me: 'These days I say to my son, you went on your first job when you were just six.' In his place I might have done what I had been ordered to do. I would never have disclosed to my young son that I had once left him in a car in the care of his uncle while I went off to execute someone.

Of all the men I talked to, or about whom I'd been told stories, no one so encapsulated the immense contradictions of Mafia life than Greg Scarpa. He was a captain in the Colombo crime family, a passionate family man and a killer of such notoriety that he was known and feared as 'the Grim Reaper'.

The shadow he cast over those nearest to him hung over them forever and devastated their lives.

I met his daughter Linda on Staten Island.

She had never forgotten the morning her father's car was ambushed by a group of masked gunmen less than two hundred years from their home. There were ferocious volleys of gunfire. Scarpa's attackers were being repulsed and Linda could hear it all. By a coincidence she had followed her father's car to the road junction where he was attacked. She had her baby son in her car.

She had been unable to tell whether her father had been hit, and in the general confusion of the attack one of the gunmen ran away from her father's car, crossed to the other side of the road and came face to face with Linda. He stared directly at her.

Scarpa made it out alive and returned home in a fury, promising retribution. That was his dominant mood. He was, his daughter told me, anxious to be seen as a devoted father, always at home for family dinner at six thirty. He would then leave the house in his non-stop pursuit of enemies of the Mob. His cruelty was legendary, and fearsome punishments were carried out not only on his enemies but also on anyone of whom he disapproved.

When Linda was a schoolgirl, word reached her father that she had been caught smoking cannabis with a friend. Scarpa pursued the boy and had him mercilessly beaten up. He then had the boy brought home so that his daughter could see how severe his punishment had been.

I was horrified at hearing that story. Linda shook with emotion as she recalled the incident. She told me her friend's face had been reduced to a pulp and bleeding mess. The boy could hardly open his eyes.

Linda didn't say much more about the incident. I concluded that she had drifted into a long, questioning silence. Why had her father done that to a schoolboy unable to defend himself? And by what code did he feel it appropriate to show his daughter what he had done?

In her sitting room one afternoon we sat and watched old video images showing her father's more paternal side. At Linda's sixteenth birthday party he was every bit the proud patriarch, a generous host, strolling among his many guests, smiling broadly and dancing with his daughter. It appeared picture-perfect. But Linda was tearful as she remembered those happier times. She had not seen the video for many years. She said she never looked back at old pictures like those. The walls of her sitting room were bare. She explained that she had decided to hang no pictures with reminders of the past. We felt the need to apologise for showing her the video of the sixteenth birthday.

It took me some time to stop replaying parts of Linda's story in my mind. I'd heard nothing quite like it before. What was so appalling to me was his daughter's memory of her father's insistence on all the trappings of a warm family life that he managed to combine with such outrageous brutality.

There were, in my excursions into Mafia-land, lighter moments. I was shocked at the extent to which we were able to wring doses of uncanny good humour from conversations with men guilty of the most terrible crimes.

I set off one morning to interview Ron Previte, who had agreed to talk about his years in the Philadelphia Mob. He had distinguished himself by betraying his friends and, according to him, making a sizeable sum from selling information to the law enforcement authorities. He recalled several incidents with pride.

We met in the office of a run-down car repair business where Previte appeared to be among admirers. Their smiling faces suggested a genuine approval of everything he said about his worst offences. What I remember most, though, is not only the easy-going manner in which he almost dismissively described his days as a mobster, but his first words to me. 'We were talking about you last night,' he said as I introduced myself. I was more than a little puzzled and I suppose I showed it. How on earth did I become a topic of conversation between Ron Previte and his friends? 'We were wondering whether she did that thing with the sword,' he enquired. It took me a few moments to work out that he was referring to the Queen's role in conferring a knighthood. I was not too sure what I should say, especially as Prince Charles had presided at my ceremony.

I decided it would be useless to confuse the issue further. He didn't wait for my reply. 'We simply thought,' he went on to explain, 'that in our line of business we would never allow someone to wave a sword about so close to our necks.'

On the morning of the day I was flying back to London after a ten-day trip absorbing much more than I wished to know about life in the Mafia, I met one of the most notorious characters from the Philadelphia Mob, Ralph Natale.

It had not been easy to pin him down, but he eventually agreed to see us one Sunday morning in a Brooklyn bar.

It was well before opening time, and the dim half-light of the bar seemed to make it an appropriate setting to meet our man and talk about his career. There was little traffic about; Brooklyn had yet to wake up. Someone in our team, speaking softly, made the observation that Natale had not turned up on his own. I eventually spotted two or three men in the vicinity of the bar, nervously pacing around the near-deserted street, trying without success to look as if they were not there. The surrounding area rendered them too conspicuous for that.

Sitting on opposite bar stools I thought I might shock Natale by asking him bluntly if he could tell me why he had killed thirty-three men. Hardly pausing and looking directly at me he replied: 'Because they were trying to kill me.'

After that admission I struggled to get too much more out of my mobster killer. I remember asking a few questions about whether he was plagued by feelings of remorse, and did he find it easy to sleep at night given the enormity of what he had done as a member of the Philadelphia Mob. His reply stays with me today. 'I have no problem sleeping at night. Of course, at my age I get up two or three times a night to go to the toilet. Other than that I sleep soundly.'

* * *

I spent two weeks in the American South in 2017, making a programme about Martin Luther King to mark fifty years since he was shot and killed in Memphis in April 1968.

Over many years I have studied many aspects of King's life and work. I have always been moved beyond words by his leadership of the civil rights movement and the tenacity, the courage and the bravery of his great army of supporters, black and white, who were prepared to put their lives on the line in the cause of overcoming the curse of racism and a country's racist laws. I was amazed at King's determination, under sustained pressure, to stick to a policy of non-violence.

I remember from newsreels the quiet dignity of Rosa Parks' refusal to give up her seat to a white passenger on the bus in Montgomery, the unbelievable success of the bus boycott, the march on Washington and Dr King's 'I have a dream' speech.

In the course of reporting at various times for ITN, *Channel 4 News*, the *Tonight* programme and working on documentaries for ITV, I have been to the church in Memphis where one rainy night Dr King made his last prophetic speech. I am always moved to tears to hear him talk about having gone to the mountain top and seen the Promised Land and about the realisation that he may not get there.

I have been to Selma, Alabama, where people attempting to do nothing more than to march peacefully to the state capital in Montgomery, to plead for the right to vote, were set upon by state troopers on horses, riot police and dogs, and beaten bloody as they attempted to cross the Edmund Pettus Bridge.

I remember how that savage attack on defenceless marchers shocked America and the world, and finally shamed the White House into action.

President Lyndon Johnson, a Southern Democrat, who had some time before voted against an anti-lynching law – *against* an anti-lynching law – went up to Capitol Hill to suggest that Selma must not be repeated and that it was necessary to 'give negroes the vote'.

All these things I knew. What I had not appreciated until my most recent visit in 2017 was the extent to which hate – deeply ingrained in the minds of the entire criminal justice system and in the minds of Americans mainly in the South – informed the segregated past. American segregationists were not concerned with merely keeping black Americans from lunch counters and coffee shops. They were not really concerned with keeping them away from their golf courses and country clubs. They wanted black Americans gone altogether. They despised them. They were not truly American, and as a consequence should have no part in the life of the country.

In the eyes of many whites, black Americans polluted the integrity of the white race.

When the authorities turned their fire hoses on the marchers in Selma, the intent was not simply to stop them getting across the bridge or to bruise and offend their dignity. It was naked brutality, sanctioned by the state and aimed at eviscerating black Americans of all humanity.

Consider this.

The fire hoses were sufficiently powerful to tear bricks from mortar. And here's a fact that in the overall immensity of the story I had forgotten until it was told to me again in 2017.

On Bloody Sunday in 1965, hundreds of local people from Selma came to watch the action. The violence was initiated and orchestrated by the state and it assumed that it had community support. People were well aware of the symbolic relevance of the ghastly events unfolding before their very eyes.

Whenever I have undertaken one of those long journeys across the American South, the highways heavily wooded on both sides of the road, I've always itched to get back to the bright lights of big cities before the dark of evening. In states like Mississippi, Georgia, Louisiana, Alabama and Arkansas, I associated such areas deep in the countryside with the obscene ritual of lynching.

Bryan Stevenson, who leads the Montgomery-based Equal Justice Initiative, an organisation that has studied and published an authoritative work on the history of lynching in America, explained to me that black Americans were not always put to death through stealth in the lonely countryside but were lynched on courthouse lawns, in broad daylight and again with crowds looking on.

This had little to do with mere discrimination or a denial of the right to vote. It was, rather, a clear expression of what some Southern states, their sheriffs and governors, saw as the fate marked out for black Americans.

They should never be afforded equality. They were seen as inferior, fit to work the land but not to live in ordinary communities.

On my most recent visit to states in the American South I could not resist the view that although the era of lynching has passed, its legacy lives on and stains the continuing discussion about the problems of race in America today.

My time was spent mainly in the South, but the issue of race is as pronounced as it was across the country in Dr King's day. It is the running sore in American life. It lives on today in the white supremacist policies of the Ku Klux Klan and the tribalism evident in all almost every political debate. At the highest political levels the Klan appears to have acquired a new respectability. Its members no longer need to hide their faces, march with burning crosses or disguise their true identity in white robes.

Its echoes are heard every time a white policeman shoots an unarmed black man and no one is prosecuted. And how could it be explained that in 2018 police were called to a Starbucks coffee shop in an upmarket neighbourhood of Philadelphia because two black men occupied a table while they waited for a colleague? The men had earlier been refused permission use the toilet. The colleague for whom they were waiting arrived in time to see them handcuffed and taken away by police. The reason for the arrest could not have been clearer. They were guilty of being black and sitting in a Starbucks coffee shop.

One media professor in the city called it 'a ritual that is consistent and longstanding as America: the erasure, the criminalisation of brown people in public spaces'.

Long after slavery was abolished, black people driving across America were advised to avail themselves of a guidebook called *The Negro Motorist Green-Book*. It listed the limited number of places where black drivers could buy petrol, go into a restaurant or find a bed for the night. It has become better known recently because of the Oscar-winning film *Green Book*. On my recent visits to the American South, I've heard it argued with only the slightest touch of sarcasm that perhaps the time had come for such a guidebook to be republished.

Such questions of concern frame the persistent theme of the movement Black Lives Matter and, whether politicians choose to admit it or not, they are central to the players in the NFL 'taking a knee' – going down on one knee during the playing of the American national anthem before the start of games.

It is decidedly not about a lack of respect for flag or country. It is about the continuing battle for equality – a battle that rages unabated – and those who portray it as something else are guilty of the same deliberate blindness to the inequality that caused the footballers to protest in the first place.

I was fortunate to be in Washington in November 2008 when Barack Obama was elected president, the first black man to be so. On the Mall the morning after the election, and on the day of his inauguration, Washington was enveloped by the kind of celebration the city had never seen before.

In a country where black people were once paraded in chains to be bought and sold and after decades stained with the blood of sacrifices made in the cause of basic human rights, a black man had made it to the White House, the highest office in the land.

The celebratory mood was not universal and did not last too long.

Even before the election an ugly rumour had surfaced. Something called the 'birther movement' began to suggest that Obama was not American and should not be allowed to run for president. It might have been thought that such a blatant lie would be given no political space. But it was. It proved to be no barrier to Obama's detractors.

The sponsors of the 'birther movement' knew it was fraudulent, but their mini-campaign continued to wind its weary way right up to election day and beyond. It was just another way of emphasising (perhaps to those who were *unaware* of the fact) that Obama is part-Kenyan and black.

There was another twist.

Some congressional leaders began to suggest that there should be concerted opposition to any legislative proposition put forward by the Obama administration. Then came the call from the right-of-centre Tea Party about 'taking our country back'. Back from whom, I wondered.

That code was not difficult to decipher.

It expressed a determination to make sure that a black man is never again elected president of the United States and that every effort should be made to ensure that Obama would be a one-term president.

Congress was as good as its word. It proceeded to block the most important elements of Obama's proposed legislation. It killed his plan for affordable health care a full year before his second term was up. It blocked Obama's constitutional right to appoint a Supreme Court Judge. At least the Senate Republican leader, Mitch McConnell, did nothing to disguise his hatred of the Obama administration. In August 2016 he recounted: 'One of my proudest moments was when I looked Barack Obama in the eye and said, "Mr President, you will not fill the Supreme Court vacancy."'

One year later, when the Ku Klux Klan, with its poisonous

message of race hatred, clashed with demonstrators opposed to their views in Charlottesville, Virginia, Obama's successor as president, Donald Trump, could not bring himself to oppose the views of white supremacists. He responded by saying that there were good people on either side. American political commentators rushed to explain why. The president had been careful in his phrasing because he had no wish to 'alienate his base'.

A year later the White House press office struggled to explain why a black woman, who turned on the president after losing her job in the West Wing as a senior adviser, was described by the president as 'crying lowlife' and 'a dog'. Such language from the holder of the highest office in the land – so common, so coarse and misogynistic and so entirely without shame and deliberately demeaning – is surely without precedent.

I have already commented that when President Lyndon Johnson made the speech to Congress paving the way for the eventual passing of the Civil Rights Act in 1965, he ended by saying 'and we shall overcome'. It is reported that Dr Martin Luther King was moved to tears. What, I wonder, would he have made of the words another president said after Charlottesville?

In the days after those two black men were arrested and taken out by police from a Starbucks coffee shop in Philadelphia, the company, with a sharp eye on its public face, announced that it was initiating a new training course for members of its staff. I had the mischievous thought that I would have loved to be in the audience on the first day of such an uplifting seminar. It would in all probability have begun with the announcement: 'Ladies and gentlemen, the first thing I would like to say to you today is that in the United States many citizens are white, but in case you haven't noticed some are black. And they are citizens too.'

One snapshot of race relations in America today can be seen not only in the widespread practice of gerrymandering, where areas populated mainly by black Americans are deliberately tacked on to large white conurbations so that the black vote can be contained or marginalised, but by the determined efforts to stop black Americans registering to vote. That is still in the twenty-first century a common practice.

American prisons still hold a disproportionately high number of black prisoners. The author of a recent book, *The New Jim Crow*, says there are more black Americans in prison, on probation and parole today than there were in slavery at the beginning of the American Civil War.

Progress is not an accident but a necessity, was the opinion of philospher Herbert Spencer, but the lack of progress is not an accident either.

11

The Politics of Black and White

'And we are here as on a darkling plain
Swept with confused alarms of struggle and flight,
Where ignorant armies clash by night.'

Matthew Arnold, 'Dover Beach'

As an ITN reporter, I pursue interviews with a wide assortment of world leaders. I once spent months setting up a meeting with the Libyan leader Muammar Gaddafi. Today every time I read about the tribal revolt that toppled him and its role in helping to create the crisis of Arab and African migrants seeking refuge in Europe, I remember the long, rambling conversation we had in a multicoloured tent in the grounds of his house in Tripoli. He talked about his country's tribal complexity and the necessity of his absolute control.

The main problem in arranging to see the Libyan leader was that none of his officials appeared willing or able to suggest to Gaddafi he should keep an appointment. To put it another way, he was in no way constrained by time. Scheduled arrangements were unknown. An agreement about an interview was vaguely possible but it was impossible to commit the president to a specific time and place.

So it was with Gaddafi.

I had gone to Tripoli on the strict understanding that my time in the country was limited. I freely used the excuse that

I was required back in London on a certain date to read the news. That ruse was never challenged, and it worked regularly in my favour. It made no impression on the colonel. On the afternoon we were supposed to meet, one of his aides telephoned me to say that he would take me to lunch and that we would then follow the colonel on a drive across the desert to Libya's border with Tunisia.

Gaddafi wanted to demonstrate Libya's improving relations with neighbouring Tunisia. He would do this by demolishing a small, undistinguished looking border post. My memory is that the border post had long ceased to function as anything vaguely official. I do not recall the presence of any other camera crews on the journey or at the border, and concluded that the demonstration would be purely for the benefit of ITN.

Once at the border the colonel got into a JCB truck with a swivelling front end and got to work attempting to destroy the hut marking the line in the sand between Libya and Tunisia. It appeared that Gaddafi had never driven such a truck before. He had several swings at destroying the border post but kept missing it entirely. It took several attempts and nearly half an hour before the thing crashed into an untidy heap.

There was a distinctly comic look to the entire cameo, but his aides looked on soberly and we felt that laughing too openly would break the mood.

I had no idea why we had been invited to watch the colonel at work and thought that my interview would follow. Instead we were informed that, having come such a long way from the capital and with evening approaching, Gaddafi had decided to spend the night in the desert and we were invited to do the same. The Libyan leader apparently did that quite regularly to burnish his credentials as a Bedouin.

By then I had lost my patience at all the waiting around watching the desert theatricals, and I announced that I would be going back to Tripoli. I did accept a large drink before the journey back to the capital.

The drama continued the following day. When by mid-morning I was informed there was still no word about the Gaddafi interview, I said that I was thinking of leaving Libya for London on a flight that night. That ultimatum did the trick. I would see the Libyan leader that afternoon.

It was as fine a bit of theatre as I've seen.

Gaddafi insisted on being interviewed in a tent in the grounds of his house. It was situated at the end of a long dirt track some distance from the house, and we set up our camera to record the scene of the Libyan leader walking towards the tent. It was an image we never got.

About thirty minutes after his expected arrival and with our camera still looking down the dirt track, my attention was drawn to a rustling in the bushes around the tent, a few yards from where we stood. I was not overly alarmed but slightly shocked to see two or three men in military fatigues, crawling on their stomachs commando-style and carrying AK-47 machine guns. They came within a few feet of me, looked around, and wordlessly and slowly, still crawling through the undergrowth, made their way back whence they had come.

They had, I must assume, been securing the area around the tent before their leader's arrival. He duly appeared, walking not along the dirt track on which our camera had been trained for more than half an hour, but from a stubbly growth of plants to the side of his tent. Attired in his customary flowing white robe, and with a faint smile, he brushed past a sunflower to greet us.

My interview with Colonel Gaddafi was interesting more for the fact that we eventually got to him than for its substance. He stuck to his lines. He was not a sponsor of terrorism in the Middle East or in any other part of the world. He had never supplied weapons to the IRA, although he did support political movements fighting for equality and for a fairer say in the way their countries were administered. Libya, he told me, had a leading role to play in promoting a pan-African approach to solving the problems in the region. He seemed very assured in that belief and it was clearly an assertion of national pride.

The formal part of our conversation over, Gaddafi was apparently in no rush to leave. He enquired about my work in England and wanted to know how I came to settle there. I replied that it was too long a story to tell and that its origins lay in the fact that Trinidad had until independence been a British colony.

The colonel suddenly became more animated in tone. 'Oh, you must tell me all about it. I know a lot about colonialism. You should come to work for me.' I said nothing, but he launched into a lecture about Libya's history and went on to explain why he had to be so tough in dealing with the various tribal divisions in his country. He implied that Libya's colonial masters had left the country in a mess he needed to clear up.

For years I thought very little about my off-camera conversation with Gaddafi. I spoke of it as one of the more amusing episodes in my travels as a journalist. That is, until it became clear how the political disorder and general chaos in Libya after Gaddafi have played a significant role in igniting a refugee crisis that cripples Europe and is quickly changing the political outlook in European countries.

It began with the decision by the French, British and American NATO alliance to topple Gaddafi with absolutely no thought of what would follow. Bombing a country from twenty thousand feet might have many military attributes. Having people on the ground to assist in building a new order is quite another story. The vacuum was filled by anti-Gaddafi tribes and a conglomeration of gun-toting militias, all seeking to establish their own areas and plunging the country into anarchy. That chaos was the spur for West African and Arab refugees in their hundreds of thousands to try to reach the Libyan coastline to be taken on board boats to cross the Mediterranean and into Italy. Human trafficking is one of the largest industries in Libya today.

From Italy economic migrants hope to reach other parts of Europe; Italy complains about its inability to take any more people and the issue of immigration has become the most toxic on the Continent. Far-right, anti-immigration political parties battle for the kind of prominence never thought possible. In the Czech Republic, Sweden and Slovenia migrants face increasing hostility. Hungary passed a law making it a criminal act to help undocumented people.

The tone in Britain is not very much better. I feel a very personal sense of shame that I didn't pay more attention to what has now commonly been called the Windrush scandal. It seems to me that it arose out of the former prime minister when home secretary's desire to create what was deliberately styled and called a 'hostile environment for illegal immigrants'.

I could not understand the need for sending vans around to parts of the country where there may or may not have been illegal immigrants but where there certainly were immigrants.

I never understood – and it's a problem of language here – why it was necessary to create a 'hostile environment for illegal immigrants'. Why *hostile*? Every country has a duty to control the number of people who come into it. You can't be a proper country unless you have proper immigration policies, so I take that as written, and you must take steps to keep out people who shouldn't *be* in the country. But why *hostile* environment? You could call it effective. You could call it robust. You could say it's something which must be done as a country. But why deliberately *hostile*? I was shocked by that. I was particularly shocked that it was happening to West Indians who had made Britain their home in the 1950s. A number of them were treated abominably on discovering that they had no British passports, although they'd lived in this country the whole time. They were deprived of their ability to find employment. They lost their entitlement to health care and, in many instances, they were deported and denied re-entry to the United Kingdom when they returned from trips abroad. I thought this was unthinkably horrid.

And one of the reasons I felt this so strongly was that throughout my early life in Trinidad I was acutely aware of the great attachment West Indians had for Britain. It was not just Britain, it was the mother country. All eyes were focused on what went on in the mother country and many people aspired to live there. My mother talked endlessly about Winston Churchill and his oratory during the Second World War, and I remembered many years later that when Churchill died John F. Kennedy memorably said how 'Churchill mobilised the English language and sent it into battle'.

These were stories we West Indians thrived on. We thought that Britain identified itself not only with its ability to survive the Blitz with that bulldog spirit but also with the nobler virtues of humanity. I was told as a child stories about the finer qualities of British parliamentary democracy. I was schooled on the notion that people might have the biggest fight on the floor of the House of Commons but at the end of the day they would let bygones be bygones and have a drink in the bar together. These things we were constantly told about what a great country it is.

I remember the pride with which West Indians would tell you: 'We have a son who is reading medicine in London' or 'We have a daughter who is studying at the London School of Economics'. There was a pride in having that connection with London.

The people who embarked on the journey to England on the *Windrush* in 1948 would have been brought up with a strong, unbreakable faith in British justice, in British decency, in British humanity and in the fairness, the *fairness*, of British life. The Windrush scandal turned all that around and I was shocked by the way it happened.

British exploits were painted to us in glowing primary colours. Thus Captain Cook's voyages of exploration, and

Nelson's valour at the battle of Trafalgar. And when in 1797 Trinidad was wrested from its Spanish occupiers, the advancing British naval force never needed to fire its guns. Spain surrendered meekly.

Fast-forward to the twentieth century and West Indian men were recruited to join Britain's fight against Nazi Germany in the Second World War. Some West Indian women paid their own way to travel to London to assist in the war effort. Tiny, impoverished islands subscribed to a Spitfire fund to build more planes to combat German might. In my later life I knew a handful of men who had served with distinction in the RAF. I have never forgotten the modest pride with which they talked about their service to Britain.

The Home Office has since scrambled to try to correct the appalling errors made in rendering thousands of people stateless and desperate. Such attempts, though obviously important, should never have been necessary in the first place. It should never have come to this. The scandal of the Windrush generation sadly changed a number of basic perceptions of English life. Many have been changed utterly.

In a frequently depressing catalogue of journalistic reflections from more than fifty years, there have been, to my great good fortune, a number of bright and shining moments. They light up the international landscape and restore faith in the ability of a few good men to alter the tide of events for the better.

Sometimes a single voice is all that it takes to express succinctly and without flourish the pent-up emotion of a multitude.

Acknowledgements

I owe much to many people.

I never cease to thank Radio Trinidad for the latitude and freedom it gave me to try my hand at a variety of projects. I was for a while a horse-racing commentator, though I was never very good at it. I was even less so covering water polo. I hope I was better at it with football, cricket and tennis, and only wish that I had known as much about those sports then as I do now.

My agent Anita Land was cheerully practical and encouraging when my resolution to finish the book faded, as was Robert Caskie. I was always happy to share his sunny optimism about my work. If this chronicle of my long and disjointed career as a journalist has any rigour and coherence, credit must go the the patient and quiet brilliance of my editor, Alan Samson, and his excellent colleagues at Orion – Lucinda McNeile, Hannah Cox, Helen Ewing, Steven Marking, Tom Noble, Paul Stark, Maura Wilding, Elizabeth Allen, Ellie Freedman and Zoe Yang. Their wise and smiling confidence was pointed and valuable.

I am grateful to Pippa Stephens who has worked for so many years as my Personal Assistant, and to ITN and Getty images and to the independent production company Plum for providing many of the pictures in this book, and to Kate Sangway for her help.

ITN editors David Nicholas, Stuart Purvis, Richard Tait,

David Mannion, Nigel Dacre and Deborah Turness are among the finest in the industry. Their trust was the crucial element in my survival. They gave me the time and the space and the choice of assignments to do what Nigel Ryan suggested. For a long time I was asked by ITN, by *Channel 4 News* with whom I spent two memorable years, and by the Granada Television show *Tonight* – edited for many years by James Goldston and Jeff Anderson – to pursue and to conduct nearly all big-name interviews. My colleagues on the *Tonight* programme were unfailingly serious with their help and their time – among them Michael Lewis, Alison Kirkham, Amy Frith and Louise Ryder.

Travelling, frequently at a moment's notice, to far-flung corners of the world became part of my life. I revelled in it. Every technical director, producer, fixer, scriptwriter and every member of every camera crew with whom I've worked gave me the full quota of their generosity and the strength and warmth of their guiding hands. I could have accomplished little without them.

The roster of star talent at ITN when I joined was awesome. I was terrified walking into the place for the first time. The great Robin Day had worked there. So had the multi-talented Christopher Chataway. Presenters in my time included that master of the art of every branch of journalism Alastair Burnet, Reginald Bosanquet, who commanded an extraordinary national following, Anna Ford, Robert Kee, Leonard Parkin, Andrew Gardner, Ivor Mills, Rory McPherson, Sandy Gall and a galaxy of other journalists of proven talent . . . Peter Sissons, Peter Snow, Julian Haviland, Jon Lander, Michael Nicholson, Robert Southgate, Robert Hargreaves, Anthony Carthew, Gerald Seymour, Keith Hatfield, Geoffrey Archer, Michael Brunson, Ray Maloney, Martyn Lewis, Sarah Cullen, Carol Barnes, Joan Thirkettle and much later Alastair Stewart and Jon Snow. I must also note that *News on Ten* had the finest writers in our industry for many years. Mine were Simon Holdrich and David Stanley.

Without exception they and many others gave me their friendship and advice, frequently laced with good wine at lunches and dinners in London, Paris, Moscow and Washington.

All journalism depends for its survival on the willingness of experts to talk-to reporters and to share with us, on the record or in non-attributable conversations, their views about how we might begin to understand and to explain to our audiences those complex issues in domestic and international politics. The list of those who gave me their time and the benefit of their knowledge would easily trace a line halfway around the globe. Ambassadors and senior diplomats at British embassies abroad found time to see me and to offer guidance. So did scores of foreign government officials.

The editors and producers with whom I worked were among the finest in our trade. My numerous trips to America to report on American presidential campaigns, deliberations at the United Nations and East–West summits were made with the invaluable assistance of Alexandra Henderson. Graham Walker and Cliff Bestall introduced me to the complexities of South African politics. Angela Frier was my indefatigable producer in Baghdad before the first Gulf War and during the second in Kuwait.

I owe much to the kindness and help of friends, John Morrison, John Mahoney, Tony Millett, Maggie Eales, Richard Clemmow, Jamie Donald, Garron Baines, Sue Inglish, Helen Armitage, Chris Hulme, Jim Akhurst, Simon Bucks and Mike Nolan and a host of others.

I would hate to be held to account for the errors I made and the missteps I took in my career. Their names are legion for they are many. More often than not I simply got things wrong and was not sufficiently wise to predict what the poet Henry Wadsworth Longfellow called 'the shadowy future'.

At the end of long, tense days, I waited impatiently to see members of the team again to have the cathartic download of a discussion about our triumphs and our failures over drinks and long rambling dinners. I recall those days with pleasure. If in the course of these adventures I managed to help explain the thinking and action of presidents or prime ministers, and if my work aided any understanding of how government policies affect the lives of the mass of ordinary people, I am immensely proud. I could not have done any of it without the help of others.

I could fill a small book to describe the extent to which I'm indebted to so many people. On one of my earliest visits to Pakistan the late President Zia ordered that I be ushered in through the ambassador's entrance to his official residence. That presidential order had been given because my colleague Sandy Gall had known the Pakistani president for many years and had warmly commended me to him. I remember with mischievous glee the baffled look on the faces of the actual ambassadors in what was their waiting room. They could make no sense of my appearance in their group and I thought it rather fun to deny them the courtesy of an explanation.

Similar acts of collegiate generosity burn themselves into the memory. A few days before I was given my very first shift as an ITN news presenter, the senior technical director Diana Edwards-Jones approached me in a corridor just off the newsroom to say that she'd been told I was about to be assigned to read the early evening news. She had a suggestion. 'I'm here on duty over the weekend. Why don't you come in and we can have a few practice sessions to see if you are any good?' It would be a travesty, obvious to anyone who worked at ITN at the time, if I did not add that those were emphatically not the words Miss Edward-Jones used. Her language was more colourful, famously salty and her exhortations, delivered in the rolling cadences of her native Wales, were punctuated by a volley of adjectives not to be found in any version of the Church of England's Book of Common Prayer. 'You old fart' was I think, one of her more polite addresses and she added for good measure that the rehearsals would prove if I 'was any bloody good'.

It was more than a thoughtful gesture. In her role as senior studio director Diana may have been asked or even instructed to invite me to do those trial runs. To make that assumption, though, would be to would miss the point. The result was that after a few practice sessions under her expert supervision I was not a failure when I read the early evening news for the first time. Her advice sustained me for years.

There were times when I was carried by nothing else than the brilliance of colleagues. Two days after President Ceauşescu of Romania was overthrown I anchored *News at Ten* from the capital, Bucharest. The sudden collapse of a Stalinist police state had been greeted with relief in many parts of the country but marked by a descent into lawlessness in others. We were advised to choose a broadcast position at ground level outside the British Embassy because it was feared that the sight of television arc lights at a more elevated location might attract the attention of rooftop snipers.

It was a cold December night and it had been snowing. With minutes to go before the news began we lost all contact with studio control in London. ITN was on the point of deciding to cancel the feed from Bucharest and to fall back on the emergency plan of doing the entire bulletin from London. With minutes to go our engineer in Bucharest, Peter Heaps, scraping away at the snow with his bare hands, found and repaired the faulty line. It was held in place throughout our broadcast.

Ten years after I joined ITN I was seconded to be part of the team responsible for the start of a sixty-minute news programme for the new Channel 4 television station. It gave me the opportunity to work with many of the finest editors and journalists in the industry and it allowed me to travel to places to which I might never have been assigned in the normal course of ITN news gathering. News broadcasts on all the major television outlets in Britain have occasionally changed broadcast times. From its inception *Channel 4 News*, anchored brilliantly first by Peter Sissons and now by my friend Jon Snow and colleagues, has kept its originally scheduled start time of seven o'clock in the evening. I was fortunate to have been part of the team from the beginning.

I discovered the simple truth that the major issues governing the relationship between nation states are more complex than they may at first appear. Few things in politics are susceptible to facile responses. The finest statesmen and the most talented diplomats wind and twist their way in and out of impenetrable situations in unpredictable ways and we, the watching press, do not always correctly interpret their motives or their actions. Thus, my predictions about how political crises might be resolved have often been wide of the mark. But I gave serious thought to the assignments I was given and, even though on reviewing them have concluded that, given another chance, I might have done things differently, I can say hand on heart that I gave them my best shot at the time.

I do in moments of reflection trawl through all the stories I've been part of for a scintilla of proof that as a journalist I may have done some good or anything worthwhile, something useful to someone other than my bosses at ITN or to the enhancement of my own career.

I recall an incident in Hong Kong many years ago that still brings a smile of pleasure. One morning we were taken out into the harbour to see the latest batch of Vietnamese refugees seeking asylum in the colony. They had undertaken a hazardous journey and fought off the piratical attentions of unscrupulous middlemen to reach this point and were a thoroughly miserable sight. On floating barges, they were men, mostly, in what looked like wraparound, loose fitting undergarments, squatting on their haunches and gazing blankly out to sea, images of utter hopelessness unrelieved by the dazzling sunlight bathing the South China Sea. A capable interpreter and self-appointed spokesman for the group explained to me when we had boarded why they had decided to try their luck in Hong Kong. They had come from Vietnam where their prospects had not been good. Once on dry land they'd be consigned to detention centres. The only means of escape would be to contact someone, somewhere else in the world, willing to sponsor a trip to a more hopeful destination.

I got to talking to the self-appointed spokesman after my formal interviews were done and I asked whether he had any relatives abroad. He explained, much too vaguely I felt, that his brother lived somewhere in the Los Angeles area and that he was hoping somehow to get in touch with him. At my urging he gave me, partly from memory and with the help of a tiny scrap of paper, what he thought was his brother's address and I offered to write a letter to America on his behalf. I did that as soon as I got back to my hotel and promptly forgot about it.

Many months later, to my home address in west London there came a badly typed and discernibly irate message from a Vietnamese man living in Los Angeles. It began by chiding me for getting his address so badly wrong but went on to say that, after a considerable delay for which I was partly to blame, he and his brother had been reunited. I was delirious with joy. I had at long last done something of palpable benefit to another human being in the margins of my work as a journalist.

Such moments were rare.

If, on the other hand, I can lay claim to anything resolutely professional, then the credit for that must be shared by an army of colleagues. I thank them all and will be forever grateful. I hope they feel that this book is partly theirs, too.

I do often wonder, though, what my devoted parents would have made of it all.

Index

Abrahams, Harold, 78
Abramowitz, Alan I., 20
Adams, Sir Grantley, 55
Affordable Health Care Act, 21, 300
Afghanistan, 14, 96, 127, 174, 176–7,
   181–2, 242, 244
African National Congress (ANC),
   200–5, 208–9, 214–16, 220–2,
   231–4, 236–7
Al-Hadithi, Naji, 255, 273–4
Albanian Communist Party, 155
Alite, John, 290–2
Allitt, Beverley, 279–80
al-Qaeda, 241–3, 246
Amin, Idi, 83, 169–70
Anne, Princess, 95–6
Aquino, Cory, 157–9
Arafat, Yasser, 144, 149–52
Arbatov, Georgi, 179
Argentina, 103, 107, 109–11
   see also Falklands War
Aristotle, 51
Arlott, John, 41, 66
arms control, 176–7, 179–80
Arnold, Matthew, 42
Atwell, Winifred, 75
autographs, 67
Aziz, Tariq, 270

Bad Girls, 164–5
Baer, Frederick, 283–4
Bailey, E. McDonald, 77
Baker, James, 143, 270
Batista, Felix, 158

BBC World Service (Bush House),
   44–5, 56, 72–82, 84, 100, 115,
   134, 142, 160, 169–70
Beaujolais nouveau, 171–2
Beethoven, Ludwig van, 34
Begin, Menachem, 144–5
Beijing Olympics, 110
Bell, Christopher, 56
Bell, Sir Ronald, 92–3
Belleek bombing, 125–6
Bellow, Saul, 57
Berlin Olympics, 3
Berlin Wall, fall of, xiv, 179, 214
Berlioz, Hector, 34
Bestall, Cliff, 193–4, 311
Bhutto, Benazir, 181
Biko, Steve, 211, 233
Black Lives Matter, 299
Black Sash, 189
Blair, Tony, 243–5, 247
Bloody Sunday, 112
Boesak, Allan, 195–6
Bosanquet, Reginald, 91, 310
Botha, P. W., 204–5, 208, 212–14,
   223
Botha, Pik, 195
Brezhnev, Leonid, 174–8
Buckhurst, Lord, 48–9, 52–3
Burke, Edmund, 44
Burnet, Alastair, 91, 310
Bush, George H. W., 2, 254
Bush, George W., 2, 16–17, 241–5,
   247
Bush House, see BBC World Service

Buthelezi, Chief Mangosuthu, 200–3
Butler, Lord, 245
Bye, Phil, 261
Byron, Lord, 42–3

calypsos, 42, 50
Cape Town University, 234
Caradon, Lord (Hugh Foot), 77
Cardus, Neville, 41
Caro, Robert, 18
Carrington, Lord, 142–6
Carter, Jimmy, 166
Castro, Fidel, 151
Ceauşescu, Nicolae, 313
Challenger disaster, 166
Chamberlain, Neville, 144
Channel 4 News, 152–5, 314
Charles, Prince, 295
Charleston, South Carolina, 22–3
Charlottesville, Virginia, 301
Cheney, Dick, 243, 246
Chinese Communist Party, 110
Churchill, Winston, 32, 44, 94–5, 308
CIA, 244, 246–7, 274
Clark, Sheriff Jim, 8
Clarke, Thurston, 17
Clinton, Bill, 2, 13, 16
Clinton, Hillary, 13
Clive, Robert (Clive of India), 44
Cod Wars, 141
Cohen, Roger, xi–xii
Coleridge, Samuel Taylor, 42
Columbus, Christopher, 25
Common Market, *see* European Economic Community (EEC)
Commonwealth, 74, 171, 202
Commonwealth Games, 77–8, 100
Constantine, Sir Learie, 46–7, 49
Coogan, Tim Pat, 132
Cook, Captain James, 308
Cook, Robin, 243
Cooke, Sam, 55
Corrigan, Mairead, 129–30
Craig, William, 115–16

cricket, 41, 47, 50, 55, 64–6, 77, 86, 100–1, 103, 105–7, 111, 133
  and apartheid, 185–6
Cromwell, Oliver, 25
Cry Freedom, 211
Cuba, 25, 54, 169
Cushing, Cardinal Richard, 10
Cyprus, Turkish invasion of, 99

Davis, Sammy, Jr, 55
de Gaulle, General, 171
de Klerk, F. W., 208, 213–15, 223–4, 234, 236–7
de Kock, Eugene, 233–4
de Paor, Liam, 116
Dearlove, Sir Richard, 244
death row prisoners, 280–9
Dialogue, 79–80, 82
Dickens, Charles, 42–3
Diderot, Denis, xiv
dietary supplements, 66–7
D'Oliveira, Basil, 185
Drake, Sir Francis, 43
Duarte, Jessie, 236
Duterte, Rodrigo, 159
Dutton, Jim, 261

Edwards-Jones, Diana, 312–13
Eisenhower, Dwight D., 17, 54
Eliot, George, 42
Eliot, T. S., 55, 138
Ellison, Ralph, 19
Europa Hotel, Belfast, 121–4
European Economic Community (EEC), 74, 171–4

failure, fear of, 31
Falklands War, 144–9
Faulkner, William, 11
football, 100–1, 103, 107–11, 229
Ford, Anna, 91, 310
Forsyth, Bruce, 97
Freedom Riders, 10
Freeman, Morgan, 282
Frier, Angela, 256–8, 261

Frost, Robert, 87

Gaddafi, Muammar, 151, 303–6
Gairy, Eric, 27
Gall, Sandy, 91, 310, 312
Galtieri, General, 144
Gandhi, Mohandas, 197
Gardner, Andrew, 91, 310
Garner, Eric, 23
Gerasimov, Gennady, 179
Ghana, 75
Gibson, William Clyde, 284–5
Glaspie, April, 255–6
Goethe, Johann Wolfgang von, 34
Goldberg, Anatol, 76
Good Friday Agreement, 133
Gorbachev, Mikhail, 166–7, 179–80
Gordon, Ken, 37
Green Book, 299
Greenidge, Gordon, 65
Grenada, American invasion of, 27

Hall, Wes, 65
Handel, George Frideric, 52
Hasssan, Nael, 252–4, 271–2
Hastings, Warren, 44
Hazlitt, William, 42
Heaps, Peter, 261
Henbolt, Henry, 41
Henderson, Alexandra, 147, 311
Henderson, Sir Nicholas, 147
heroin, 181–2
Hirohito, Emperor, 127
Hitler, Adolf, 3, 144, 266
Hong Kong, 276, 315
horse racing, 101
horse shows, 95
Huddleston, Bishop Trevor, 77
Hussein, King of Jordan, 252
Hussein, Saddam, 137, 241, 243–52,
  254–6, 259–61, 264–77

Inkatha, 200–1
IRA, 114, 120, 125, 129, 305
Iraq War (second Gulf War), 14, 137,

240–9, 273–4
Islamic State, 182, 241
Israel–Palestine conflict, 142–4
ITN, 82–6, 88–94, 134–7, 160–5,
  167–70, 310–11
  and launch of Channel 4, 152–4
  Saddam Hussein interview, 256–8,
    262, 267–8
  sports coverage, 100–3

Jackson, Rev. Jesse, 23, 167
Jagan, Cheddi, 55
James, C. L. R., 42–3
Jay, Douglas, 74
Jefferson, Thomas, 2
John Paul II, Pope, 117
Johnson, Lyndon B., 18–19, 23, 296,
  301
Johnston, Willie, 108

Kaunda, Kenneth, 151
Keats, John, 42
Kennedy, John F., 2, 5, 10, 17, 54,
  308
Khan, Imran, 182
Khrushchev, Nikita, 54
King, Billie Jean, 105
King, Martin Luther, 3, 11, 18–19,
  23–4, 167, 216, 296, 298, 301
Kipling, Rudyard, 43
Ku Klux Klan, 8, 11, 298, 300
Kuwait, 249–50, 252–5, 262, 265,
  267–70, 274

Lamb, Charles, 42
Lancet, The, 69
Larkin, Philip, 31
Lazarus, Emma, 16
Lebanon, 71
Lie, Trygve, 152
Lincoln, Abraham, 2, 23
Lindley, Richard, 82
literature and poetry, 28–9, 42–3
Lloyd, Clive, 65
Louis, Joe, 3

Lugenpresse (lying press), xii
lynching, 11, 18, 296–8

McCain, John, 8–9
McConnell, Mitch, 300
McDonald, Eunice, 59, 65
McDonald, Lynette, 59, 65
McGuinness, Martin, 133
Machel, Samora, 151
MacLeod, Ally, 108–9
McManus, Paul, 285–8
Mafia, 288–95
Magee, John Gillespie, Jr, 166
Mandela, Nelson, 200, 202–5, 208–9,
    212, 215–39
Mandela, Winnie, 216, 231
Manning, David, 244
Manningham-Buller, Eliza, 244
Mannion, David, 218
Marcos, Ferdinand, 157–9
Margaret, Princess, 44
Marr, Andrew, 82
Marshall, Malcolm, 65
Martin, Dean, 55
Mathis, Johnny, 55
Mawhinney, Brian, 118
May, Theresa, 307
Mayer, Jane, 244
Mercer, Derrik, 153–4
Milton, John, 42–3
Monaghan bombing, 119
Monday Club, 92–3
Montgomery, Alabama, 8, 12, 15,
    18, 23
Mount Hope Hospital, 63
Mubarak, Hosni, 252
Mugabe, Robert, 151
Muhammad, Prophet, 6
Murillo, Rosario, 155
Murray, Deryck, 65

Nash, Johnny, 55
Natale, Ralph, 295
National Health Service, 58
Nelson, Admiral Lord, 43, 309

New Jim Crow, The, 302
News at Ten, 83, 91, 98, 133, 136,
    160–5
    and Mandela's release, 218–19
news journalism, 73–4, 82–3
    and fake news, xi–xii
    and government statements, 126–7
    stake-outs, 95
    war reporting, 139–41
NFL, and 'taking a knee', 299
Nicaragua, 155–6
Nicholas, David, 100–1, 103, 154
Nicholson, Michael, 99
Nietzsche, Friedrich, 34
Nobel Peace prize, 130
Northern Ireland, 29, 71, 86–7, 99,
    111–33, 163, 167
    army press officers, 124–6
    and integrated schooling, 118–19
    and mixed marriages, 119–20
    parades and flying of flags, 132
    peace initiatives, 129–31
    power sharing, 116
    religious divide, 117–20
Nzo, Alfred, 230

Obama, Barack, 2–24, 167, 299–300
Obama, Michelle, 12–13
O'Neill, Terence, 118
Ortega, Daniel, 155–6
Ouspensky, Nicholai, 179
Owens, Jesse, 3

Packer, Kerry, 105–7
Paisley, Rev. Ian, 115, 118, 133,
    172–3
Pakistan, 181–2
Palin, Sarah, 9
Panama Canal, 29
Paris Olympics, 78
Parks, Rosa, 296
Peace People, 129–30
Pearl Harbor, 241
Pearish, Rick, 288
Pérez de Cuéllar, Javier, 147–9

Pettus, General Edmund, 8
Philippines, 157–9
Phillips, Captain Mark, 95
Plato, 51
Platters, The, 55
Plock, Vike Martina, 73
Pol Roger champagne, 95
Port of Spain Country Club, 35–6
Powell, Colin, 246–7, 268
Power, Samantha, 247–8
Previte, Ron, 294–5
Profile, 77
Purvis, Stuart, 218, 252, 310

Race Relations Act, 93
Race Relations Board, 80–1
Radio Trinidad, 33–4, 37, 45–53, 56, 60, 87
Raleigh, Sir Walter, 43
Reagan, Ronald, 2, 16, 26–7, 149, 166–7, 179–80
Renwick, Robin, 148
Rhodes, Cecil, 234
Rice, Condoleezza, 246
Richards, Vivian, 65
Robbie, Ian, 202
Roof, Dylann, 22
Roosevelt, Franklin D., 2, 17
Royal Ulster Constabulary, 115
rugby, 100, 103, 224, 227
rum shops, 63, 68
Rumsfeld, Donald, 245–6, 248–9
Runcie, Dr Robert, 71
Ryan, Nigel, 83–4, 93, 170

Sadat, Anwar, 143
Sanford, Ronald, 282–3, 288
Sankara, Thomas, 151
Save the Children, 96
Scarpa, Greg, 292–4
Schwarzkopf, General Norman, 254–5
Scoon, Paul, 27
Selma, Alabama, 8–10, 12, 15, 18, 23, 296–7

September 11 attacks, 7, 241–2, 244, 246
Shakespeare, William, 43, 231, 247
Sharpeville massacre, 197
Shaw, George Bernard, 28
Shawshank Redemption, The, 282
Shelley, Percy Bysshe, 42
Sheppard, Rev. David, 77
shoes, 61
Simpson, John, 256–7
Sin, Cardinal, 157–7
Sinatra, Frank, 55
Sissons, Peter, 310, 314
Sisulu, Walter, 215, 226
slavery, 23, 35, 49–50, 71, 299
Snow, Jon, 27, 311, 314
Sobers, Gary, 65
Solzhenitsyn, Alexander, 76
South Africa, 184–208
  Bantustans, 190, 200
  black-on-black violence, 233
  black townships, 197–200, 203, 205–7, 210, 215
  colour classifications, 193–5
  international licences, 191–3
  land ownership, 237–8
  latrines report, 206–7
  Pass Laws, 187–9
  post-Mandela era, 234–8
  tri-cameral legislature, 189–90, 195–7, 200, 203–5, 208
  white opposition to apartheid, 211–13
South African Broadcasting Corporation (SABC), 217–18, 220
Soviet Union, xiv, 76, 166–7, 174–82, 214
Spencer, Herbert, 302
Spenser, Edmund, 42
sports reporting, 100–11
Stalin, Joseph, 266
Star Wars nuclear shield, 167, 180
Starbucks, 298–9, 301
Statue of Liberty, 16
Stevenson, Adlai, 53–4

Stevenson, Bryan, 298
Stewart, Jon, 22
Suzman, Helen, 211

Tair, Richard, 178
Taliban, 182
tennis, 101, 103–5
Tennyson, Alfred, 28, 43, 56, 78
Thackeray, William Makepeace, 42–3
Thatcher, Margaret, 27, 179, 202
This Is Your Life, 71
torture, 91, 111, 127, 211–12, 233, 246–9
Treaty of Rome, 171
Treurnicht, Dr Andries, 192
Trinidad, 25–70, 306
    attachment to Britain, 43–4, 71–2, 308–9
    carnival, 42, 64
    emigration, 29, 37–40, 56, 58
    family life, 59–70
    independence conference, 45–52
    international outlook, 168–9
    media self-censorship, 79–80
    race relations, 35–7
    village life, 63–4
Trinidad and Tobago Television, 79–80, 82
Truman, Harry S., 17
Trump, Donald, 21–2, 301
Truth and Reconciliation Commission, 211–12, 233–4
Tutu, Archbishop Desmond, 218–19, 229–30, 232–3, 238

Ulster Defence Association, 120
United Nations, 54, 73, 146–9, 152, 182, 214, 254
    and Iraq War, 246–9
United States of America, 1–24, 296–302
    'birther movement', 300
    gun ownership, 7–8
    Obama inauguration, 1–24, 299–300

police killings, 23
presidential campaigns, 166
rise of Tea Party, 20–1, 300
voting rights, 10–11, 23–4, 302
University of the West Indies, 80

Venezuela, 37–9, 156
Victoria, Queen, 234
Videla, Jorge, 109–11
Vieira de Mello, Sérgio, 247–8
Vienna OPEC siege, 137
Vietnam War, 99, 242, 288
Vietnamese boat people, 314–15

Walcott, Clyde, 50, 64–6
Walcott, Derek, 72
Wallace, George, 8
Washington, George, 15
Weekes, Everton, 50, 64–6
Wellington, Duke of, 228–9
West Indies Federation, 55
West, Fred and Rose, 279
whisky, 68, 78, 130, 260
Wihaib, Haitham Rashid, 276–7
Wilkinson, Peter, 109
Williams, Betty, 129–30
Williams, Eric, 48–53
Wilson, Woodrow, 19
Windrush scandal, 307–9
Wolfe, Tom, 5
Wolfowitz, Paul, 242
Woods, Donald, 211
Wordsworth, William, 43
World Series Cricket, 105–6
Worrell, Frank, 50, 64–6
Wright, Rev. Jeremiah, 12

Yad Vashem Holocaust Museum, 143–4

Zia ul-Haq, Muhammad, 151, 181, 312
Zorin, Valerian, 54
Zulu people, 201–3

Picture Credits

The author and publisher would like to thank the following for use of the images listed below:

Section 1
ITN pp.5(t,b), 6-7; Getty/Keystone p.2(b); Getty/Rolls Press p.3; Claire Mead p.4; Shutterstock/Ken McKay p.8.

Section 2
Getty/David M. Benett p.6; Getty/Dave Hogan pp.2, 3; Getty/David Munden p.5; Getty/Photoshot p.8(b); Getty/Pool p.4; Plum Pictures pp.1(t, b); 7; Shutterstock/Daily Mail p.8(t).